EVIDENCE-BASED PRACTICE PROCESS IN SOCIAL WORK

Evidence-Based Practice Process in Social Work

CRITICAL THINKING FOR CLINICAL PRACTICE

Antonio R. Garcia, PhD, MSW and
Jacqueline Corcoran, PhD, LCSW

OXFORD
UNIVERSITY PRESS

Oxford University Press is a department of the University of Oxford. It furthers
the University's objective of excellence in research, scholarship, and education
by publishing worldwide. Oxford is a registered trade mark of Oxford University
Press in the UK and certain other countries.

Published in the United States of America by Oxford University Press
198 Madison Avenue, New York, NY 10016, United States of America.

© Oxford University Press 2024

All rights reserved. No part of this publication may be reproduced, stored in
a retrieval system, or transmitted, in any form or by any means, without the
prior permission in writing of Oxford University Press, or as expressly permitted
by law, by license, or under terms agreed with the appropriate reproduction
rights organization. Inquiries concerning reproduction outside the scope of the
above should be sent to the Rights Department, Oxford University Press, at the
address above.

You must not circulate this work in any other form
and you must impose this same condition on any acquirer.

Library of Congress Cataloging-in-Publication Data
Names: Garcia, Antonio R., 1978– editor. | Corcoran, Jacqueline, editor.
Title: Evidence-based practice process in social work : Critical thinking
for clinical practice / [edited by] Antonio R. Garcia, Jacqueline Corcoran.
Description: New York, NY : Oxford University Press, [2024] |
Includes bibliographical references and index.
Identifiers: LCCN 2023032529 (print) | LCCN 2023032530 (ebook) |
ISBN 9780197579848 (paperback) | ISBN 9780197579862 (epub) |
ISBN 9780197579879
Subjects: LCSH: Evidence-based social work. | Social service—Practice.
Classification: LCC HV10.5 .E937 2024 (print) |
LCC HV10.5 (ebook) | DDC 361.3/2—dc23/eng/20230801
LC record available at https://lccn.loc.gov/2023032529
LC ebook record available at https://lccn.loc.gov/2023032530

DOI: 10.1093/oso/9780197579848.001.0001

Printed by Marquis Book Printing, Canada

CONTENTS

About the Authors vii

SECTION I: GATHERING EVIDENCE 1

1. Introduction: Overview of the Evidence-Based Practice Process 3

2. Client Assessment and the Development of PICO Questions 15

3. Locating Research to Inform Practice Questions 30
   With Sherry Morgan

SECTION II: CRITIQUING THE EVIDENCE 43

4. Randomized Controlled Trials and Alternatives for the EBP Process 45

5. The Role of Systematic Reviews in the EBP Process 61

6. Qualitative Research and the EBP Process 79
   With Holly Bell

SECTION III: IMPLEMENTING THE EVIDENCE 99

7. Introduction to Implementation Science 101
   With Sean E. Snyder and Courtney Benjamin Wolk

8. Identifying and Addressing Common Barriers to Applying the EBP Process 117
   With Courtney Benjamin Wolk and Sean E. Snyder

9. Adaptation 163

10. Evaluating Client Progress: Review and Critique of Methods to Evaluate Practice 173

11. Review and Conclusion 215

Index 231

ABOUT THE AUTHORS

Unless otherwise noted, all chapters were coauthored by Garcia and Corcoran

Sherry Morgan, PhD, MS, RN
Graduate and Clinical Research Liaison
Penn Libraries
University of Pennsylvania

Holly Bell, PhD
Retired Research Scientist
University of Texas, Austin

Sean E. Snyder, DPA, MSW, LCSW
Program Manager
Pennsylvania Hospital | Penn Medicine

Courtney Benjamin Wolk, PhD
Assistant Professor
University of Pennsylvania

SECTION I
GATHERING EVIDENCE

CHAPTER 1

INTRODUCTION

Overview of the Evidence-Based Practice Process

> *Tyrone is a 12-year-old African American male who has witnessed domestic violence and experienced multiple forms of child maltreatment, including emotional abuse, sexual abuse, and physical abuse. Tyrone meets DSM-5 criteria for PTSD and exhibits symptoms of depression. Like Tyrone, many African American students enrolled in his local charter school reside in underserved and impoverished neighborhoods. Students referred to school social work services may present behavioral problems in class such as falling asleep or acting out, and struggling to pay attention. They may have low self-esteem, and trouble coping with stress. Camille, one of our second-year MSW students who interned at the local charter school, presented this case in our direct practice research class. Camille first learned about trauma-focused cognitive behavioral therapy (TF-CBT) during her first-year field placement as an MSW intern. She cofacilitated a weekly skills group for school-aged children, following the TF-CBT components, including psychoeducation and parenting skills, relaxation techniques, affective expression and regulation, and cognitive coping and processing.*

As a social worker, what would you do? How would you begin to address the issues of concern in this case? What questions would you ask, and how would you ask questions in a way that evokes clients' "true" feelings and experiences? What information would you want to gather from them? What would your assessment entail? How do you rely on assessment data to search for the best available evidence to find interventions to address issues of concern? What if more than one evidence-informed intervention would "work"? What if there are no effective and culturally applicable interventions that address need? What else should you do to inform intervention and case planning? What if you don't have the capacity or training to implement evidence-informed interventions to mitigate risk factors for this case and other cases you are assigned to? What if you are unable to implement the intervention to fidelity? How do you ensure that what you are doing will meet client goals and address their issues of concern? How do you grapple with simultaneously assessing client values or preferences, best available evidence, and your own judgment and biases? These are just some of the questions that even the most seasoned social workers struggle to address.

This textbook aims to show students and even veteran social workers how to engage with the evidence-based practice (EBP) process to grapple with these questions. While the synergy to shift toward a paradigm of using evidence to inform practice decisions started in medical contexts back in the early 1990s (Mykhalovskiya & Weir, 2004), professionals across the social sciences and social work spectrum, perhaps more than ever, are faced with growing pressure to demonstrate that what they deliver to clients addresses their issues of concern and enhances well-being. The mounting pressures, however, are likely mitigated as new clinical social workers gain more familiarity and comfort with the EBP process (Oh et al., 2020). In subsequent chapters, we walk you through the steps in detail, focusing more on clinical contexts rather than macro/policy-oriented spaces. In our experience, we have found most students are nervous and even terrified of even thinking about research. By the end of the semester, our students, by and large, feel more confident to apply the EBP process in practice.

The steps of the EBP process have been detailed ad nauseum. However, most students and practitioners have little idea about how to carry out these steps with their client systems. *Evidence-Based Practice Process in Social Work: Critical Thinking for Clinical Practice* addresses several gaps or limitations in the literature, contextualizing the EBP process and operationalizing the steps with detailed instructions and case studies. We will present case studies, such as the one presented at the beginning of this chapter, that focus on diverse systems (e.g., child welfare, behavioral health, criminal justice, health) and populations (children and families, adults, older adults), focusing on the diverse and oppressed populations to whom social work is committed. The book will detail how to engage critically with the EBP process for each case presented. A systematic review of teaching methods for the EBP process has demonstrated the necessity of a case-based approach to learning this material and becoming competent through practice (Scurlock-Evans & Upton, 2015). Other case examples are provided throughout the text as necessary to illustrate points. In this book, and in contrast to some other works, we focus on simplifying the process and locating it within the helping phases of direct and clinical practice. (Note that although the EBP process can also inform macro practice, the state of knowledge at the moment is that not many macro interventions are subject to research, meaning there is often little evidence to draw from in decision-making.) In addition to nuts-and-bolts instructions and illustrative cases, we end each chapter with activities. Instructors can scaffold the learning and use the tools and templates to show the practical application of the process. Many of the activities ask students to draw on their current cases so that a bridge is drawn between research and practice.

The book is divided into three major sections. Section I includes a brief overview of the EBP process (Chapter 1), methods on how to conduct assessments and to rely on assessment data to develop well-formed practice-driven research questions (Chapter 2), and subsequently locate relevant research studies to address those questions (Chapter 3). In this section, we also offer a brief overview of why engaging in the EBP process is important and what the EBP process entails, pointing you in the direction of where in the book the steps are elaborated. Section II, Chapters 4–6, focuses on the types of research designs (i.e., randomized controlled trials [RCTs], systematic reviews, qualitative research) that will inform how you intervene or what intervention you ultimately decide to implement. The impetus to weigh the evidence, client preferences, and your capacities as a clinician is underscored. In Section III, Chapters 7–9 focus on what factors may impact your ability to implement the intervention plan and under what circumstances you may need to adapt it. Chapter 10 focuses on the different methods you can use to monitor client progress, and Chapter 11 offers a review of key concepts and additional case studies to reflect on. Figure 1 delineates the organization of the book.

We argue that the EPB process should be integrated into routine practice. Therefore, some topics we cover are given much more depth of information in other parts of your social work education curriculum. For instance, in Chapter 2, we discuss assessment and goal-setting as an essential step in the EBP process, even though these topics are covered in other courses, such as foundation direct practice and human behavior in the social environment. In this book, they are discussed as Step 1 in the EBP process when questions about *how* best to meet goals arise from a practice situation. In Chapters 4, 5, and 6 we review research designs and their threats, recognizing that these topics are covered in much greater detail in research methods courses.

Practice-based questions relevant to a community or agencies serving that community can be addressed through EBP. Therefore, we want to emphasize the many ways this book can be used in a supplemental way. That is, the *Evidence-Based Practice Process in Social Work: Critical Thinking for Clinical Practice* can be used as a supplemental text for foundation research, or as its own text in a research elective on EBP for clinical practice/research for clinical practice. Administration and planning courses connect particularly well since the EBP process can be applied to clientele problems and programs. Additionally, the implementation issues presented in Section III of this book involve agency and program administration.

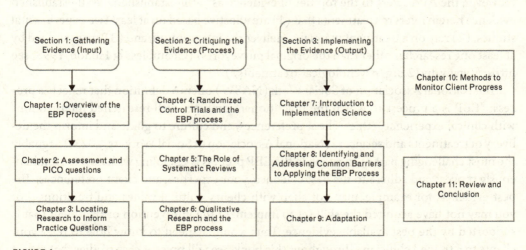

FIGURE 1 Organizational Structure of Chapters within Each Section

DEFINING EPB AS AN OUTCOME VERSUS A PROCESS

To begin, we should delineate the difference between EBP as an outcome versus EBP as a process. Think of an outcome as a conclusion about the state of science for a particular intervention or treatment. The next question becomes, what kind and amount of accumulated studies meets criteria to be considered an *evidence-supported or informed* intervention (Parrish, 2018) or *empirically supported* intervention (ESI) (Drisko & Friedman, 2019)? Different organizations and databases define the compilations of "evidence" in various ways. Drake and colleagues (2001), for example, assert that ESIs "are interventions for which there is consistent scientific evidence showing that they improve client outcomes" (p. 180). According to the California Evidence-Based Clearinghouse (CEBC, 2006–2020), an intervention does not receive a "well-supported by research evidence" rating unless it meets the following criteria:

- At least two rigorous RCTs with nonoverlapping analytic samples that were carried out in usual care or practice settings have found the program to be superior to an appropriate comparison program on outcomes specified in the criteria for that particular topic area.
- In at least one of these RCTs, the program has shown to have a sustained effect at least one year beyond the end of treatment compared to a control group.
- The RCTs have been reported in published, peer-reviewed literature.

See https://www.cebc4cw.org, and refer to Chapter 3 for an example of using the CEBC to find evidence for a particular question. While the CEBC definition offers more specificity, it discounts the value of clinical expertise and client expectations and values (Wike et al., 2014).

Interventions that are referred to as "empiricallysupported treatments" (also called ESIs) by the American Psychological Association (APA) have a similar criterion as the CEBC. However, the APA refers to the top tier of evidence as "well-established." Well-established evidence herein refers to treatments that (1) are effective based on at least two experimental studies, (2) rely on a treatment manual to deliver the intervention, and (3) are examined by at least one researcher other than the original purveyor(s) (Chambless & Hollon, 1998; see https://www.div12.org/psychological-treatments/).

The National Association of Social Work (NASW) offers a definition that reflects a process: "EBP is a process in which the practitioner combines well-researched interventions with clinical experience, ethics, client preferences, and culture to guide and inform the delivery of treatments and services" (National Association of Social Workers, 2023). Arguably the most challenging part of engaging in the EBP process is grappling with how to simultaneously process and adhere to the best evidence, your expertise, and client preferences. The best evidence, for example, may not align with clients' cultural values and traditions—or you may not have acquired the skill set to implement the intervention or treatment that is supported by the best available evidence. Thus, you may need to know how to refer your clients to a trained clinician. Throughout this book, we will present case studies that reflect these challenges and offer recommendations for addressing them. Indeed, as a social worker, it is your ethical responsibility, as stipulated in the Code of Ethics (Section 5.02), to

- Monitor and evaluate policies, the implementation of programs, and practice interventions.
- Promote and facilitate evaluation and research to contribute to the development of knowledge.
- Critically examine and keep current with emerging knowledge relevant to social work and fully use evaluation and research evidence in their professional practice.

Besides our ethical imperative to engage in the EBP process, continued mandates by funders and policymakers highlight the importance of increasing clinicians' understanding of research knowledge, how to translate the EBP process into practice, and ultimately how it affects client outcomes (Wike et al., 2014). Other advantages of the EBP process for social work include preparing a skilled workforce and improving the professional credibility of social work, particularly within interdisciplinary teams (Bertram et al., 2015). In Grady et al.'s (2018) study of social worker use of the EBP process, an advantage named was that clients may have more buy-in to interventions that have research support and have helped many participants. Some of the advantages and disadvantages of ESIs have been discussed in Scurlock-Evans and Upton's systematic review (2015), and we address some of the main myths about ESIs in Table 1.1.

A BRIEF OVERVIEW OF THE EVIDENCE-BASED PRACTICE PROCESS

Here we offer a brief overview of the EBP process to provide you with an idea as to how the EBP process unfolds. More details and examples will be provided in subsequent chapters. Listed below are the critical steps of the EBP process, albeit before Step 1, we advocate for including the assessment process as a critical first step.

1. Engage in client assessment.
2. Rely on data gathered from the assessment to formulate a direct practice research question to answer practice needs.
3. Search for evidence to answer the question.
4. Critically appraise evidence for
    a. Impact: Does the study demonstrate the intervention of interest addresses issues of concern?
    b. Rigor of study: Can you trust or rely on findings to inform practice?
    c. Applicability: Do study findings apply to your target population and issues of concern?
5. Select and implement intervention: Select the intervention based on available evidence, client values, and practice wisdom. What is the most appropriate plan to implement the intervention selected?
6. Client monitoring, evaluation, and feedback: How much change do we need to know success is achieved?

TABLE 1.1 The Evidence Based Practice Process: Myths and Facts

Myths and Objections	Facts
ESIs are excessively rigid and authoritarian.	The EBP process drives program, policy, and planning decisions, which aids in the accountability in implementation and fidelity of services and increases cost-effectiveness of services.
ESIs are based on studies of clients not typical of social work practice.	The EBP process can use research that is conducted "in the field" of practice settings. Client characteristics and preferences are one aspect of the process.
ESIs are restrictive and highly structured and devalue the professional expertise.	The EBP process helps to promote lifelong learning. Provider expertise is a part of the process.
ESIs ignores client perspectives, values, and preferences.	ESIs use definitions that include not only clinical expertise but client values and preferences as well.
ESIs ignore cultural or social contexts.	The EBP process protects clients by providing comprehensive and explicit tools for making critical practice decisions aligned with clients' culture, values, and preferences.
ESIs are about forcing social workers to select their interventions from lists of empirically supported treatments.	The EBP process is a mutual decision-making process, that takes into account the ethics of the profession, client values, preferences, and characteristics, as well as practitioner and agency context and resources.
ESIs are too mechanistic and too entrenched in positivism.	Part of the EBP process is exploring with clients their views and preferences.
The therapeutic alliance is the single most important factor for change.	Research can inform us about the importance of the therapeutic alliance. Wampold (2015) argues that the therapeutic alliance is crucial, as long as the practitioner is following a structured treatment.
ESIs ignore social justice issues.	The EBP process offers a systematic and critical appraisal process so that marginalized clients obtain services that are relevant and effective versus those that are untested. Interventions to improve access are also researched and can be used in decision-making.

STEPS 1 AND 2: CLIENT ASSESSMENT AND DEVELOPMENT OF WELL-FORMED QUESTIONS

While Gambill (2019, 2006) and other authors (Rubin & Bellamy, 2022; Wike et al., 2014; Wodarski & Hopson, 2012) illustrate how to develop well-formed questions, they do not explain what typically needs to occur beforehand. How do social workers generate the information needed to develop a question? Herein lies the importance of how to conduct a thorough contextual or ecological client assessment in Step 1. To effectively engage in the EBP process, practitioners need solid clinical and assessment skills and the ability to synthesize assessment and research studies (Drisko & Grady, 2019; Grady et al., 2018).

In the case study presented at the beginning of the chapter, the DCFS social worker spent days collecting information from the family and providers across the different systems involved with the family—TANF, homeless shelter, child psychiatrist, school counselor, and teachers. Social workers are trained to conduct ecological assessments, incorporating all the systems at play to identify needs and strengths to capitalize on. We argue that the assessment drives or informs how the practice-based research question is formulated. Your research question must include critical information about client demographics, lived experiences, issues of concern to grapple with, strengths, and intended outcomes. Next, keywords from your question must be included in your subsequent search for evidence. We have found that many students struggle with developing well-formed questions (Step 2), often because they have not acquired a holistic understanding of clients' lived experiences. They may have limited knowledge or experience in (1) conducting assessments that consider context, place, and culture, and (2) interpreting information gathered from assessments to develop well-formed questions. Thus, in Chapter 2 (part of Section I), we will discuss in detail what to include in an assessment.

Based on the assessment, the next step, also covered in Chapter 2, is to develop well-formed practice-relevant research questions. Questions should be clear, well-articulated, researchable, and measurable and should include the following components, as highlighted by Gambrill and Gibbs (2015) and Gambrill (2019):

1. Describe the population (P),
2. Highlight the intervention you are considering to address the issue of concern (I),
3. Compared to another intervention or services as usual (C), and
4. Hoped for outcomes (O).

In Chapter 2, we will cover how to use information gathered from your assessment to develop a PICO question—This process is illustrated below for the case study presented at the beginning of this chapter. You may often not know what intervention (I) to consider. In these cases, your research question may need to articulate a broad question initially and your intervention selections can be refined after you have conducted a literature review search.

Camille identified the population as African-American, fifth to eighth graders, ages 10–15, who have been exposed to a traumatic event, and show symptoms of PTSD and depression. Before selecting the intervention of concern, she conducted a preliminary search using Google Scholar and PsycINFO to determine which interventions are effective in a school setting for school-aged children. She found that cognitive behavioral intervention for trauma in schools (CBITS) and TF-CBT were two effective interventions. CBITS is the intervention of concern and will be compared to TF-CBT. The hoped-for outcomes include decreased trauma-related symptoms and improved strategies for problem-solving, coping and relaxation skills. The question for research is, among middle school-aged children ages 10–15 who have been exposed to trauma and show symptoms of PTSD and depression, is CBITS more effective in reducing trauma-related symptoms and promoting problem-solving, coping, and relaxation skills compared to TF-CBT?

STEP 3: SEARCH FOR EVIDENCE TO ANSWER THE QUESTION

In Step 3, social workers are tasked with "locating research to inform practice questions" (see Chapter 3). While strategies to search for evidence are covered by others (e.g., see Gambrill's [2019] *Critical Thinking and the Process of Evidence-Based Practice*), we will briefly illustrate how to string together the best search words, to ensure all information related to your target population are addressed. We often refer to this stage as the INPUT stage, as the idea here is to gather all the relevant information you can find relevant to your PICO question. In addition to describing a systematic search process for scholarly articles, we will also illustrate in Chapter 3 the process for searching for reliable external sources, such as websites and evidence-based clearinghouses. In reference to Camille's case, some of the search terms she used in Google Scholar and PsychInfo included "trauma interventions and children," "middle school-aged children and exposure to trauma," "CBITS," "evaluation of CBITS," "effectiveness of CBITS and TF-CBT," and "evaluation of CBITS in schools."

STEP 4: CRITICALLY APPRAISE EVIDENCE—PROCESS STAGE

After searching, you may have gathered a variety of different sources from your scholarly research: reviews, theoretical articles, quantitative articles, and qualitative articles in addition to clearinghouse databases and other external resources. How do you begin to PROCESS all the information at your disposal? Step 4 involves "weeding out" the information that is not effective, valid, and applicable. At this stage, many students find it difficult to simultaneously make choices between studies that, for example, show effectiveness but are not applicable for the target population or are not as "rigorous" as other studies. The articles you choose will inform what intervention you select to meet your client's goals. One of our goals is to increase your competence and ability to understand and interpret findings from various methods so that you feel confident in the intervention you decide to implement. For Camille's case, she came across a meta-analysis of 74 studies looking at trauma-related interventions for children exposed to violence (Miller-Graff & Campion, 2016). Most of the studies reviewed by Miller-Graff and Campion (2016) evaluated cognitive behavioral therapy (CBT) treatments, which were "well represented" and showed "medium to large effect sizes" (p. 237). Another meta-analysis specifically looked at the effectiveness of TF-CBT as a treatment for PTSD and depression for children and adolescents (Lenz & Hollenbaugh, 2015). She also found a systematic review of TF-CBT (Cary & McMillen, 2012). While both TF-CBT reviews suggest that TF-CBT is more effective for reducing symptoms of PTSD and depression when compared to either no treatment, such as waitlist, or alternative treatments like standard care, she found very few studies that looked promising for CBITS. For example, a 2003 RCT found that while students assigned to CBITS had significantly lower scores of PTSD and depression than those assigned to a wait-list-delayed intervention comparison group 3 months later, the sample included only Latino students in two large East Los Angeles middle schools (Stein et al., 2003). Another RCT focused solely on students with PTSD symptoms following Hurricane Katrina (Jaycox et al., 2010). One-group post-test studies, again with Latino youth, were then conducted on CBITS (Allison & Ferreira, 2017; Santiago et al., 2015). Examining the RCT studies on TF-CBT, samples included African American youth within Tyrone's age group (e.g., Cohen et al., 2011; Deblinger et al., 1996; Deblinger et al., 1999). Here, it is equally important to consider if the evidence applies to the contexts, circumstances, and sociodemographics of your clients.

Rather than only provide a review of the different types of research design and pros and cons of each design, we will illustrate in Section II (Chapters 4–6) the process for how to disentangle multiple sources of evidence and weigh the evidence with regard to how effective and applicable it is for your clients, and when and under what circumstances to use the evidence in practice. We provide an overview of RCTs (Chapter 4), systematic reviews (Chapter 5), and qualitative research designs (Chapter 6). Each chapter will include case studies, examples, and illustrations of how to use evidence from studies that rely on these designs, underscoring in each step how to critically engage with the EBP process.

STEP 5: SELECT AND IMPLEMENT THE EVIDENCE—OUTPUT STAGE

Now that you have weighed the evidence, it is time to select and implement the intervention and develop a plan to ensure your clients have access to and engage in the intervention. In other words, it is time to OUTPUT the valid, reliable, and practical plan of action. We have found that little attention is devoted to teaching students how to grapple with barriers to implementing the plan of action or intervention (Step 5). While implementation science is a growing field across many disciplines, education and training in MSW graduate programs are either not offered or is limited in scope. As future practitioners, students must learn to identify, grapple with, and address barriers that are likely to prevent them from implementing evidence-informed intervention and service plans. To that end, Chapters 7 and 8, in Section III, focus on implementation. After providing an overview of implementation science in Chapter 7, we draw on recent research studies that shed light on promising strategies to mitigate implementation barriers in Chapter 8. Implementing an ESI requires being aware of the multiple and intersecting contextual factors that impact your ability to follow through with a case plan as intended. Relatedly, in Chapter 8, we delve into what agency leaders need to do to support staff and create the optimal conditions necessary to implement a new ESI.

As for Camille's case, she decided it would be in Tyrone's best interest to refer him to a clinician trained to implement TF-CBT. While she is privy to some of the skills required to deliver TF-CBT, she is not fully trained or certified to deliver the intervention. She reported the findings to her supervisor, who considered hiring a certified clinician to deliver TF-CBT at the charter school. As we move forward, we will present scenarios highlighting even more complexity that would require that would require you to wrestle with what the evidence tells you to do versus what can be implemented ... In other cases, you may find you need to adapt interventions or modify the EBP process to fit the needs and characteristics of the target client system. We grapple with the complexity of adaptation as part of the implementation process in Chapter 9.

STEP 6: MONITOR CLIENT PROGRESS—EVALUATION STAGE

At this stage, you now better understand how to apply research concepts to practice and know strategies to address implementation barriers. As for the final step of the EBP process, covered in Chapter 10, it is your ethical responsibility to determine whether the interventions or approach improve the well-being of our clients. Students are often intimidated by the idea of monitoring their practice (Step 6). In Chapter 10, we offer a brief review of methods (e.g., rapid assessment, individualized rating scales, goal attainment scaling, standardized scales) that could be implemented to monitor and evaluate client progress and guidance on how to select which method would be most rigorous, feasible, and appropriate for the circumstances of your clients. Throughout each step of the process, client preferences, beliefs, and cultural traditions will be equally considered with the "evidence" to produce the intervention that will benefit the client or population in need.

In Camille's case, Tyrone agreed to answer items from the same measures administered to participants in Allison and Ferreira's (2017) CBITs study: the Child Posttraumatic Symptom Scale (CPSS) and the Short Mood and Feelings Questionnaire (SMFQ). At minimum, Camille will administer as an interview the measures at three time points during the 10-week intervention—before he begins treatment, during the fifth session, and at the end of the last session.

CONCLUSION

This introductory chapter has covered the EBP process and its importance for social work, as well as provides an overview of the book. The aim of the book overall is to build student and practitioner knowledge and skills in a scientific, data-driven approach and critical appraisal. The EBP process values these skills and their inter-marriage with practitioner and agency context and client characteristics and preferences.

FOR YOUR PRACTICE

1. What are the steps of the EBP process?
2. What is the difference between the EBP process and ESI?
3. Name one of the critiques of the EBP process and one way to address it.
4. What is one challenge that may come up for you when engaging in the EBP process after graduation, and how would you address it?

NOTE FOR INSTRUCTORS OR PROGRAM DIRECTORS

For most of the proceeding chapters, we include exam questions for students. If you would like to receive an answer key, please contact Antonio Garcia via email at antonio.garcia080818@gmail.com.

REFERENCES

Allison, A. C., & Ferreira, R. J. (2017). Implementing Cognitive Behavioral Intervention for Trauma in Schools (CBITS) with Latino youth. *Child and Adolescent Social Work Journal, 34*(2), 181–189. https://doi.org/10.1007/s10560-016-0486-9

Bertram, R., Chamin, L., Kerns, S., & Long, A. (2015). Evidence-based practices in North American MSW curricula. *Research on Social Work Practice, 25,* 737–748. https://doi.org/10.1177/1049731514532846

California Evidence-Based Clearinghouse (CEBC). (2006–2020). *Overview of the CEBC scientific rating scale.* https://www.cebc4cw.org/files/OverviewOfTheCEBCScientificRatingScale.pdf

Cary, C. E., & McMillen, J. C. (2012). The data behind the dissemination: A systematic review of trauma-focused cognitive behavioral therapy for use with children and youth. *Child and Youth Services Review, 34,* 748–757.

Chambless, D., & Hollon, S. (1998). Defining empirically supported therapies. *Journal of Consulting and Clinical Psychology, 66,* 7–18. https://doi.org/10.1037/0022-006X.66.1.7

Cohen, J. A., Mannarino, A. P., & Iyengar, S. (2011). Community treatment of posttraumatic stress disorder for children exposed to intimate partner violence. *Archives of Pediatrics and Adolescent Medicine, 165*(1), 16–21. https://doi.org/10.1001/archpediatrics.2010.247

Deblinger, E., Lippmann, J., & Steer, R. (1996). Sexually abused children suffering posttraumatic stress symptoms: Initial treatment outcome findings. *Child Maltreatment, 1*(4), 310–321.

Deblinger, E., Steer, R. A., & Lippmann, J. (1999). Two-year follow-up study of cognitive behavioral therapy for sexually abused children suffering from post-traumatic stress symptoms. *Child Abuse and Neglect, 23*(12), 1371–1378. https://doi.org/10.1016/S0145-2134(99)00091-5

Drake, R. E., Goldman, H. H., Leff, H. S., Lehman, A. F., Dixon, L., Mueser, K. T., & Torrey, W. C. (2001). Implementing evidence-based practices in routine mental health service settings. *Psychiatric Services, 52*(2), 179–182. https://doi.org/10.1176/appi.ps.52.2.179

Drisko, J., & Friedman, A. (2019). Let's clearly distinguish evidence-based practice and empirically supported treatments. *Smith College Studies in Social Work, 89*(3-4), 264–281. https://doi.org/10.1080/00377317.2019.1706316

Drisko, J. W., & Grady, M. D. (2019). *Evidence-Based Practice in Clinical Social Work.* Springer.

Gambrill, E. (2006). Evidence-based practice: Choices ahead. *Research on Social Work Practice, 16,* 338–357.

Gambrill, E. (2019). *Critical thinking and the process of evidence-based practice.* Oxford University Press.

Gambrill, E., & Gibbs, L. (2015). Developing well-structured questions for evidence-informed practice. In K. Corcoran & A. Roberts (Eds.), *Social workers' desk reference* (3rd ed.). Oxford University Press.

Grady, M. D., Wike, T., Putzu, C., Field, S., Hill, J., Bledsoe, S. E., Bellamy, J., & Massey, M. (2018). Recent social work practitioners' understanding and use of evidence-based practice and empirically supported treatments. *Journal of Social Work Education, 54*(1), 163–179. https://doi.org/10.1080/10437797.2017.1299063

Jaycox, L. H., Cohen, J. A., Mannarino, A. P., Walker, D. W., Langley, A. K., Gegenheimer, K. L., . . . Schonlau, M. (2010). Children's mental health care following Hurricane Katrina: A field trial of trauma-focused psychotherapies. *Journal of Traumatic Stress, 23*(2), 223–231. https://doi.org/10.1002/jts.20518

Lenz, A. S., & Hollenbaugh, K. M. (2015). Meta-analysis of trauma-focused cognitive behavioral therapy for treating PTSD and co-occurring depression among children and adolescents. *Counseling Outcome Research and Evaluation, 6*(1), 18–32.

Miller-Graff, L. E., & Campion, K. (2016). Interventions for posttraumatic stress with children exposed to violence: Factors associated with treatment success. *Journal of Clinical Psychology, 72*, 226–248.

Mykhalovskiy, E., & Weir, L. (2004). The problem of evidence-based medicine: Directions for social science. *Social Science and Medicine, 59*(5), 1059–1069. https://doi.org/10.1016/j.socscimed.2003.12.002

Oh, H., Poola, C., Messing, J., Ferguson, K., & Bonifas, R. (2020). Correlates of attitudes toward evidence-based practice among MSW students preparing for direct practice. *Journal of Social Work Education, 57*(7), 1–13. https://doi.org/10.1080/10437797.2020.1714521.

National Association of Social Workers. (2023). https://www.socialworkers.org/News/Research-Data/Social-Work-Policy-Research/Evidence-Based-Practice.

Parrish, D. E. (2018). Evidence-based practice: A common definition matters. *Journal of Social Work Education, 54*(3), 407–411.

Rubin, A., & Bellamy, J. (2022). *Practitioner's guide to using evidence based practice* (3rd. ed.). Wiley.

Santiago, C. D., Kataoka, S. H., Hu-Cordova, M., Alvarado-Goldberg, K., Maher, L. M., & Escudero, P. (2015). Preliminary evaluation of a family treatment component to augment a school-based intervention serving low-income families. *Journal of Emotional and Behavioral Disorders, 23*, 28–39. https://doi.org/10.1177/1063426613503497

Scurlock-Evans, L., & Upton, D. (2015). The role and nature of evidence: A systematic review of social workers' evidence-based practice orientation, attitudes, and implementation. *Journal of Evidence-Informed Social Work, 12*, 369–399.

Stein, B. D., Jaycox, L. H., Kataoka, S. H., Wong, M., Tu, W., Elliott, M. N., & Fink, A. (2003). A mental health intervention for schoolchildren exposed to violence: A randomized controlled trial. *Journal of the American Medical Association, 290*(5), 603–611. https://doi.org/10.1001/jama.290.5.603

Wampold B. E. (2015). How important are the common factors in psychotherapy? An update. *World psychiatry: official journal of the World Psychiatric Association (WPA), 14*(3), 270–277. https://doi.org/10.1002/wps.20238

Wike, T. L., Bledsoe, S. E., Manuel, J. I., Despard, M., Johnson, L. V., Bellamy, J. L., & Killian-Farrell, C. (2014). Evidence-based practice in social work: Challenges and opportunities for clinicians and organizations. *Clinical Social Work Journal, 42*(2), 161–170. https://doi.org/10.1007/s10615-014-0492-3

Wodarski, J., & Hopson, L. (2012). *Research methods for evidence based practice.* Sage.

CHAPTER 2

CLIENT ASSESSMENT AND THE DEVELOPMENT OF PICO QUESTIONS

Lucas, an 8-year-old, white male, came into foster care 18 months ago. His older brother, who is now 10 years old, disclosed that he had been sexually victimized by his and Lucas's father. Lucas and his two other siblings denied experiencing or witnessing sexual or physical abuse. At the time of the disclosure, his mother did not believe the abuse had occurred and refused to have her husband leave the home. As a result, Lucas and his siblings were removed from the home and placed in separate foster care homes about 25 miles apart.

Lucas quickly became attached to his foster mother, a single woman with no other children in the home. He began weekly individual therapy (nondirective play therapy), had mentoring services, and started having weekly supervised visits with his biological family. During the visits, Lucas hid underneath the table and often became oppositional with his mother. When she asked him to do something, he would respond "no" or dismiss what she said; at times, he wouldn't talk at all. After visits with his family, his foster mother reported "tearful" episodes. Other times, Lucas would act angrily—pinching the family dog and breaking his toys. However, he would recover within a few hours after being with his foster mother again.

After Lucas's father was incarcerated for the sexual abuse, Lucas's mother moved into a one-bedroom apartment and started working 50 hours a week at a local restaurant. When asked why she wasn't following through on the Child Protective Services treatment plan to regain custody of her children, which entailed individual therapy for herself and family therapy, she said, "I have to work if I'm going to support my kids. I can't get a bigger place that'll fit all of us without making some money first." About 6 months into the placement, Lucas became clingy with his foster mother. He constantly asked where she was going and what time she would return. He started having unrealistic fears. He was terrified of thunder and lightning and scared of the dark; he often hid under his covers or bed at night. Although his appetite was normal, he complained of stomachaches before bedtime and had difficulty concentrating on school assignments or chores at home. The foster mother reported that she was concerned about his excessive worrying and fears. At this time, she began relaxation techniques with him at bedtime.

After 1 year, Lucas's biological mother had made little progress with her goals and was granted a 6-month extension to achieve these goals. At the 6-month point, however, she voluntarily gave up her parental rights. At this time, a year after the onset of his symptoms, Lucas still experienced fears and worries, especially those revolving around his foster mother. He told his daycare staff, case manager, and teacher that he was "scared she will be in a car wreck or something would happen to her" when he went to school. Lucas still had visits with his biological mother; however, they were less frequent due to her lack of consistency and his adverse reactions afterward. During visits, she would tell him she wants him back and will fight for him. Lucas talks little about his family to his foster mother, caseworker, or therapist. He reports being "happy in his foster home" and wants to know why it takes so long for his adoption. Despite his lack of focus at times due to his worry, he is still able to maintain a B average. He has some friends with whom he plays at school and daycare; however, he does not refer to them when he is not with them. Lucas recently underwent a physical examination and was found to be a healthy 8-year-old boy.[1]

The topic of this chapter is client assessment, which we argue is the first step of the evidence-based practice (EBP) process and leads to the development of PICO questions, which are also covered in this chapter. Before Step One (developing well-formed questions), holistic information must be gathered on client strengths and needs as well as context, place, and culture and then interpreted and synthesized to develop goals. From there, EBP process questions can be posed on *how* to best meet these goals.

We recognize there are many ways to approach assessment. See Franklin and Jordan (2020) for an entire volume focused on clinical assessment tools and Thomlison (2015) for family assessment. Assessment also depends on the theoretical lens being applied. Additionally, agencies have their own assessment and intake forms, depending on the agency's purpose, the clientele served, and the social worker's role at the setting. In this chapter, we discuss two main approaches for assessment: the *Diagnostic and Statistical Manual of Mental Disorders* (DSM) and the risk and resilience biopsychosocial-spiritual framework. We go from the processes of gathering assessment data and beginning to formulate goals as a way to inform PICO questions. We focus mainly on questions involving interventions but also explore others that may be relevant, using the case of Lucas to illustrate the material.

THE DSM

The *Diagnostic and Statistical Manual of Mental Disorders* (DSM), published by the American Psychiatric Association (APA), is the preeminent diagnostic classification system among clinical practitioners in the United States. The DSM, which catalogs, codes, and describes

---

1. Case drawn from Corcoran (2011).

various mental disorders, was first published in 1952 and has undergone continual revisions during the past 50 years. The latest version is DSM 5, published in 2013 (APA, 2022). The DSM represents a medical perspective, only one of many possible perspectives on human behavior. Much of the terminology from the DSM has been adopted by mental health professionals from all fields as a common language with which to discuss disorders.

The definition of "mental disorder" used by the American Psychiatric Association (2022) is a syndrome related to a clinically significant disturbance in a person's thinking, emotional regulation, or behavior that reflects an underlying mental functioning dysfunction having to do with psychological, biological, or developmental factors. This medical definition used in the DSM-5 TR focuses on underlying disturbances within the person and is sometimes referred to as the *disease model* of abnormality. This implies that the abnormal person must experience changes within the self (rather than environmental change) to be considered normal or healthy again.

The challenge is teaching social workers competence and critical thinking in the diagnostic process, while also considering diagnosis in a way consistent with social work values and principles. These values include a strengths-based orientation, concern for the worth and dignity of individuals, and an appreciation for the environmental context of individual behavior.

The DSM classification system is a product of the psychiatric profession and does not fully represent the knowledge base or values of the social work profession (see Corcoran & Walsh, 2022, for a discussion of critiques). Still, it is extensively used by social workers (and many other human service professionals) nationwide for the following reasons (Kirk, et al., 2017): reimbursement of services from third-party payers, so social workers can claim expertise similar to that of the other professions and can converse in a common language about disorders. Recall from Chapter 1 that the EBP process first caught on in medicine. Therefore, clinical disorders as problems identified from the assessment fit very well in a medicalized profession that is primarily defined in terms of disorders. However, that does not mean that the DSM-defined disorders are the only issues that social workers can grapple with using the EBP process. Some of these include symptoms that may not meet DSM criteria though they impact well-being, exposure to trauma and violence, adverse educational outcomes, unemployment, lack of access to services, and agencies that are not optimized to implement the EBP process for diverse populations. We will elaborate on a number of examples of these in the coming chapters.

Considering the case at the start of the chapter, the following DSM diagnoses were given to Lucas (Corcoran, 2011):

Z65.3: Problems related to other legal circumstances:
   His custody is with child protective services, and he is in the middle of a legal process where hopefully, he will be adopted by his foster mother.

309.81 (F43.10): Posttraumatic Stress Disorder
   Criterion A is exposure to trauma: Lucas learned that his father had sexually abused his brother, as well as was separated from his family due to safety concerns by child protective services and placed into foster care.

> *Criterion B: Marked psychological reactions to internal or external cues that symbolize or resemble an aspect of the traumatic events:*
>
> The cue seems to be his foster mother leaving, which may resemble the abandonment Lucas experienced. Lucas experiences intense fear that something terrible will happen to his foster mother and she won't return.
>
> *Criterion C: Persistent avoidance of cues and memories:*
>
> A symptom that infers avoidance is when he hides from his biological mother during visits.
>
> He also seems to avoid discussing his family with his foster mother, caseworker, or therapist.
>
> *Criterion D: Negative alterations in cognitions and mood associated with the traumatic event(s), beginning or worsening after the traumatic event(s) occurred, as evidenced by two (or more) of the following:*
>
> 1) Persistent and exaggerated negative beliefs or expectations about oneself, others, or the world: "Something bad is going to happen to my foster mother" (e.g., the world is dangerous)
>
> 2) Persistent negative emotion state: fear
>
> *Criteria E is marked alterations in arousal and reactivity associated with the traumatic event(s), beginning or worsening after the traumatic event(s) occurred, as evidenced by two (or more) of the following:*
>
> The foster mother reports that he has difficulty concentrating on school and chore tasks.
>
> He has irritable or angry outbursts, which he exhibits after visits with biological mother.

BIOPSYCHOSOCIAL-SPIRITUAL ASSESSMENT

While social workers may be required to rely on the DSM, we encourage using other assessment tools that, when used in conjunction with the DSM, will unveil a more holistic understanding the of clients' strengths and issues of concern, and the underlying causes and circumstances of those concerns. Indeed, the social work profession is distinguished by its holistic attention to the biological, psychological, and social influences on people's functioning, and a biopsychosocial-spiritual assessment is widely used in social work agency settings. There are a number of specific questions/items that are addressed under each of the factors, depending on the purpose of the agency and the role of the social worker. For example, an agency that specializes in housing will attend to clients' resources and supports and not delve heavily into the biological realm except where it may affect the goal of housing, such as a chronic medical condition that handicaps the person from regular employment or that requires a certain housing situation.

We tout a universal assessment involving a risk and resilience perspective on the biopsychosocial-spiritual domains of functioning. "Risk and resilience" considers the balance of risk and protective processes at the biological, psychological, and social levels that interact to determine an individual's propensity toward *resilience*, or the ability to function adaptively and achieve positive outcomes despite stressful life events. The "strengths" perspective underlies the concept of "resilience," or the skills, abilities, knowledge, and insight that people accumulate over time as they struggle to surmount adversity and meet life challenges. It refers to clients' ability to persist despite their difficulties (Saleeby, 2012).

On the other hand, risks can be understood as hazards or problems at the biological, psychological, or social levels that may lead to poor adaptation (Bogenschneider, 1996). *Protective factors* may counterbalance or buffer the individual against risk (Pollard et al., 1999; Werner, 2000), promoting successful adjustment in the face of risk (Dekovic, 1999). Risk and protective factors are sometimes the converse of each other. For instance, at the individual level, a difficult temperament is a risk factor, and an easy temperament is a protective factor. Indeed, researchers have found many pairs of risk and protective factors that are negatively correlated with each other (Jessor et al., 1997).

The biopsychosocial emphasis expands the focus beyond the individual to recognizing systemic factors that can create and ameliorate problems. The nature of systems is that the factors within and between them influence each other. For instance, a particular risk or protective factor may increase the likelihood of additional risk and protective factors. Wachs (2000) provides the example of how an aversive parenting style with poor monitoring increases children's risk for socializing with deviant peers. If parents are overwhelmed by many environmental stressors, such as unemployment, lack of transportation and medical care, and living in an unsafe neighborhood, their ability to provide consistent warmth and nurturance may be compromised. This phenomenon also operates for protective factors. For example, adolescents whose parents provide emotional support and structure the environment with consistent rules and monitoring tend to group with peers with similar family backgrounds. Supportive parenting will, in turn, affect individual development in which a child learns to regulate emotional processes and display cognitive and social competence (Wachs, 2000). Systemic influences also play themselves out from the perspective of a child's characteristics. A child with resilient qualities, such as social skills, effective coping strategies, intelligence, and self-esteem, is more likely to attract high-quality caregiving, and attachment patterns formed in infancy tend to persist into other relationships across the life span.

Although precise mechanisms of action are not specified, data have begun to accumulate about the number of risk factors that are required to overwhelm a system and result in adverse outcomes (e.g., Fraser et al., 1999; Kalil & Kunz, 1999). The cumulative results of different studies seem to indicate that four or more risk factors represent a threat to adaptation (Epps & Jackson, 2000; Frick, 2006; Runyan et al., 1998; Rutter et al., 1979). However, risk does not proceed in a linear fashion, and all risk factors are not weighted equally (Greenberg et al., 2001). Risk and protective factors play a role in multiple types of problems. In a prevention and intervention sense, these common risk factors occurring across multiple domains can be assessed as targets for reduction or amelioration, and these protective factors are good targets for enhancement (Corcoran & Nichols-Casebolt, 2004). See Table 2.1. Table 2.2 is a risk and resilience assessment for the case of "Lucas."

Social workers' knowledge of risk and resilience influences helps focus attention on relevant areas of the client's life and keeps a systemic and strengths-based perspective.

TABLE 2.1 Risk and Resilience Biopsychosocial-Spiritual Assessment

Factor	Risk	Protective
Biological		
Genes and Heritability • Not generally known, since family environment interacts with genetic predispositions and a genetic vulnerability may be activated by adverse environmental events		
Temperament • provides the foundation for personality, involving qualities that are biologically driven, observed from infancy, and moderately stable across the life span • involves activity level, intensity, attention span, quality of mood, adaptability, flexibility, and rhythmicity	Irritability Risk-taking (for conduct disorder)	Behavior inhibition (for conduct disorder but risk for anxiety)
Physical Health • includes prenatal health	Medical problems Pregnancy and birth complications	Good physical health Regular prenatal care
Developmental Stage	Adolescence for depression in females Young adulthood for onset of mental disorders	Personality disorders may recover in middle age
Psychological		
IQ	Low IQ Learning disorders	Average or high IQ Absence of learning disorders
Self-Efficacy and Self-Esteem	Low self-esteem and efficacy	High self-esteem and efficacy
Self-Regulation and Emotion Regulation	Dysregulation	Ability to regulate
Coping Strategies	Avoidance, including substance use Rumination	Problem-solving Ability to identify and express feelings Seek social support
Spiritual	Lack of meaning	Religious involvement Beliefs that provide meaning Mindfulness and other spiritual practices
Social		
Family	Poor attachment bonds Lack of supervision and monitoring Harsh or inconsistent parenting Two-parent family Isolation of nuclear family	Secure attachment Supervision and monitoring Warm, consistent, authoritative parenting Single-parent household Extended family involvement

TABLE 2.1 Continued

Factor	Risk	Protective
Traumatic and Stressful Life Events, Loss	Frequent moving Abuse Loss Stressful life events Intimate partner violence	Stability Safety
Neighborhood	Unsafe Availability of alcohol outlets and drug dealing Segregated Crowding Lack of organized community activities	Safe Spacious Caring neighbors Integrated Community activities
Ethnicity and Culture	Ethnic minority risk for discrimination, segregation, health disparities, etc.	Culture can be source of identity and support
Sexual Identification and Orientation	LGBTQ at risk for anxiety, depression, suicidality, bullying, violence	Straight, cis-gender
Welfare, Tax Policies, and Legal Sanctions	Current US safety net inadequate	Safety nets can meet some basic needs Child support laws Earned income tax credits
Social Class	Poverty	Mid- to- higher SES

Source: Corcoran and Nichols-Casebolt (2004); Corcoran and Walsh (2019)

TABLE 2.2 Risk and Resilience Assessment for "Lucas"

Biopsychosocial Risk and Resilience Influences Applied to Case of "Lucas"

Risk Influences
Biological
Criminality on paternal side (sexual abuse of child)

Psychological
Anxiety

Social
Family separation
Foster care transition
Brother's sexual abuse
No permanency plan as of yet

Protective Influences
Biological
Physically healthy

Psychological

Social
Relationship with siblings
Good relationship with foster mother
Supportive teachers and daycare
Academically on par

Knowledge gained from such an assessment will inform the PICO question and provide a balanced, holistic appraisal of the client situation.

FORMULATING GOALS FROM ASSESSMENT

One of the critical purposes of assessment is to formulate goals for intervention, although specific goals may also emerge after we find a research-supported intervention, which may guide goals. For instance, if family systems therapy is indicated for a certain child problem, the plan would be to improve parents' ability to work together in the session to change the family's habitual way of responding. Symptom relief, the child's behavior, per se, is not the goal; it is seen as a byproduct (Nichols & Davis, 2020).

Social workers are also interested in providing intervention at the appropriate system level, particularly if a number of agency clients are afflicted. For instance, a school social worker tasked with talking to students individually after in-school suspensions (which are overrepresented among Black youth and those with disabilities) may formulate a practice-based question on how to prevent such incidences. If answers have to do with schoolwide intervention, such as training teachers in skills that may de-escalate child problem behavior, then the involvement of school administration and staff would be necessary, rather than working with the individual child one-by-one.

In the case of Lucas, a foremost goal is to work on adoption rather than an approach that might medicalize his anxiety. When we operate solely along the lines of the DSM system, we are interested in what is the best treatment for reducing Lucas's PTSD symptoms, whereas the social work perspective is that symptoms often arise out of a situation that needs change, and we should address the risks at that level.

FORMULATING PICO QUESTIONS

Once an assessment has been conducted and you have identified both problems and strengths, how will you address the areas of concern and goals you've identified? What interventions will be effective? You are now ready to formulate a PICO question so that you can initiate the EBP process and discover the answer you are seeking to help a particular client or clientele. The acronym PICO is described and detailed in Table 2.3. Inspired by Gambrill (2020), we expand on the formulation of PICO questions in this chapter, offering examples and activities to solidify your learning.

TABLE 2.3 **PICO Question Guide**

Population of Clients	Describe your target **population** and its key elements: • Age • Gender • Race/Ethnicity • Socioeconomic status • Diagnoses (mental health and/or medical) • Issue of concern
Intervention of Concern	What **intervention** are you considering?
Compared to What	Are you going to **compare** this intervention to another? • Alternative intervention • Treatment as usual • No comparison (why?)
Outcomes	What is the desired **outcome**? • When deciding on an outcome, it should be specific, definable, and measurable.
Type of Studies	Randomized control designs, systematic reviews of intervention studies

DEFINING PICO

First, we define the elements of the PICO as applied to the case of Lucas:[2]

- Describe population of clients (P): children in the foster care system long-term and suffer from anxiety and/or PTSD.
- Intervention of concern (I): *intervention for anxiety and PTSD from maltreatment and being separated from family; permanency planning policies that reduce anxiety/PTSD*
- Compared to what (C): *the intern didn't have a particular comparison in mind; she might be interested in "compared to child welfare casework as usual."*
- Hoped-for outcomes (O): *reduction in anxiety symptoms and posttraumatic stress; permanency planning.*
- Type of studies (T): *RCTs, systematic reviews of RCTs/quasi-experimental.*

The typical practice-based question involves finding an effective intervention, but other kinds of PICO questions that are relevant to agency practice are listed and defined with examples in Table 2.4.

[2]. We use the common parlance "PICO question," although we add a "T" so we can be explicit about the type of research studies that will answer the particular question in mind.

TABLE 2.4 Other Types of PICO Questions

Types of PICO Questions	Definition	Example
Prevalence	How many people at a local, state-wide, national, or international level, suffer from the problem that plagues your client(s)? This question is particularly useful at the needs assessment and program planning stage.	With the case of Lucas, a prevalence question might be, *how many children have been in foster care for over two years? How many children in foster care suffer from anxiety and/or PTSD?*
Prediction/Correlational	What factors contribute to a problem?	*What are the risk factors for anxiety and PTSD developing in children living in foster care?*
Measurement	What is the best (feasible, economical, reliable, and/or valid) instrument to screen, assess, or evaluate a particular problem.	*What is the most accurate instrument to assess change in trauma and anxiety over time in children in foster care?*
Lived Experience	What are the needs, experiences, and perceptions of the people suffering from the problem or experiencing the phenomenon of interest?	*According to youth and foster parents, what is the impact of permanency policies on children and families? How do foster parents describe how they manage their children's anxiety and PTSD symptoms?*
Cost-Effectiveness	Seek to understand the costs of a certain program or intervention and the savings that are realized from its implementation. Cost-effectiveness research involves an economic analysis to determine if the program is worth implementing.	*How much does it cost to keep children in long-term foster care? What are the costs associated with permanency planning options?*

CONCLUSION

We have covered assessment, a critical stage of the helping process, because we want to emphasize how the EBP arises naturally from assessment. During assessment, social workers synthesize various data—observation, client report, collateral reports, clinical impressions, the case record, standardized assessment, supervisor input, and agency expertise—to understand the presenting problem and pinpoint some general goals for action. The process of synthesis involves the same discernment used to decide how to weigh the evidence to answer your practice question.

At the point in the helping process of the culmination of assessment, goal-setting, and intervention planning, the EBP process is activated to answer the question of *how*: given that we have identified a particular problem in assessment, *how* will we address it, informed by the available research knowledge base?

This chapter has reviewed two assessment approaches: (1) clinical diagnosis per the DSM due to its ubiquitous placement in US mental health services; and (2) the biopsychosocial risk and resilience model due to its ability to capture environmental influence and strengths/resources, as well as problems and risk. Another primary source of assessment information is offered through the use of standardized scales. We discuss them in Chapter 10 to evaluate client progress, but the reader should also understand how these tools can be used as an evidence-based way to screen and assess client problems.

At the end of the chapter, we discussed the variety of PICO questions that can be asked in social work practice and illustrated these with a case, recognizing that intervention questions are the most common (also see additional practice with PICO questions in Chapter 11). We encourage you to practice formulating questions from client assessment in the activities presented at the end of the chapter.

FOR YOUR PRACTICE

ACTIVITY #1:

What are the advantages and disadvantages of using the DSM perspective with Lucas?

ACTIVITY #2:

What are the advantages and disadvantages of using the risk and resilience biopsychosocial framework for assessment with Lucas?

ACTIVITY #3:

Directions: The table below is a blank form that you can use for examining risk and protective factors in your clients. A goal section has been added as a column if the formulation lends itself for avenues to pursue intervention. Conduct an assessment of a client case using this framework. What are its advantages and disadvantages when you apply it to a case? What is a PICO question that emerges from this assessment?

ACTIVITY #4:

Consider another assessment system you have been taught in your social work program. What are the advantages and disadvantages compared to the ones that have been presented here?

Template for Biopsychosocial-Spiritual Risk and Resilience Assessment and Goal-Setting

Factor	Risk	Protective	Possible Goals
Biological			
Genes and Heritability			
Temperament			
Physical Health			
Developmental Stage			
Other			
Psychological			
IQ			
Self-Efficacy and Self-Esteem			
Self-Regulation and Emotion Regulation			
Coping Strategies			
Other			
Spiritual			
Social			
Family			
Traumatic and Stressful Life Events, Loss			
Neighborhood			
Ethnicity and Culture			
Sexual Identification and Orientation			
Welfare, Tax Policies, and Legal Sanctions			
SES			
Other			

ACTIVITY #5:

Examine your agency intake form in light of information from this chapter. What are the advantages and disadvantages of using the agency intake form? Does it delve into client strengths? Could it lead to goals that can be rephrased into PICO questions?

ACTIVITY #6:

Identify the following types of PICO questions from this list:

- intervention
- prevalence
- measurement
- the lived experience
- prediction/correlational
- cost-effectiveness

   a. Do adolescents with greater family involvement in an intensive outpatient dual diagnosis treatment program have better outcomes on relapse prevention than adolescents whose families are not involved in their treatment process?
   b. Which treatment is more effective in reducing PTSD symptoms in adolescents with complex trauma who have no supportive caregiver: trauma focused-cognitive behavior treatment (TF-CBT) or eye movement desensitization and reprocessing (EMDR)?
   c. What are the needs and experiences of pregnant, low-income women with intimate partner violence?
   d. What is the prevalence of anxiety in patients with cancer undergoing radiotherapy?
   e. What assessment tools would help social workers in the emergency room working in pediatrics screen for mental health and substance use problems?

ACTIVITY #7:

For your area of interest, complete hypothetical PICOs for the following:

• Prevalence
• Measurement
• Lived experience
• Prediction/correlational
• Cost-effectiveness

ACTIVITY #8:

Multiple Choice Questions

1. A student is interested in how to engage Black parents in their elementary children's day treatment to attend family sessions because attendance at parent contacts is low. Most of the children have been diagnosed with ADHD, along with other diagnoses. Which of the following PICO questions addresses this topic of interest?
   A. How does a day treatment facility engage parents who are Black to attend parent sessions when their elementary-age children are in treatment services?
   B. What is the lived experience of Black parents whose children are diagnosed with ADHD?

Assessment and the PICO Questions • 27

C. What is the level of attendance and treatment completion in Black families who are referred for treatment for ADHD?
   D. What instruments should a day treatment program use to assess stressors and barriers to attending parent sessions for Black parents?
   E. These are all potential PICO questions to address this topic.
2. What type of PICO question is this: What is an effective psychosocial treatment for elementary-age children diagnosed with ADHD and have trauma histories in day treatment?
   A. Intervention
   B. Prevalence
   C. Measurement
   D. Cost-Effectiveness

ACTIVITY #9:

Translating Agency Needs into Answerable Questions

Interview your field instructor, executive director, or other person involved in the administration of your agency and find out the types of answers they would like to know about the clientele being served. Because they likely have not been taught to formulate PICO questions, translate their issues of concern into PICO questions.	
Issues of Concern	PICO questions

REFERENCES

American Psychiatric Association. (2022). *Diagnostic and statistical manual of mental disorders* (5th edition, text revision [DSM-V-TR]). APA.

Bogenschneider, K. (1996). An ecological risk/protective theory for building prevention programs, policies, and community capacity to support youth. *Family Relations: Journal of Applied Family and Child Studies*, 45, 127–138.

Corcoran, J. (2011). *Mental health treatment for children and adolescents.* Oxford University Press.

Corcoran, J., & Nichols-Casebolt, A. (2004). Risk and resilience ecological framework for assessment and goal formulation. *Child and Adolescent Social Work Journal*, 21(3), 211–235.

Corcoran, J., & Walsh, J. (2019). *Mental health in social work: A casebook on diagnosis and strengths-based assessment* (3rd ed.). Allyn & Bacon.

Corcoran, J., & Walsh, J. (2022). *Clinical assessment and diagnosis in social work practice* (4th ed.). Oxford University Press.

Deković, M. (1999). Risk and protective factors in the development of problem behavior during adolescence. *Journal of Youth and Adolescence, 28*(6), 667–685.

Epps, S., & Jackson, B. (2000). *Empowered families, successful children*. American Psychiatric Publishing.

Franklin, C., & Jordan, C. (2020). *Clinical assessment for social workers: Quantitative and qualitative methods* (5th ed.). Oxford University Press.

Fraser, M. W., Galinsky, M. J., & Richman, J. M. (1999). Risk, protection, and resilience: Toward a conceptual framework for social work practice. *Social Work Research, 23*(3), 131–143.

Frick, P. J. (2006). Developmental pathways to conduct disorder. *Child and Adolescent Psychiatric Clinics of North America, 15,* 311–331.

Gambrill, E. (2020). Posing well-structured questions for evidence-informed practice: Step 1. In L. Rapp-McCall, K. Corcoran, & A. Roberts (Eds.), *Social workers' desk reference* (4th ed., pp. 701–709). Oxford University Press.

Greenberg, M., Speltz, M., DeKlyen, M., & Jones, K. (2001). Correlates of clinic referral for early conduct problems: Variable-and person-oriented approaches. *Development and Psychopathology, 13*(2), 255–276.

Jessor, R., Van Den Bos, J., Vanderryn, J., Costa, F. M., & Turbin, M. S. (1997). Protective factors in adolescent problem behavior: Moderator effects and developmental change. In G. A. Marlatt & G. R. Van Den Bos (Eds.), *Addictive behaviors: Readings on etiology, prevention, and treatment* (pp. 239–264). American Psychological Association.

Kalil, A., & Kunz, J. (1999). First births among unmarried adolescent girls: Risk and protective factors. *Social Work Research, 23*(3), 197–208.

Kirk, S., Gomoroy, T., & Cohen, D. (2017). *Mad science: Psychiatric coercion, diagnosis, and drugs*. Routledge.

Nichols, M. P., & Davis, S. D. (2020). *Family therapy: Methods and concepts* (12th ed.). Pearson.

Pollard, J. A., Hawkins, J. D., & Arthur, M. W. (1999). Risk and protection: Are both necessary to understand diverse behavioral outcomes in adolescence? *Social Work Research, 23*(3), 145–158.

Runyan, D. K., Hunter, W. M., Socolar, R. R., Amaya-Jackson, L., English, D., Landsverk, J., Dubowitz, H., Browne, D. H., Bangdiwala, S. I., & Mathew, R. M. (1998). Children who prosper in unfavorable environments: The relationship to social capital. *Pediatrics, 101*(1 Pt 1), 12–18. https://doi.org/10.1542/peds.101.1.12

Rutter, M., Maughan, B., Mortimore, P., Ouston, J., & Smith, A. (1979). *Fifteen thousand hours: Secondary schools and their effects on children*. Harvard University Press.

Saleeby, D. (2012). *The strengths perspective in social work practice* (6th ed.). Pearson.

Thomlison, B. (2015). *Family assessment handbook: An introductory practice guide to family assessment* (4th ed.). Cengage.

Wachs, T. (2000). *Necessary but not sufficient*. American Psychological Association.

Werner, E. (2000). Protective factors and individual resilience. In J. Shonoff & S. Meisels (Eds.), *Handbook of early childhood intervention* (2nd ed., pp. 115–133). Cambridge University Press.

CHAPTER 3

LOCATING RESEARCH TO INFORM PRACTICE QUESTIONS

With Sherry Morgan

> *A second-year field student was placed in a community outpatient mental health clinic serving primarily low-income people of color. The student was seeing youth and their families and was finding that anxiety among youth was a common presenting problem. At intake, clients met with a psychiatrist and intake specialist and were assigned to a therapist; however, the waitlist was over 3 months for an appointment. There was no limit to the number of sessions a client could receive, but the treatment plan was updated every 15 sessions/4 months. At every treatment plan update, the same scales and measures were again given to assess treatment progress. The student developed a PICO question: What is an effective intervention for low-income youth of color aged 8–17 receiving treatment for anxiety in an outpatient mental health setting?*

Now that we have provided an overview of how to develop PICO questions, the next logical question is how you might locate and access the research to answer the question. This chapter covers fundamental information about the technical aspects of finding studies and databases that will answer your practice-based questions. We start with library databases and then get into evidence-based repositories, using the case above as an example.

SEARCHING LIBRARY DATABASES

In this section, we discuss the main library databases available, focusing mainly on PubMed, as that might provide the most accessibility to published journal articles when you're a practicing social worker. We cover how to conceptualize search terms, formulate search strings that are applied to the databases, and track and organize the search.

DATABASES AVAILABLE

Since social work is an interdisciplinary field, a variety of electronic databases are potentially useful for your search, depending on your topic. PubMed is the premier health sciences database produced by the National Library of Medicine, which is part of the National Institutes of Health. PubMed will be helpful if you have a practice question that involves a medical or mental health topic. While you can read titles and abstracts, you will only be able to obtain access to some articles. An occasional free full-text option is on the site, and a Google search may also turn up some full-text options. Additionally, you can reach out directly to the author and express interest in his or her work and request a specific article.

The following are other databases that may be useful in your search for studies:

Cumulative Index to Nursing and Allied Health Literature (CINAHL): nursing
PsycINFO (Psychological Abstracts): psychology
Sociological/Social Services (Social Work) Abstracts: social work, human services, and related areas, including social welfare, social policy, and community development, and other related journals on a variety of social work topics
Digital Dissertations/Dissertation Abstracts Online: Dissertations and some theses
ERIC (Educational Resources Information Center): Education

You will only use some of the databases listed here. In fact, you may include others relevant to your topic. For instance, if your PICO involves older adults, you would likely include Age Line.

CONCEPTUALIZING SEARCH TERMS

When conceptualizing search terms, the student should know that each database has its own vocabulary for subject or thesaurus terms. In PubMed/Medline, this vocabulary is called *Mesh Terms* or Medical Subject Headings. Let's say a student in a school setting with pregnant and parenting teens wants to see what studies have been done on preventing repeat childbearing related to her PICO question, *What are the school-based services that can prevent pregnancy in teens that are parents*? Here are official Mesh Terms gathered from PubMed that represent the concept "teen pregnancy" aligned with the *Participant's* aspect of the PICO question.

"Pregnancy in Adolescence"[Mesh]; "Adolescent Fathers"[Mesh]; "Adolescent Mothers"[Mesh]

> "Pregnancy/prevention and control"[Mesh]; "Contraception"[Mesh]; "Contraceptive Agents"[Mesh]

Once you have identified the controlled vocabulary terms representing each PICO concept, brainstorm and collect as many synonyms or related terms as possible. In the example, for participants, the keywords to consider are: *teenage/adolescent parents*; *teen/adolescent pregnancy*, and *teen/adolescent childbearing*. Synonyms for pregnancy prevention with teen parents are: *secondary pregnancy prevention*; *contraception*; *contraceptive*; *birth control*; and *family planning*. Intervention research can also be called *treatment outcome research*, or *controlled research*, such as *RCTs (Randomized Controlled Trials)*. Other terms for the outcome are *repeat* or *subsequent childbearing*. With the teen pregnancy concept, you can combine both these official and unofficial keywords using the Boolean connector "OR":

> "Contraception"[Mesh] OR "Contraceptive Agents"[Mesh] OR "Pregnancy/prevention and control"[Mesh] OR "Pregnancy prevention" OR contraception OR contraceptive OR "birth control" OR "family planning"

FORMULATING SEARCH STRINGS

Each database has its system for formulating search strings in which terms and keyword phrases are combined. A commonality is their reliance on Boolean logic, which sets up the relationships between keywords and concepts. The most commonly used are: AND, OR, and NOT. The AND connector narrows the domain.

The Boolean connector "OR" broadens to collect a comprehensive list of citations. You can put together all the keywords/phrases of a particular aspect of PICO together, such as participants, using OR. For instance, in the example above, you would put teen* OR adolescen* together since you're interested in this age group. The entire string together may comprise the following:

> ("teenage parents" OR "adolescent parents" OR "teen pregnancy" OR "adolescent pregnancy" OR "teen childbearing" OR "adolescent childbearing" OR "Pregnancy in Adolescence"[Mesh] OR "Adolescent Fathers"[Mesh] OR "Adolescent Mothers"[Mesh])

The Boolean connector NOT removes a concept from results. For example, let's say we are interested in the postpartum experience but *not* when women are pregnant. It would then be postpartum NOT pregnan*. One potential consequence of using NOT is mistakenly eliminating articles that talk about both (if that's not what you want). Once you have combined all terms representing your first concept, you can add a second and subsequent set of terms representing other concepts.

The next step would be to connect these terms to other aspects of the PICO with the AND connector. The search strategy can be constructed by combining both sets with a different Boolean connector, "AND"; this will reduce the number of citations that result from searching each set of terms separately as the following:

(teen• OR adolescen*) AND (pregnan* OR parent*)

When we want to combine two conceptual sets, we use both OR and AND commands.

An example of a search in PubMed that combines two conceptual sets of terms based on our current topic is represented here.

("teenage parents" OR "adolescent parents" OR "teen pregnancy" OR "adolescent pregnancy" OR "teen childbearing" OR "adolescent childbearing" OR "Pregnancy in Adolescence"[Mesh] OR "Adolescent Fathers"[Mesh] OR "Adolescent Mothers"[Mesh]) AND ("Contraception"[Mesh] OR "Contraceptive Agents"[Mesh] OR "Pregnancy/prevention and control"[Mesh] OR "Pregnancy prevention" OR contraception OR contraceptive OR "birth control" OR "family planning")

Another principle for developing search strings are *wild-card truncations*, in which words can be truncated with an asterisk to indicate that any version of a keyword—plural, variations of the term, verb tense—is an option for the search. For example, the terms "pregnant" and "pregnancy" can be represented by "pregnan*". Understand that an asterisk cannot be added to subject headings, only to keywords that are synonyms or related terms.

This is also a time to use the expertise of a research librarian or other information specialist who may be assigned to a social work program. The research librarian can help create search strings for each of the databases you're interested in searching, and they will amplify your search terms by combining them with Boolean connectors. Adjustments must be made as appropriate for each database. The use of filters/limits for publication date, age, type of research, and language will differ across databases; the librarian will also assist you in this.

You can use the unofficial keywords in other databases from the above example of a PubMed search. Please note that you must also find the official vocabulary terms within each database to add to the keywords. Remember that conceptually related terms are combined using the Boolean connector "OR," while the Boolean connector "AND" combines each separate set of associated terms. Below is an example of replicating as closely as possible the search that was done in PubMed above in the combined Sociological Abstracts/Social Services database. Adjustments across other databases will be necessary to reflect their official vocabulary.

(MAINSUBJECT.EXACT("Adolescent Pregnancy") OR MAINSUBJECT.EXACT("Adolescent Parents") OR MAINSUBJECT.EXACT("Adolescent Mothers") OR MAINSUBJECT.EXACT("Adolescent Fathers") OR "teenage parents" OR "adolescent parents" OR "teen pregnancy" OR "adolescent pregnancy" OR "teen childbearing" OR "adolescent childbearing")

AND

(MAINSUBJECT.EXACT("Birth Control") OR MAINSUBJECT.EXACT("Family Planning") OR "Pregnancy prevention" OR contraception OR contraceptive OR "birth control" OR "family planning")

Limits applied

Databases:

- Sociological Abstracts

Narrowed by:

Year: 2017; 2018; 2019; 2020; 2021; 2022;

Location: United States—US; New York; California; Canada; Chicago Illinois; Missouri; Ohio; Texas; Washington DC; Ann Arbor Michigan; Houston Texas; Illinois; Iowa; Mississippi; New Mexico; St Louis Missouri; Utah; Wisconsin; Wyoming;

Language: English;

Source type: Scholarly Journals; Conference Papers & Proceedings

---

Please note that the search strategy is in a version that combines the Sociological Abstracts and Social Services databases available through ProQuest, a publisher of databases. This example includes the Main Subjects found in the database's thesaurus as well as the same keywords used in the PubMed search strategy. In addition, several limits were applied to narrow the results (year, language, location, source type). The second involves filter features by type of study, age, gender, etc. Filter features for PubMed, such as RCTs and meta-analysis, are on the left of the search bar.

We have emphasized in this book that we want to assess studies for their validity and how they control bias. In a similar process, we avoid introducing bias into the studies we choose by filtering out in advance articles that will take more effort. Therefore, students should refrain from limiting articles to "full-text," as many good articles are not free and downloadable but can be found through library subscriptions (if available to you) or through Interlibrary Loan services, which are efficient about obtaining electronic scans and sending them quickly.

ORGANIZING AND TRACKING THE SEARCH

It's easy to get overwhelmed and confused when working in different databases and formulating search strings for each one. You'll have to devise a method to track the searches and the studies you read. These are some of the basic steps to follow, no matter what kind of system you use.

RECORD THE SEARCH STRATEGY FOR EACH DATABASE

There may have been several versions of the search strategy. If you are inundated with "hits" (let's say more than 200), your search terms may be too broad. On the other hand, you may have no hits on the various databases or very few; in this situation, there may not be studies in the area you have chosen, but another possibility is that you have not included the appropriate search terms or you may have made your terms too narrow. A revised version of the terms may lead to finding more studies. This is why adjusting search strategies is often necessary, but make sure you track the different versions to make your search transparent and possibly return to a particular strategy that yielded the type of articles you seek. Keeping a chart (see Table 3.1) helps ensure you conduct a thorough search. It is also a document that can be incorporated into your final paper to demonstrate that you have followed a standardized process for finding relevant articles.

RUN THE SEARCH STRATEGY

To summarize briefly, here are the types of studies that you may find:

- Reviews (see Chapter 5).
- Quantitative studies, which include surveys on the topic, and intervention research, which involve RCTs (see Chapter 4).
- Theoretical or conceptual framework articles that discuss the theory underlying a topic or the application of theory to a population or problem.

Most of the time, you'll be able to screen out articles that do not fit the criteria just by skimming the title and the abstract of studies. Get the full-text version of the articles that pass through the screening process. Most university libraries have subscription services to many journals, but it still might be necessary to order a couple of articles from the interlibrary loan system. You will find that many of the research articles you download or

TABLE 3.1 Terms Used in Search Strategies by Database

Official Terms and Keyword Terms Used in Database Searches

Concepts	PubMed Medical Subject Headings (MeSH Terms)	PsycInfo Thesaurus Terms	CINAHL Subject Terms	Keywords Used in All Databases
"Adolescent Pregnancy"**	"Pregnancy in Adolescence"[Mesh] OR "Adolescent Fathers"[Mesh] OR "Adolescent Mothers"[Mesh]	MAINSUBJECT.EXACT ("Adolescent Pregnancy") OR MAINSUBJECT.EXACT ("Adolescent Fathers") OR MAINSUBJECT.EXACT("Adolescent Mothers")	(MH "Pregnancy in Adolescence+") OR (MH "Adolescent Mothers") OR (MH "Adolescent Fathers")	"teenage parents" OR "adolescent parents" OR "teen pregnancy" OR "adolescent pregnancy" OR "teen childbearing" OR "adolescent childbearing"
"Pregnancy Prevention"**	"Contraception"[Mesh] OR "Contraceptive Agents"[Mesh] OR "Pregnancy/prevention and control"[Mesh]	MAINSUBJECT.EXACT ("Birth Control") OR MAINSUBJECT.EXACT("Contraceptive Devices") OR MAINSUBJECT.EXACT ("Family Planning")	(MH "Contraception+") OR (MH "Reproductive Control Agents+")	"Pregnancy prevention" OR contraception OR contraceptive OR "birth control" OR "family planning"
Limits/Filters	English; 2012-2022; Article Type: Review	English; 2012-2022; Methodology: Literature Review	English; 2012-2022; Publication Type: Review	

*Please note that all terms representing each concept (official vocabulary and keywords for each database) must be connected using the Boolean connector OR.

**Please note that each set of terms representing a concept (all official and keyword terms that have been ORed together) must be connected using the Boolean connector AND; Limits/Filters can then be applied to the results.

36 • EVIDENCE-BASED PRACTICE PROCESS IN SOCIAL WORK

TABLE 3.2 Tracking the Search Process

Name of database	Number of Hits After Deduplication	Number Screened Out by Title and Abstract	Number of Full Text Articles Obtained	Number Ordered from Interlibrary Loan	Number of Articles that Fit Criteria
PubMed	107 (originally 107)	85	15	7	12
PsycInfo	25 (originally 41)	19	3	0	2
CINAHL	12 (originally 39)	10	1	1	1
Total	144	114	19	8	15

order from interlibrary loan have varying degrees of usefulness. Upon closer examination, some articles are off your topic area and not useful for your review. But other articles will not only offer important information but also lead you to other important articles. Indeed, you often find more relevant articles through this "snowball technique" (Ridley, 2012) than through database searches. The Scopus database also has a function wherein you can see which authors have cited that particular study when you type it into the search window. That will also put you in touch with the most recent studies. Table 3.2 shows a method for tracking the results of your search.

EVIDENCE-BASED REPOSITORIES

We start by reminding you of the compilations of ESIs, as they can be valuable sources, particularly when you no longer are a student and lose access to library databases. We cover the American Psychological Association's Division 12 Task Force compilation and the California Evidence-Based Clearinghouse (CEBC) here.

APA DIVISION 12 TASK FORCE

The American Psychological Association's (APA) Division 12 Task Force assigns the following designations:

> Well-Established (Strong): at least two group-design experiments, conducted by independent investigatory teams show statistically significant findings over medication, psychosocial placebo, or another treatment. Alternatively, the treatment may be equivalent to an already established treatment in experiments with sufficient statistical power to detect moderate differences. Furthermore, treatment is manualized, targeted for a specified problem, outcome measures are reliable and valid, andappropriate data analysis is also used.
> Probably Efficacious (Moderate): an intervention is either superior to a wait-list control group in two experiments, equivalent to an already established intervention,

or superior to a pill placebo, psychological placebo, or another intervention in a single experiment.

Possibly Efficacious (Weak): at least one study must indicate that a treatment is superior without conflicting evidence.

The link to their database, which is organized by DSM mental health disorders across the lifespan, can be found here: https://div12.org/psychological-treatments/. Access to treatment manuals is also part of this compilation. We note some flaws with the vote count method used to determine these various designations, which we explain in more detail in Chapter 5.

Using the same criteria for empirically supported treatments and specific to child problems, the *Journal of Child and Adolescent Clinical Psychology* also publishes periodic reviews of mental health problems in youth:

ADHD (Evans et al., 2014)
Autism (Smith & Iadarola, 2015)
Disruptive disorders (Kaminski & Claussen, 2017; McCart & Sheidow, 2016)
Self-injury (Glenn et al., 2019)
Trauma (Dorsey et al., 2017)
OCD (Freeman et al., 2018)
Depression (Weersing et al., 2017)
Youth who are ethnic minority with a mental disorder (Pina et al., 2019)

Returning to the case, the student relied on Pina et al. (2019), who reviewed, using American Psychological Association Division 12 criteria for empirically supported treatment, the child and adolescent treatment literature to find those that were endorsed for ethnic minority youth. For anxiety, the authors found that cognitive behavioral therapy (CBT) applied to Latinx youth was a *well-established* treatment. For Black adolescents, Ginsberg and Drake (2002) implemented a group CBT intervention in the school setting. Adaptations included making the session length shorter, having fewer sessions, using relevant situations as illustrations for techniques, and excluding the parent component due to the parents' work schedules and transportation barriers. In a small pilot study, this adapted group CBT intervention was found to be more effective than an attention-support control condition on anxiety; therefore CBT was categorized as *experimental*.

When the student examined the various studies, she was not able to locate a treatment manual, but she did discover that the basis for some of the treatments were the following books:

- Josephs, S. (2017). *Helping Your Anxious Teen: Positive Parenting Strategies to Help Your Teen Beat Anxiety, Stress, and Worry*. New Harbinger Press.
- Rapee, R., Wignall, A., Spence, S., Lyneham, H., & Cobham, V. (2008). *Helping your anxious child* (2nd ed.). New Harbinger Press.
- Wignall, A., Rapee, R., & Lyneham, H. (2008). *Helping your anxious child children's workbook* (2nd ed.). Centre for Emotional Health: Macquarie University, Sydney University.

The intern found that PDF copies of the first two were about $11, which was an affordable cost for the agency, and with the purchase of Rapee et al. (2008), the child's workbook was free. As these were designed as self-help workbooks and because she'd had a course in CBT during her MSW program, the student felt confident that, with supervision, she could lead her clients through this empirically-supported, structured approach. Given the waitlist, she believed that a group treatment might be a more cost-effective way to deliver services, and indeed Ginsberg and Drake (2002) had tested a group model with African American youth. Given the problem of inconsistent attendance that the supervisor had warned her about, the student thought starting with a large group size (say 10–12) might help overcome the problem of absences. The treatment had also been telephone-delivered, so she thought that might be a way around transportation problems and other barriers to treatment, such as parents' schedules, to catch up youth on any missed treatment.

CALIFORNIA EVIDENCE-BASED CLEARINGHOUSE (CEBC)

Another resource to refer to when working with children and families is the California Evidence-Based Clearinghouse (CEBC). The CEBC website (https://www.cebc4cw.org/) contains a database with all the ratings it has given to programs implemented for children, youth, and families involved in the child welfare system or who are at-risk for child welfare involvement. Broadly, programs aim to address a wide range of issues of concern (e.g., anger management, anxiety, depression, disruptive behavior, domestic violence, home visiting to prevent child maltreatment, parent training, substance abuse, trauma treatment, neglect, and abusive behavior). As noted, many programs target adults/caregivers, as it is imperative to address their issues of concern so that they in turn are supported and equipped to parent safely. Refer here for a complete list of topic areas: https://www.cebc4cw.org/search/by-topic-area/. As explained by Garcia and colleagues (2019), the registry includes a wealth of information about the components and goals of each program, its target population, key research findings, and information about the intervention developers. With such valuable information, the registry serves as a resource to find an ESI and access guidance on what steps to take to initiate the implementation process. Each program is critically reviewed, relying on extant research findings, and subsequently ranked on its level of effectiveness, with 1 being *Well-Supported by Research Evidence*, 2 signaling a program that is *Supported by Research Evidence*, 3 meaning a program has *Promising Research Evidence*, and NR meaning not able to be rated. The program is also ranked by level of relevance: (1) *high* ranking represents programs that are commonly used to meet the needs of youth and families who receive child welfare services, (2) *medium* ranking indicates the program is designed to serve clients who are similar to child welfare populations (in terms of history, demographics, or presenting problems) and likely include current and former child welfare services recipients, and (3) *low* ranking suggests the program is designed to service clients with little or no apparent similarity to clients in the child welfare services population.

There are several options to access the evidence you need via the CEBC website:

1. An alphabetical list of programs is available (click on the "Programs" tab). You can also search for a program if you have a few programs already in mind and want to search for evidence supporting the implementation of a program.
2. You can click on the "Topic Areas" tab. Within each tab, you will find a list of ESIs to review and consider for implementation. There are also advanced search options, as illustrated below.

Referring to the case study presented at the beginning of this chapter, evidence suggests parental depression is a risk factor for child maltreatment. How can we support low-income youth of color who experience anxiety? The CEBC registry would be a helpful resource to address this question. After clicking on the tab *find a program*, (1) go to the advanced search engine, and enter anxiety as the *keyword*; (2) check "Well-Supported by Research Evidence" under the drop-down menu for *scientific rating*; (3) check anxiety treatment for child and adolescent under "topic areas"; and (4) denote any age between 8 and 17 in the "age of child" tab. Child welfare relevance is not applicable here; thus, there is no need to denote a selection for this field. After clicking on search, one ESI is generated: Coping Cat (Children experiencing problematic anxiety).

SUMMARY

This chapter focused on the search process, beginning with library databases. Information on technical details of using official and unofficial terms and building search strings was discussed. PubMed was emphasized, since that database offers more access than others after graduation. Evidence depositories were also covered as a resource available for students and practitioners to access empirically supported treatments available for different problem areas.

FOR YOUR PRACTICE

1. Use a PICO question of interest and develop synonyms for each PICO element.

PICO Element	Your PICO	Synonyms
Participants		
Intervention		
Control/Comparative conditions		
Outcomes		
Type of study		

2. Choose a relevant library database. Find the Subject/Thesaurus terms in that database to use for the PICO elements.

PICO Element	Your PICO	Subject/Thesaurus Terms
Participants		
Intervention		
Control/Comparative conditions		
Outcomes		
Type of studies		

3. Considering what you have been working on in #1 and #2, what delimiters/filters would you use in that database search?
4. Construct a search string in that database that includes the subject/thesaurus terms and your "unofficial" keywords for your PICO question, using Boolean operators and the delimiters/filters.
5. Run the search string in the database, tracking the number of "hits" it receives. Is the number manageable (<100)? If not, construct another search string that has a narrower scope. Redo the search you have constructed if necessary.
6. Track the search process for that particular search/database.

Data and Search String	Number of hits after deduplication	Number screened out by title and abstract	Number of full text articles obtained	Number ordered from interlibrary loan	Number of articles that fit criteria

7. Use the same PICO or a different one, and look up one of the depositories of ESTs. Which depository did you choose and why? Did you find the answer to your PICO? What is it?

REFERENCES

Dorsey, S., Mclaughlin, K., Kerns, S., Harrison, J., Lambert, H., Briggs, E., . . . Amaya-Jackson, L. (2017). Evidence base update for psychosocial treatments for children and adolescents exposed to traumatic events. *Journal of Clinical Child & Adolescent Psychology, 46*(3), 303–330.

Evans, S., Owens, J., & Bunford, N. (2014). Evidence-based psychosocial treatments for children and adolescents with attention-deficit/hyperactivity disorder. *Journal of Clinical Child & Adolescent Psychology, 43*(4), 527–551. https://doi.org/10.1080/15374416.2013.850700.

Freeman, J., Benito, K., Herren, J., Kemp, J., Sung, J., Georgiadis, C., Arora, A., Walther, M., & Garcia, A. (2018). Evidence base update of psychosocial treatments for pediatric obsessive-compulsive disorder: Evaluating, improving, and transporting what works. *Journal of Clinical Child & Adolescent Psychology, 47*(5), 669–698. https://doi.org/10.1080/15374416.2018.1496443

Garcia, A. R., DeNard, C., Morones, S., & Eldeeb, N. (2019). Mitigating barriers to implementing evidence-based interventions: Lessons learned from scholars and agency directors. *Children and Youth Services Review, 100*, 313–331.

Ginsburg, G. S., & Drake, K. L. (2002). School-based treatment for anxious African-American adolescents: A controlled pilot study. *Journal of the American Academy of Child & Adolescent Psychiatry, 41*(7), 768–775. https://doi.org/10.1097/00004583-200207000-00007

Glenn, C. R., Esposito, E. C., Porter, A. C., & Robinson, D. J. (2019). Evidence-base update of psychosocial treatments for self-injurious thoughts and behaviors in youth. *Journal of Clinical Child & Adolescent Psychology, 48*(3), 357–392.

Kaminski, J., & Claussen, A. (2017). Evidence base update for psychosocial treatments for disruptive behaviors in children. *Journal of Clinical Child & Adolescent Psychology, 46*(4), 477–499. https://doi.org/10.1080/15374416.2017.1310044

McCart, M. R., & Sheidow, A. J. (2016). Evidence-based psychosocial treatments for adolescents with disruptive behavior, *Journal of Clinical Child & Adolescent Psychology, 45*(5), 529–563. https://doi.org/10.1080/15374416.2016.1146990

Pina, A. A., Polo, A. J., & Huey, S. J. (2019). Evidence-based psychosocial interventions for ethnic minority youth: The 10-year update. *Journal of Clinical Child & Adolescent Psychology, 48*(2), 179–202. https://doi.org/10.1080/15374416.2019.1567350

Rapee, R., Wignall, A., Spence, S., Lyneham, H., & Cobham, V. (2008). *Helping your anxious child* (2nd ed.). New Harbinger Press.

Ridley, D. (2012). *The literature review: A step-by-step guide for students.* Sage Publications.

Smith, T., & Iadarola, S. (2015). Evidence base update for autism spectrum disorder. *Journal of Clinical Child & Adolescent Psychology, 44*(6), 897–922. https://doi.org/10.1080/15374416.2015.1077448

Weersing, V. R., Jeffreys, M., Do, M.-C. T., Schwartz, K. T. G., & Bolano, C. (2017). Evidence base update of psychosocial treatments for child and adolescent depression. *Journal of Clinical Child & Adolescent Psychology, 46*(1), 11–43. https://doi.org/10.1080/15374416.2016.1220310

SECTION II
CRITIQUING THE EVIDENCE

CHAPTER 4

RANDOMIZED CONTROLLED TRIALS AND ALTERNATIVES FOR THE EBP PROCESS

> *Morris is a Black 6-year-old male receiving social work services at a charter elementary school. Morris was referred due to inattention, inability to complete tasks, and angry outbursts. Two years ago, his older brother was murdered in their neighborhood.*

Before we illustrate how to engage in the EBP process, we offer a brief review of randomized controlled trial (RCT) research designs, and what you need to be mindful of when deciding to rely on the evidence generated by an RCT study. We also cover the other designs that you may seek out to answer practice-based questions, particularly when RCTs are not available.

REVIEW OF RCTS

The RCT is the most robust study design when examining the impact of an intervention (Wodarski & Hopson, 2012). You will also hear it called "the gold standard of research." An RCT study involves randomly assigning clients to the novel treatment condition or to a control group, which may receive no treatment at all or treatment as it is usually practiced (treatment as usual). Participants in each condition complete the same pre- and post-measures, and those data are compared to see whether the treatment group is significantly more likely to achieve intended outcomes. Except for those randomly assigned to receive the novel treatment, each participant is exposed to the same conditions, thus ruling out potential threats to internal validity.

As a refresher, internal validity refers to the extent to which the tested intervention changed the dependent variable. The randomization process in RCT controls for other factors or client circumstances that may have caused the change. In other words, RCTs allow for greater control over these factors, which may include history, attrition (dropping out of the study), and selection bias, as some of the most common. Table 4.1 summarizes these with examples, but please consult your research methods textbook for more detail.

You will likely not run an RCT for your own practice, but, if you are interested, we refer you to *Randomized Controlled Trials: Design and Implementation for Community-Based Psychosocial Interventions* (Solomon et al., 2009). Our focus here is on how to read, summarize, and critique articles that publish the results of RCTs, as these studies may help inform the development of the intervention plan for your client(s).

READING AND SUMMARIZING AN RCT

Sometimes reading academic articles that describe an RCT can become overwhelming, and it's easy to get bogged down in the amount of detail and trying to understand the statistics. It is helpful, at least initially, when you're learning how to be a consumer of this research, to learn how to summarize and pull out the main points. By deconstructing studies in what at first seems like a laborious way, you will become more adept at reading and understanding this research. Table 4.2 details the elements of a template we have developed throughout the years, focusing on the following:

1. The purpose of the study and its hypotheses. A hypothesis is a prediction about what the results of your research will show. In other words, it is an educated guess about what is expected to happen when the independent variable—the intervention—and the dependent variable—what the intervention is believed to influence, such as depression—are studied together.
2. Theoretical or conceptual framework undergirding the study. A theory attempts to describe phenomena or to explain relationships. In other words, why is one factor related to another? The theory for an intervention being tested could be CBT, interpersonal therapy, psychodynamic therapy, family systems therapy and so forth.
2. The research design is the "how" of the study, specifically the decisions the researcher makes about where, when, and in what format to collect the data (Corcoran & Secret, 2013). The RCT seeks to establish a cause-and-effect relationship between the independent and dependent variables.
3. Sampling involves how people are selected and recruited to be part of the study.
4. Measurement involves how the dependent variable is operationalized.
5. What were the statistical results of the hypothesis testing? All statistical analysis is based on one idea: did our result happen due to chance (a random occurrence) or because we indeed have found something that, at least statistically, is meaningful (Corcoran & Secret, 2013)? The level at which we call a relationship or a difference in our data statistically significant or not is called the *p-value*, the *alpha level*, or the *significance level*. The value of a probability falls between 1 and 0. The convention in the sciences is to use a minimum p value of .05. In other words, we have less than a 5% probability (1 in 20) that the relationship occurred by chance. These results will determine the impact of the intervention for your PICO question, which we will go over with the case example featured in this chapter.

TABLE 4.1 Threats to Internal Validity

Validity Type	Threat	Example
History	Changes in experimental subjects over time might not be due to the intervention, but instead to events that happened over the intervention period.	The initiation of the Black Lives Matter movement might have accounted for change and not any intervention that was being delivered at the time.
Attrition	Individuals who complete treatment may be different from those who do not.	People who stick with treatment might have other resources and supports that affect their ability to be involved in treatment which could cause change rather than the intervention itself.
Selection	Involves discrepancies in how people are assigned to treatment conditions. Other preexisting conditions between the experimental and control may account for treatment effects instead of the intervention itself.	This is a typical shortcoming of quasi-experimental designs in that groups are chosen for their convenience; therefore, they may differ on characteristics that are important for change and these might account for results rather than the intervention.
Maturation	Naturally occurring changes over time, such as growth or maturity, could be confused with a treatment effect.	Children may become better at emotional regulation because of maturation rather than an intervention.
Regression	If the most "at-risk" group is selected for investigation, some improvements will occur through time as extreme scores have a tendency to regress toward the average.	A youth who scores very high on a trauma symptomology report one day may naturally score closer to the mean score the next time being tested rather than the reduction occurring because of intervention.
Testing	Testing can alter behavior and how people think and respond to questions; in other words, improved posttest scores may be related to the experience of the pretest and not the intervention.	This factor occurs particularly in knowledge-building questionnaires. If MSW students are tested at the beginning of their research course for their knowledge of research concepts, they might do better on the posttest at the end of class because of their familiarity with those particular questions rather than the intervention (the course).
Instrumentation/ Measurement procedures	Changes in calibration of measurement due to fatigue of data collectors, changes in testing procedures, and changes in manner of explaining instructions	At the beginning of an intervention, the clinicians at an agency were administering the measures to the families they saw and were explaining the directions, but over time, the administrative staff at the front desk were administering measures and simply handing them along with the intake package for family members to fill out.

TABLE 4.2 RCT Study Summary Template

Author(s) (year) Purpose and hypotheses Theoretical orientation	Research design	Sampling: How were participants selected?	Measure	Results [related to hypotheses]
The first column addresses the purpose of the study, or its *research question*, the hypotheses, and the theoretical framework undergirding the study. Sometimes students have a difficult time finding the theoretical framework, but if it is not obvious—usually it's named in the title and the abstract—then there may not be a conceptual framework to name. The research question and hypotheses are usually found at the end of the literature review that builds into an argument for the particular question, and before Methods.	The design is an RCT. You can name if a follow-up period is being studied beyond posttest.	The total *n* of the sample. The sampling method for an RCT is usually one of convenience. It's hard to recruit participants for intervention research, so whoever met the inclusion criteria and provided informed consent was part of the study. Also discussed where the sample was recruited from. A snapshot of the main demographic characteristics (e.g., gender, race/ethnicity, and SES) is also provided here.	This includes standardized scales that measure the constructs selected for the study.	Results should be assessed along whether they do or do not support the hypotheses that the researchers planned in the beginning. Sometimes they are "partially supported." Because MSW students haven't learned a lot of statistical information, we suggest relying on the abstract and discussion section to get this information rather than getting bogged down into technically sophisticated statistical terms that the MSW student would not typically have learned. Are the results clinically important? In other words, is there a difference on people's scores on a tool that uses depression self-report that means something? A meaningful finding, for instance, might be that people move out of a moderate level of depression into a range of mild, rather than only reducing their depression score by 2 points.

48 • EVIDENCE-BASED PRACTICE PROCESS IN SOCIAL WORK

CRITICAL APPRAISAL

The next part of the EBP process involves critical appraisal of the evidence provided by the RCT. In her book, Gambrill (2018) offers a checklist of items to consider when assessing an RCT. We embedded her checklist as headings into the critical appraisal tool we adapted from the Cochrane Collaboration (Table 4.3). External validity refers to the degree to which the methods, intervention, and setting of an experiment approximate and generalize to real-life practice—your clientele and setting, for example (Corcoran & Secret, 2013; Wodarski & Hopson, 2012).

Critical Appraisal for Quantitative Study (Adapted from Cochrane Collaboration)

Were they properly randomized into groups using concealed assignment?

How was randomization performed?	Randomization is often performed with a computerized method off site by a statistician. A "low tech" method is when sealed envelopes contain the treatment condition to which the participant is being assigned. Both these methods take personal interest of the research team in results away from decisions about which people should be put in certain conditions. Participants can't be treated differently if the research team does not know the condition to which they are assigned.

Was everyone involved in the study (participants and researchers) "blind" to treatment? In other words, were they not privy about which interventions participants received?

Was randomization blind?	When individuals enter treatment, the researchers who are interested in the study outcome should not be the ones to assign the persons to condition and should not know who has been assigned to the treatment condition. This method helps to ensure that the research team doesn't do anything to influence the results, even unconsciously. Similarly, although not always possible, participants should be shielded from knowing that they are in the "experimental" condition. They may respond positively, sensing that they are being treated in a special way.
Were assessments administered blind?	Were administrators of measures blind to the treatment condition participants were randomized to?

Were intervention and control groups similar at the start of the trial?

Baseline imbalances between intervention and control groups tested? If yes, were there imbalances?	Even with randomization to conditions, it is sometimes possible that, due to chance, participants with certain characteristics, such as more males, for example, end up in one condition over another. For that reason, researchers routinely test to see if there are differences between participants at the beginning before treatment starts.

Fidelity: Was the treatment implemented as it was designed?

How was fidelity assessed?	Fidelity is defined as the treatment being implemented as it was designed. The reason for attention to fidelity is that we have to be able to say, at the end of the treatment, that it was the treatment itself that accounted for the change that occurred. There are many ways that studies report on fidelity. They usually start with the credentials and training of the interventionists and then report on training and supervision in the intervention that is being delivered. Sessions are often videotaped and a subset randomly selected so that observers can code the clinician's interactions along a checklist for fidelity.

What was the result of fidelity testing?	These involve numerical results of fidelity, including correlations.

Are all the participants who entered the trial accounted for at its conclusion?

Differential attrition between groups?	Does dropout from treatment, which is almost inevitable to some degree, happen at a different rate in the experimental versus the comparison condition? If we only examine the results of the people that finished treatment, the "completers" may have additional resources than those who dropped out, which may account for improvement, beyond the treatment itself. We can also take care of this problem in the statistical analysis (see intent to treat).
Intent to treat?	Intent to treat involves analyzing the data from all those that started treatment, irrespective of whether they finished. They are typically assigned a no-change score to make sure that findings aren't inflated.

CRITICAL THINKING: IMPACT, RIGOR OF STUDY, AND APPLICABILITY

When guiding students to engage in critical thinking during this stage of the EBP process, we encourage them to consider the extent to which the studies they review are valid and applicable, and whether the results are impactful and show that the intervention achieves intended outcomes. Note that we use the example of an RCT here and follow the process all the way through, but you will typically look at more than one study to decide how to best answer your PICO question.

- **Impact:** Impact is straightforward—Did the study or group of studies find that the intervention has a positive impact or achieve intended outcomes? In rendering your own conclusion, think about why or how the independent and dependent variables are linked.
- **Rigor of study**: How well can you trust or rely on the findings? In other words, is the study rigorous? You will want to ask yourself how well the research design of any given study you review controls for threats to internal validity. RCTs, by design, control for these threats. For external validity, please see your foundation research methods text. We center here on the generalizability of the research to your population of interest.
- **Applicability:** Are the people participating in the RCT and their contexts like the clients you work with? Applicability has to do with whether the sample under study reflects your target population. Do sample characteristics—age, gender, race/ethnicity, SES, life circumstances, issues of concern, etc.—align well with that of your client(s)? Consider how well the sample study represents your client population and whether the sampling method might have biased the results. Now that we have offered a summation of what to look for and critique when appraising RCTs, we turn to the case introduced at the beginning of the chapter.

STEP 1: ASSESSMENT

As highlighted in Chapters 1 and 2, we discussed the merits of adding the "assessment" phase to the EBP process. As noted by the student, Morris was assessed by the school psychologist who rendered a diagnosis of ADHD. Despite the trauma he'd experienced, she concluded that criteria for PTSD were not met. Morris is not on medication, primarily because he lacks insurance, but his mother was also hesitant about medication due to his age. Based on his trauma and Morris's symptoms of inattention and hyperactivity, the social worker wanted to know how to help the client process the trauma and learn emotional regulation.

STEP 2: DEVELOPMENT OF WELL-FORMED QUESTIONS

After conducting an assessment, we need to rely on the information to formulate a research question to inform practice. Following the PICO question formula, as described by Gambrill and Gibbs (2009), the social worker derived the following: Population is African American 6-year-old male who witnessed a traumatic event; the Intervention of concern is unknown at this time; the Comparison is no intervention; and the hoped-for outcome is decreased symptoms of ADHD (inability to complete tasks, and angry outbursts). Therefore, the PICO question is: What is an effective intervention for young Black children who have suffered a traumatic event and are diagnosed with ADHD symptoms?

STEP 3: EVIDENCE SEARCH

Next, the student began a search in Google Scholar, using a combination of the following search terms: The University EMBASE database and the Cochrane Collaboration Library were used to locate treatment outcome research and systematic reviews. Search terms that were used included: "ADHD," "inattention," "hyperactivity," "trauma," "PTSD," "children," "elementary-age," "youth," "African American," "black," "intervention," and "treatment." For illustration for this chapter on RCTs, we center here on an unpublished dissertation that reported an RCT. However, note that you may look at several studies, including systematic reviews (Chapter 5), to determine your client's optimal intervention.

The dissertation located in this illustration, Kram (2019), examined the effectiveness of child-centered play therapy (CCPT) as an intervention with children who had been diagnosed ADHD and suffered adverse childhood experiences (ACEs). Thirty-four children 5–8 years old were randomly assigned to the CCPT novel treatment group (sixteen 30-minute sessions, $n = 17$) intended to decrease inattention and impulsivity symptoms or to a waitlist control group ($n = 17$). Black children made up almost 30% of the study sample, with the intervention taking place in an elementary school located in a disadvantaged area. The student summarized the study in Table 4.3.

TABLE 4.3 RCT Summary: Kram (2019)

Author(s), purpose, year, hypotheses, and theoretical orientation	Research Design	Sampling	Measures	Results
Kirsten Kram (2019) The purpose is to examine the effectiveness of child-centered play therapy (CCPT) with young children who have experienced multiple ACEs and demonstrate symptoms of inattention and impulsivity. Hypothesis: CCPT will be more effective than the waitlist control group when used with children who have experienced multiple ACEs. Person-centered theory	RCT	Convenience sampling $N = 34$ Five Title 1 elementary schools in the southwest United States. Average age: 6.12, ranging from 5 to 8 years old. Gender: 28 males and 6 females. Race: 38.2% Caucasian, 29.4% African American, 17.6% Hispanic/Latinx, and 14.7% biracial identifying.	ACES Questionnaire ADDES-4 Home Version ADDES-4 School Version DOF Attention Deficit/Hyperactivity Problems scale	Results indicated statistically significant improvement of the CCPT treatment group over the waitlist control group.

Source: Kram (2019).

STEP 4: CRITICALLY APPRAISING STUDIES AND REVIEWS

Step 4 involves conducting a critical appraisal of the research; and in doing so, the student focused her critique on the extent to which the evidence she gathered from Step 3 is valid, impactful, and applicable.

> Impact. Teachers reported a significant reduction in inattentive and impulsive behavior in the classroom for children in the experimental condition compared to the waitlist control group.
>
> Rigor of study. The methodological quality of Kram (2019) was appraised with the Joanna Briggs tool for RCTs. See Table 4.4. It is unclear whether the waitlist control

TABLE 4.4 Critical Appraisal for Kram (2019) RCT

Were they properly randomized into groups using concealed assignment?	
How was randomization performed?	Block randomization procedures were used with an electronic random assignment software.
Was everyone involved in the study (participants and researchers) "blind" to treatment? In other words, were they not privy about which interventions participants received?	
Was randomization blind?	Yes
Were assessments administered blind?	Yes
Were intervention and control groups similar at the start of the trial?	
Baseline imbalances between intervention and control groups tested? If yes, were there imbalances?	Testing revealed no statistically significant differences.
Fidelity: Was the treatment implemented as it was designed?	
How was fidelity assessed?	Fidelity was assessed by a reviewer who coded randomly selected video sessions and coded therapist responses to CCPT categories. Then, one video was randomly selected for each child participant.
	The play therapists in this study were trained on CCPT protocol using the *Child-Centered Play Therapy Research Integrity Checklist*, received one hour of supervision per week, and completed at least two clinical play therapy courses with supervision and a practicum.
What was the result of fidelity testing?	Protocol adherence was calculated at .99, which confirms this study met criteria for CCPT protocol.
Are all the participants who entered the trial accounted for at its conclusion?	
Differential attrition between groups?	Due to change in teachers, three children's data were dropped from the analysis—one from the treatment group and two from the control group.
Intent to treat?	No intent to treat listed.

group herein included those who received some form of other treatment or support, or whether the researcher was blind to treatment conditions. The sample size is small, and more research is needed to determine whether findings are validated. Applicability. The study sample aligns with Morris's characteristics (i.e., age, race) and symptoms.

STEP 5: SELECTING AND IMPLEMENTING THE INTERVENTION

The student decided that CCPT was an optimal fit for her client and practitioner context. For client variables, both trauma/ACE and ADHD symptoms were addressed in the study for the age group of interest, and the sample had a significant proportion of Black children. The school setting was also a fit for the student's field placement at a school with the 30-minute sessions allotted, as well as the neighborhood where ACEss are not uncommon.

PROVIDER CONTEXT

The student favored the person-centered theory underlying CCPT as she found it compatible with trauma-focused care; it allows for self-determination for youth about topics for discussion and play. Provider expertise for this student comprised a year of MSW coursework, a BA in psychology, and classroom knowledge and field experience in navigating cross-cultural client–social worker interactions and relationships and delivering EBPs (in school settings). The intern had established rapport with Morris, and she'd had about seven 30-minute sessions at this point.

CLIENT VALUES AND PREFERENCES

The student asked her client whether he would be agreeable to more play therapy, and he assented with his mother's consent. This agreement from the clients was consistent with the student's clinical impression that they had built adequate rapport and that Morris enjoyed taking the lead on play and activities. His mother was also agreeable to his receiving interventions although she didn't typically have many questions about the intervention or his progress when the intern provided periodic updates.

TRAINING, SUPERVISION, AND FIDELITY

According to the California Evidence-Based Clearinghouse for Child Welfare (CEBC), play therapists who conduct CCPT as an intervention need to be licensed mental health providers with extensive training on CCPT protocol using *The Child-Centered Play*

Therapy Research Integrity Checklist. Play therapists must also complete approved coursework in CCPT or have a postgraduate certification in CCPT. The training required for certification consists of two levels, Basics in CCPT 101, which is a 12-hour training, and CCPT Practice and Application, which is an 18-hour training (Child-Centered Play Therapy, 2019). The cost of training ranges depending on the program and is around $200. Play therapists should also receive at least one hour of supervision per week to gain feedback and support. The student noted that a couple of the social workers on staff were already certified in play therapy, had the resources to receive training for CCPT, and could receive supervision.

The Play Therapy Skills Checklist and *The Child-Centered Play Therapy-Research Integrity Checklist* ensure treatment fidelity for CCPT. The *CCPT Treatment Manual* states that adherence above 90% confirms meeting criteria for CCPT protocol. The fidelity measures, *Play Therapy Skills Checklist: Instrument Used to Ensure Treatment Fidelity* and *The Child-Centered Play Therapy-Research Integrity Checklist*, are not in the public domain so they are another cost for agencies to consider.

The CEBC also suggested that the playroom should be about 12 feet by 15 feet with shelves on two walls to have adequate space for materials and toys (Child-Centered Play Therapy, 2019), which is also doable at the intern's setting. CEBC suggests that CCPT sessions should occur for 30 minutes twice a week for 8 weeks in a school setting.

ADAPTATIONS

Adaptations to the intervention include providing culturally equivalent dolls and other toys available to the client. CCPT requires three categories of toys; real life, aggressive, and creative. The student would also talk to the mother about ensuring her child made it to school every day so he could consistently attend sessions, as a barrier to potential effectiveness is his sporadic school attendance. The student was aware that Morris's mother was busy working and taking care of his two siblings, so demand would be kept low on her involvement, other than periodic updates and data collection on Morris's progress.

STEP 6: MONITOR CLIENT PROGRESS

The student planned to monitor her client's progress using the ADHD Rating Scale-IV for children. This scale would be provided to his mother (Home Version) and teacher (School Version) every week. The client's teacher is readily available and would be able to report weekly observations through the ADHD Rating Scale IV. The student's primary rationale for selecting this measure was the fact that it was freely available and accessible and would only take informants about 5 minutes to fill it out. These feasibility issues were of high consideration, although the student was concerned about the potential lack of testing with her population of interest, (young elementary-age children who are Black and have experienced trauma). For more detail, see Chapter 10.

OTHER DESIGNS

Although RCTs (and systematic reviews, covered in Chapter 5) are a first choice for evidence given the control of other factors that may account for change, they are not always available on your topic with a particular sample that reflects your client characteristics. In these situations, other kinds of designs might provide useful information for your question. Here we provide a brief overview of the designs, although your foundation research methods textbook delves into much more on this topic.

QUASI-EXPERIMENTAL DESIGNS

Quasi-experimental designs are similar to experimental designs in that they use at least two conditions, comparing an intervention to a control condition, which may be a no-treatment control or another type of intervention. However, quasi-experimental designs do not randomize participants into groups. Instead, participants are assigned to conditions, usually based on some convenience factor, such as the classroom a child attends, the county where one resides, or the people that receive services at a particular time. Although quasi-experimental designs still retain control over many threats to internal validity, selection bias looms as a central issue (Hilton et al., 2019; Monette et al., 2011). Despite this flaw, and depending on the type of quasi-experimental design (some are more rigorous than others), if there are no RCTs to answer our question, a quasi-experimental study might be the "go-to." We suggest the use of Table 4.1 as a way to summarize quasi-experimental designs, as well as RCTs. In Chapter 11, we provide an example of the EBP process using a quasi-experimental design, although with a critical appraisal tool developed to appraise the quality of this type of design.

PRE-EXPERIMENTAL DESIGNS

Pre-experimental designs are characterized by the fact that they do not have a control group to assess whether change can be attributed to the intervention itself. In other words, they are subject to many threats of internal validity. In relation to the EBP process, using other designs, such as the systematic review, RCTs, and even quasi-experimental designs to inform our practice question is preferable. Still, sometimes we rely on pre-experimental designs if no other high-quality evidence available.

In a *posttest-only* design, the researcher assesses the impact of an intervention when it is complete. We can only collect certain outcomes post-intervention, such as employment after incarceration, child abuse re-occurrence, or family reunification after a family's involvement in child welfare. One main disadvantage of posttest designs is that baseline information is not collected, so comparisons before and after intervention cannot be made.

Pretest/posttest designs are one of the most basic intervention research designs, in which a group of participants is assessed before the intervention is introduced and then after it is complete, using the same instrument. The advantage of a *pretest/posttest design* is that baseline information is known before the intervention begins. This allows the researcher to more confidently attribute observable changes to the intervention. However, many other reasons unrelated to the intervention could also explain these changes. Without a control group, you cannot necessarily claim that the changes were a result of the intervention.

SINGLE-SYSTEM DESIGNS

You likely are already interested in discovering the effect of your interventions on your clients. You probably ask them about the helpfulness of services and obtain an update on their status in your contacts. In this way, you are trying to understand whether your efforts benefit your clients. The single-system design is an extension of this natural tendency but with a more systematic method of collecting data and assessing the impact of our work. By repeatedly tracking an outcome (e.g., temper tantrums, ability to sleep through the night, arguments, positive thoughts), we determine whether—and how—we are helping clients achieve their goals. Single-system designs (also called single-case or single-subject designs) involve the social worker or student collecting data over time for a single client system on a specific outcome. A *client system* can refer to an individual client, but it could also mean a larger set of clients, such as a family or a classroom. Although the single-system design is the "lowest" form of evidence in any hierarchy, it has certain uses in informing the EBP question. It can allow for a source of in-depth information on a specialized topic or one with a better match between client characteristics and the setting.

Technically, baseline data should be collected for single-system designs comprising 5 to 10 data points without intervention (Fischer & Bloom, 1982). However, this is often unfeasible for busy practitioners and clients who need immediate intervention. Therefore, some journals, such as *Cognitive and Behavioral Practice* and *Clinical Case Studies* publish cases in which quantitative and qualitative data is collected at a single point before and after intervention is complete (pretest, posttest). These journals can provide crucial information on the use of therapeutic approaches where group data is difficult to gather, such as people who identify as transgender and or who belong to a particular ethnic minority group.

A student placed in an inpatient hospital talked with her supervisor about how to make the adults stay more focused on coping skills rather than just offering support in the groups that were the primary modality for treatment.

PICO: What type of treatment can be delivered in an inpatient hospital unit with adults who have been hospitalized to improve coping skills?

Answer: Although the student had more success finding studies examining inpatient treatment overall, she could not locate those discussing specific modalities and theories. She turned to "Brief Cognitive-Behavioral Therapy for Suicidal Inpatients," which described using an adapted version involving 10 daily sessions (Deifenbach et al., 2021). In a small study of six patients whose progress on suicidality and depression was tracked over time, the authors found important reductions in these areas. This study, which matched the student's setting and timeframe for intervention, showed her that CBT, as it was adapted in this study, could serve as a modality in the hospital where she had her field placement.

SURVEY

A *survey* gathers information about knowledge, perspectives, qualities, states, and preferences on a certain topic area. Surveys can ask participants to provide their perspectives at a single time, called *cross-sectional* research. When information is collected at two or more time points with the same participants, surveys involve *longitudinal or prospective* research. Gathering data over time allows researchers to examine whether events in the past, such as trauma, predict outcomes in the future, such as postpartum depression or pregnancy outcomes. Surveys can be self-report, where respondents read and check off items. They can also be interviewer or clinician-administered, in which they are read items and have to answer. Surveys are also subject to the sampling methods used to obtain participants who will complete them. There are two major sampling methods:

1. *Representative sample*—this sample looks like the actual population. There are equal proportions of units (males, females, people who are Black, those identifying as Muslim, those living in poverty, etc.) to that of the actual population.
2. *Unrepresentative sample*—a sample in which some characteristics are overrepresented or underrepresented relative to the total population. For example, perhaps there are more females than there are in the population.

Just as the RCT is the gold-standard study for intervention research, the gold standard of survey designs is a nationally representative study ideally, conducted over time (longitudinally). For example, the Centers for Disease Control has conducted the Youth Risk Behavior Surveillance System every two years since 1990 to assess health behaviors, such as alcohol/drug use and suicidality in US youth. Surveys may be used to answer practice questions that involve *prevalence*, as in how many people nationally suffer from a condition that we observe in our clients. We might be interested in how widespread the condition is, which may also establish whether an area is in further need. Surveys are also used for correlational studies to see how certain factors are related to, or predict, the condition. For example, we might be interested in whether teens from a minority racial/ethnic background are more or less likely to suffer from suicidality or whether other demographic patterns are more salient.

CONCLUSION

In this chapter, we briefly reviewed why an RCT is the most robust study design when examining the impact of an intervention. We presented a case study to illustrate the EBP process, how to locate and critique RCTs to inform your practice, and to determine whether indeed the novel intervention in the RCT should be implemented for your client(s). We also covered the other designs you may consult to answer practice questions without RCTs. In your practice, we hope these skills will offer a roadmap for using research to inform best practices.

FOR YOUR PRACTICE

ACTIVITY #1: MULTIPLE CHOICE QUESTIONS

1. What is the difference between randomized controlled designs and quasi-experimental designs?
   A. Random selection is involved.
   B. Both random selection and random assignment are involved.
   C. None of the above.
2. What threats to internal validity remain with an RCT?
   A. Selection
   B. Maturation
   C. Theoretically, all should be controlled.
   D. History
3. Critical appraisal of RCTs involves the following EXCEPT:
   A. What were the results of the study?
   B. What is the quality of the study?
   C. Was randomization to conditions performed in a way that minimize bias?
   D. Were measures administered by people who were blind to the treatment condition?
4. The process(es) discussed for considering the use of an RCT to answer our PICO is:
   A. Impact, rigor of study, and applicability.
   B. Internal validity and external validity.
   C. Summarizing the study.
   D. None of the above.

ACTIVITY #2:

With your peers (groups of 3–5 students), identify an issue of concern for a specific target population. In your group, reflect on a case you were assigned as an intern or practicing clinician. Engage in the six-step EBP process, locating, if possible, an RCT that applies to the characteristics and circumstances of your client.

ACTIVITY #3:

Critique an RCT, using the tools we provided in this chapter. Would you decide to select the novel intervention after considering the strengths and weaknesses of the design?

REFERENCES

Corcoran, J., & Secret, M. (2013). *The social work research skills workbook: Agency-based community research*. Oxford University Press.

Diefenbach, G. J., Rudd, M. D., Merling, L. F., Davies, C., Katz, B. W., & Tolin, D. F. (2021). Brief cognitive-behavioral therapy for suicidal inpatients. *Cognitive and Behavioral Practice, 28*(2), 224–240. https://doi.org/10.1016/j.cbpra.2020.09.010

Fischer, J., & Bloom, M. (1982). *Evaluating practice: Guidelines for the accountable professional*. Prentice-Hall.

Gambrill, E. (2018). *Critical thinking and the process of evidence-based practice*. Oxford University Press.

Gambrill, E., & Gibbs, L. (2009). Developing well-structured questions for evidence-informed practice. In A. Roberts (Ed.), *Social workers' desk reference* (2nd ed., pp. 1121–1126). Oxford University Press.

Hilton, T., Fawson, P., Sullivan, T., & DeJong, C. (2019). *Applied social research: A tool for the human services*. Springer.

Kram, K. (2019). *Child-centered play therapy and adverse childhood experiences: Effectiveness on impulsivity and inattention*. University of North Texas.

Solomon, P., Cavanaugh, M., & Draine, J. (2009). *Randomized controlled trials: Design and implementation for community-based psychosocial interventions*. Oxford University Press. https://doi.org/10.1093/acprof:oso/9780195333190.001.0001

Wodarski, J., & Hopson, L. (2012). *Research methods for evidence based practice*. Sage.

CHAPTER 5

THE ROLE OF SYSTEMATIC REVIEWS IN THE EBP PROCESS

> *Glenda interned at her university's college counseling center for her advanced year field placement. The student's supervisor shared that the administration of the center was concerned about rising rates of depression on campus, which seemed to reflect a worldwide trend. The average rate of depression among undergraduate university students is about 30%, much higher than the general population (Ibrahim et al., 2013). Clients at the counseling center ranged in age from 18 to 35 years, and were of varying ethnicities, religions, countries of origin, sexual orientation, and backgrounds. The average number of sessions available per student was 8 to 10, after which, if ongoing therapy was required, the referral coordinator helped students connect with outside providers. Glenda's supervisor said there were serious concerns about the capacity of the counseling center to serve the number of students presenting for help with depression. The administration was also concerned about the potential for suicide among students with depression.*

The most efficient way to gather studies to answer your practice question is to seek out the systematic reviews done in your area of interest. These reviews distill a large body of knowledge so that you gain a sense of the current research status of your topic. A *systematic review* aims to comprehensively locate and synthesize the research on a particular question. It uses organized, transparent, and replicable procedures at each step in the process. This chapter discusses the role of systematic reviews in the process of EBP.

Systematic reviews are considered studies in themselves rather than simply literature reviews. They involve a research question, such as *What is the effectiveness of treatment for depression in college students*? A plan for searching for studies that meet a PICO criteria is defined at the outset, along with the library databases that will be explored. A research librarian is typically enlisted so that the search terms and strings are tailored appropriately for each database. The search is comprehensive, meaning all studies on a particular topic are found, including both published and unpublished studies. The reason it's necessary to search for unpublished literature is to account for a well-known phenomenon called *publication bias*; journals are more likely to accept studies for publication that have statistically significant positive results.

Systematic reviews have methods of synthesizing results. For quantitative studies, a meta-analysis uses statistical techniques to combine results from multiple studies to produce a single overall summary of empirical knowledge on a given topic. For qualitative studies, meta-synthesis is qualitatively analyzing the studies to provide themes that cross-cut the shared body of knowledge. (See Chapter 6.)

We will start with finding, reading, and understanding systematic reviews. We will take a closer look at the statistical tool of meta-analysis in detail since that is the hardest part of reviews to understand, and you may have yet to be exposed to the concept in your previous classes. We then discuss how a systematic review can inform the case introduced at the beginning of the chapter. We conclude by discussing other reviews you may find in your searches.

HOW TO FIND SYSTEMATIC REVIEWS

Two international, interdisciplinary collaborations of scholars, policymakers, practitioners, and consumers are the go-to sources for high-quality systematic reviews, Cochrane and the Campbell Collaboration. Cochrane synthesizes results of studies on the effects of interventions in healthcare, which includes mental health. For instance, consider this student PICO question: "What are effective nonpharmacological interventions to help children and adolescents in a hospital setting manage pain related to Sickle Cell disease?" The student located the following title in the Cochrane database, which included youth and adult pain strategies, *Psychological Therapies for Sickle Cell Disease and Pain* (Anie & Green, 2015).

The Campbell Collaboration synthesizes intervention results in social care—education, aging, social welfare, crime and justice, disability, implementation and dissemination, and international development. A student in a school setting became concerned that discipline referrals often ended up with students being excluded from the mainstream classroom, usually in-school or out-of-school suspension. She became interested in exploring other possible ways of intervening. Her PICO question, therefore, was, "What are effective ways to intervene with students for discipline referrals that do not rely on suspension?" In the Campbell Collaboration Criminal Justice library, she found: *School-Based Interventions for Reducing Disciplinary School Exclusion* (Valdebenito, 2018).

The Joanna Briggs Institute (JBI), based in Adelaide, Australia, is another receptacle of high-quality systematic reviews, mainly concerning healthcare. The results of reviews done with the Institute's support are found in the journal *JBI Evidence Synthesis*, which your university library may have access to. A student in a hospital cancer ward formulated the following PICO: "What interventions are effective for gynecology oncology patients regarding their psychosocial and sexual functioning?" She found a review under their auspices, which was later published in a journal, "Effects of Psychoeducation Interventions to Improve Sexual Functioning, Quality of Life, and Psychological Outcomes in Gynecological Cancer Patients" (Chow et al., 2016).

Suppose there are no reviews under the auspices of these organizations. In that case, you can move on to other relevant academic databases, entering your topic search terms and "systematic review"/"meta-analysis" (or entering these types of studies in subject heading terms). If you find one high-quality review that addresses your PICO, you may not need to go much further in locating individual studies. However, it is more common to find related reviews rather than one entirely on target for your topic. Nowadays, it is also common for there to be multiple systematic reviews on your topic area. We cover these various scenarios later in the chapter.

META-ANALYSIS

Systematic reviews often contain a meta-analysis, which is used to statistically analyze the effects of multiple studies to produce a single, overall summary of empirical knowledge on a given topic. To combine studies quantitatively, it is necessary to obtain comparable measures across studies. For example, studies might measure clinical depression through self-report measures, such as the Beck Depression Inventory, the Patient Health Questionnaire, the Center for Epidemiological Depression Scale, and so forth. To make sense of these studies collectively, we would group these as "self-reported depression," and then we could use the study, no matter which particular measure is used. To obtain such comparable or standardized measures across studies, researchers use an *effect size* (ES). Effect sizes tell us the strength or magnitude of the difference between variables or the association between variables.

STANDARDIZED MEAN DIFFERENCE EFFECT SIZE

The most commonly used effect size, employed for studies that test intervention effects and report differences (e.g., between treated and untreated groups), is the *standardized mean difference* (SMD). The SMD, also known as *Cohen's d* (Cohen, 1969), is the mean difference between the treatment condition on a particular outcome score (e.g., depression as measured by the Patient Health Questionnaire) and the control condition on the same average outcome score and then divided by the pooled standard deviation of the two groups. Cohen's (1988) standards for interpreting the SMD are as follows:

1. a negligible finding is less than .2
2. a small finding is between .2 and less than .5
3. a medium effect is between .5 and less than .8
4. a large effect is at least .8 and above

More desirable is a large effect, but medium and even small effects can be important for social science research when results represent reduction in human suffering. You will find that many social service interventions have small effect sizes. Still, even a small effect (not negligible) can be important if the outcome is critical or difficult to change.

EFFECT SIZES FOR INDIVIDUAL STUDIES

As a student, you will probably not conduct a meta-analysis since it's a sophisticated statistical process. However, knowing how to calculate an effect size is helpful, first because it familiarizes you with the "nuts and bolts" of effect size and how it is derived. Second, studies more routinely present effect sizes in published articles, along with statistical significance, so it will assist you in knowing what authors mean when they publish effect sizes of their results.

Effect sizes are increasingly being reported because statistical significance alone possesses some limitations. As mentioned in Chapter 4, statistical significance tells us whether the results could have occurred by chance. "Vote counting" is often used when reviewing studies—simply counting up the number of statistically significant positive results—but this is a crude indicator of results. Sample size has much to do with whether we can find statistically significant results if they exist. If statistically significant results are counted up, we tend to discount smaller studies and favor the results from large studies. Relying on statistical significance further tends to make readers combine outcomes, such as anxiety, stress, and depression, rather than considering the cumulative results on each outcome separately at each relevant period (such as posttest, follow-up, and so forth). In other words, vote counting encourages the comparison of "apples and oranges."

A simplified formula to allow for hand calculation for Cohen's *d*, an effect size used for an experiment employing standardized scales, is:

$$\frac{\text{The mean of the experimental group at posttest} - \text{the mean of the control group at posttest}}{\text{Standard deviation of the mean of the control group at posttest}}$$

For sample purposes, a student formulated the following PICO: *What is the effectiveness of non-CBT interventions for depression in high school students in an alternative high school?* She located Young et al. (2018), which was an RCT, comparing interpersonal psychotherapy to group counseling. The first step in calculating an effect size is to find a table in the article that houses the specific means on standardized measurement tools between the experimental and control conditions at posttest (at the end of the intervention). In Young et al. (2018), the mean for the experimental group at posttest on the Center for Epidemiological Depression Scale (CED-S) depression score was 10.49. We note that higher scores on the CED-S are indicative of more depression.

$$\frac{\text{Mean of IPT condition at posttest (10.49)} - \text{Mean of Group Counseling at posttest (11.37)}}{\text{Standard deviation of the mean of the control group at posttest (9.28)}}$$

Subtracting the mean of the control group CED-S posttest score, which was 11.37, equals -88. We can cancel out the negative number as long as we remember the way the scale is scored. This number (.88) divided by the standard deviation of the control group (9.28) is 0.094. If we consult Cohen's (1988) standards for interpreting effect sizes, we can see that this represents a negligible effect size. In other words, there was little difference between the experimental and control group at posttest on depression scores.

The Young et al. (2018) study also contained 6-, 12-, 18-, and 24-month follow-up periods. Let's take the 24-month period, as optimally, we would like an intervention to have positive effects over a long period.

$$\frac{\text{Mean of IPT condition at posttest (9.79)} - \text{Mean of Group Counseling at posttest (7.96)}}{\text{Standard deviation of the mean of the control group at posttest (7.9)}}$$

Subtracting the control group mean score (7.96) from the experimental group score (9.79), we have 1.83, which is then divided by the standard deviation of the control group (7.9). Here we have .23, which represents a small effect size. Note that this isn't a typical pattern. A more typical pattern is for a result to be stronger at posttest, right after the intervention is over, and then for results to diminish over time. These calculations are interesting because this is not reported in the study. The authors report that the IPT condition did well at postintervention compared to group counseling but worsened at 24-month follow-up. However, the effect size pattern is that there were negligible benefits, even at posttest. Because IPT is a more resource-intensive intervention for tackling depression in the school system, the finding that group counseling might be more effective at two years out is important to know for treatment of depression in the school setting. You can see that statistical significance doesn't reveal the whole picture by itself, and effect sizes provide more information.

ODDS RATIO EFFECT SIZE

Another common effect size is the *odds ratio* (OR). This effect size is calculated when outcomes are tabulated regarding events (suicide attempts, pregnancies, number of people meeting a DSM diagnosis). An *OR* is defined as the ratio of the odds of an event (e.g., suicide attempt, pregnancy, diagnosis) among intervention group participants compared with the odds of that same event among control group participants.

$$\frac{\text{the odds of an event among an intervention condition participants}}{\text{The odds of an event among control condition participants}} = \text{Odds Ratio}$$

An odds ratio is computed by taking the number of cases that meet your criteria (for example, the number of people who meet criteria for depression) divided by the total number of participants in the experimental group (you will also recognize this as a percentage). Then compute the same for the control group. Once you have these two numbers, divide them by each other. Odds ratios have a different metric from Cohen's *d*. The *OR* is a way of comparing whether the probability of a particular event is the same for two groups. Accordingly, an *OR* of 1.0 implies that the event is equally likely in both groups; an odds ratio greater than 1.0 implies that the event is more likely in the intervention group; an *OR* less than 1.0 implies that the event is less likely in the intervention group. The closer this number is to one, the less there is an appreciable difference between the experimental and control groups.

Clarice's agency had a referral for a teenager who had been mandated to attend counseling due to a court order for sexual offending. In order to assist the therapist assigned, she searched for studies on how to reduce sexual offending effectively and found Schmucker and Lösel (2017). This review found 27 studies; on average, there was a significant reduction in recidivism for the treatment versus control group. The authors provided an odds ratio of 1.41, which meant that the odds to reoffend sexually were 1.41 times lower for treated compared to control groups. In other words, there was 26% less recidivism in the treatment condition compared to the control condition after intervention. There was a recidivism rate of 10% in treated sex offenders, and 14% in offenders in the control groups.

READING AND UNDERSTANDING A SYSTEMATIC REVIEW

We will dissect one together because systematic reviews can be difficult to read and understand. Note there is no need to read the whole study (unless you find it helpful to do so to have a sense of the whole and the context). In "For Your Practice," we display a template for students to use so that they can present in a succinct way the key information to pull out. Following is a description of each of the components of the template. In Table 5.1, there is an example of a complete systematic review summary that helps answer the PICO for the case introduced in this chapter.

PURPOSE

What is the author's overall purpose of the systematic review that was undertaken? This information can be found following the literature review, right before the methods section. Try to paraphrase, if possible, to see if you can find the essential idea. If you directly cite the purpose from the study, make sure to include quotations and a page number.

INCLUSION CRITERIA

What criteria did the researchers use to search for studies to answer the research question? This information can be found at the beginning of the methods section. Most systematic reviews will put this in the PICO format you're already familiar with. If they don't use a PICO format, you can organize their inclusion criteria in that way so you can see how it lines up with your own PICO.

- P: What was the target population for the intervention?
- I: What was the intervention being studied? What was the theory underlying the intervention?
- C: What was the intervention being compared to? Common comparisons are (1) no-treatment or waitlist control groups; (2) treatment-as-usual or placebo/attention

TABLE 5.1 Sample Summary of a Systematic Review/Meta-Analysis (PICO: Among college-aged students, what is the most effective intervention for depression?)

Author and Purpose	Inclusion Criteria	Results
Cuijpers, P., Cristea, I. A., Ebert, D. D., Koot, H. M., Auerbach, R. P., Bruffaerts, R., & Kessler, R. C. (2016). Psychological treatment of depression in college students: A meta-analysis. *Depression and Anxiety*, *33*(5), 400–414. https://doi.org/10.1002/da.22461 To examine the effectiveness of psychological treatments for depression in college-age students.	Participants: college students Intervention: a psychological therapy for depression Comparisons: RCTs with any control/comparison Outcomes: depression Studies: RCTs collected from the authors' ongoing repository of studies on depression.*	Total *N* of studies = 15, 997 participants Main effect size: $g = 0.89$ (95% CI: 0.66~1.11), which is considered a large effect. Moderator analysis: Individual more effective than group. CBT was the vast majority studied (only 4 weren't) and type of therapy didn't matter.

*The first author has conducted many systematic reviews/meta-analyses on depression.

control (meaning that the control group received some kind of attention, such as supportive counseling where people were listened to and validated for their concerns).

O: What was the outcome being addressed (the dependent variable)? What did the researchers hope to change as a result of the intervention? Sometimes there is only one outcome, but other times there are primary and secondary outcomes.

T: What type of studies were the researchers of the systematic review looking for? Only RCTs? All kinds of designs? Was there a date parameter set on the search? Was only the published literature searched or was the unpublished literature (dissertations, conference proceedings) also a focus? Were only English-language studies included or was there an attempt to find studies worldwide? Sometimes only "developed" countries are included, while other times "developing" countries are a focus of study.

RESULTS

The results section of a systematic review might become very technical if there is meta-analysis, so the student is advised to obtain the necessary results from the beginning of the results section where the studies located are described (including how many and what kind of participants, interventions, and studies were involved), the abstract, and the discussion section. The main effect size reported by the authors is also critical as it summarizes the entire body of knowledge. The same frameworks to analyze individual study effect sizes are used for the overall effect. Although authors will typically translate these numerical findings into plain English, we advise finding the exact number and using Cohen's guidelines provided to interpret the results. Occasionally, authors will overstate their findings.

Moderator analysis is often reported as a part of meta-analysis if a sufficient number of studies are included in the review. In moderator analysis, researchers can statistically examine the influence of critical variables on the overall effect size, answering such questions as how the characteristics of the participants, the intervention, or the studies influenced the effect size. In the example presented by Cuijpers et al. (2016), individual therapy was more effective than group therapy for the psychological treatment of depression in college students. Therefore, moderator analysis tells us more than just one overall effect size and provides a greater level of specificity for application.

CRITICAL APPRAISAL

Now that you have learned how to find and read a systematic review, we move to critical appraisal, which, as you know, is its own step in the EBP process. As mentioned in the descriptions of the Cochrane Collaboration, the Campbell Collaboration, and the Joanna Briggs Institute, these organizations demand high levels of rigor in their reviews, so they are typically of very high quality. Given the lengths these organizations go to preserve methodological rigor, you can assume that these reviews will demonstrate their adherence to high standards.

Aside from these, not all systematic reviews are created equal, and the term "systematic review" is now used widely. For instance, many reviews are limited to the published studies only or a specific time frame in years (say, the last 10 years). Other reviews fail to provide a synthesis of studies through meta-analysis. This could be because studies cannot be synthesized—they do not share enough similar characteristics and we would be comparing "apples to oranges"—or because the authors simply did not perform one. These reviews, therefore, rely on presenting information from studies descriptively (often in tables) and do vote counting on the number of studies with statistically significant results. As discussed earlier in this chapter, there are problems with a vote count method.

Another indicator of the quality of a systematic review was whether they developed a preset methodology and attempted to use quality standards. Protocols are sometimes registered an organization, namely PROSPERO (https://www.crd.york.ac.uk/prospero/documents/Guidance%20for%20registering%20human%20studies.pdf), Cochrane, Campbell Collaboration, or Joanna Briggs. Quality appraisal tools have been developed for systematic reviews (see list in *further resources*). However, for MSW students, it asks for a high level of technicality in the meta-analytic techniques. For this reason, we recommend the Joanna Briggs Institute rating form (see *further resources*). In Box 5.1, we spell out each of the items of this form to enable students' understanding and application, and in italics, provide the student's critical appraisal of the systematic review she found to answer her PICO.

BOX 5.1 SAMPLE: CRITICAL APPRAISAL SYSTEMATIC REVIEW AND META-ANALYSIS

STUDY SOURCE

Cuijpers, P., Cristea, I. A., Ebert, D. D., Koot, H. M., Auerbach, R. P., Bruffaerts, R., & Kessler, R. C. (2016). Psychological Treatment of Depression in College Students: A Meta-Analysis. Depression and Anxiety, 33(5), 400–414. https://doi.org/10.1002/da.22461

WAS THE PURPOSE CLEARLY STATED?

Yes, to determine the effectiveness of psychological treatments for depression in college-age students.

WAS THE SEARCH STRATEGY APPROPRIATE?

Did the authors use several, relevant academic data bases? *Yes, PubMed, PsycInfo, Cochrane until end of 2014*
Did a librarian assist in formulating search terms and strings? *Not stated*
Were the sources and resources used to search for studies adequate? (i.e., Were there two researchers working independently to screen articles with supporting information?) *Not stated.*
Was a PRISMA table used to show how many studies were screened and eliminated at each stage of the search and screening process to arrive at a final number? *Yes, p. 402*
Were there methods to minimize errors in data extraction? (i.e., were there at least two independent researchers doing data extraction?): *Yes*

HOW WAS THE QUALITY OF THE INDIVIDUAL STUDIES ASCERTAINED?

Was a particular tool used? What variables were examined? *Cochrane Collaboration tool: (1) adequate sequence generation; (2) allocation to conditions by an independent party; (3) assessors blind to outcomes; and (4) completeness of follow-up data.*
The authors concluded that "The risk of bias in most studies was considerable . . . None of the included 15 studies met all quality criteria . . . 10 met only one of the four criteria" (p. 403)
Was critical appraisal conducted by two or more reviewers independently? *Yes*
Did they do meta-analysis to combine studies? *Yes*
Were moderators examined? *Yes*

Was the likelihood of publication bias assessed? Did the researchers include unpublished studies in their inclusion criteria? Did the researchers use a statistical method for looking at publication bias (often a funnel plot is indicated)? What did they report? *"Inspection of the funnel plot suggested considerable publication bias. Egger's test of the intercept was significant (intercept: 2.14; 95% CI: 1.00~3.28; P = 0.0004). Duvall and Tweedie's trim and fill procedure indicated that eight studies might be missing due to publication bias and that the pooled effect size would decrease to g = 0.61 (95% CI: 0.37~0.85) if these presumably negative studies were included"* (p. 403).

DID THE AUTHORS PRESENT POLICY AND/OR PRACTICE IMPLICATIONS WHICH WERE SUPPORTED BY THEIR RESULTS OF THE STUDY?

Expand detection, outreach and treatment as treatment can be effective and untreated depression can severely restrict human capital. The college-age population can be reached at the beginning of their adult lives when depression sometimes emerges.

WERE THE SPECIFIC DIRECTIVES FOR NEW RESEARCH APPROPRIATE?

Higher-quality studies needed, understanding which students can potentially improve from unguided and guided self-help to meet demand.

CASE DISCUSSION

Considering the systematic review that was located and the quality appraisal, the student concluded that psychological treatment was effective at reducing depression in the college-age population. Although type of treatment was not a moderator, most treatments were identified as CBT/behavior activation. Considering the session limit at the college counseling center, the student was excited to find in Lejuez et al. (2011) that the revised behavior activation protocol had been shortened to five essential sessions. Further revised elements were less complicated and fewer forms (students already had to be organized about their schoolwork) and leading with values to guide motivation for tasks. Therefore, the <u>intervention selected</u> was behavior activation.

<u>Client characteristics</u>: The student believed that most would welcome an approach with research support after only a brief treatment period.

<u>Provider context and barriers</u>: When the student presented her findings to her field supervisor, the supervisor said that practitioners could not be told what treatment to practice,

> as they had considerable autonomy in selecting a particular approach and most preferred psychodynamic psychotherapy. The student estimated that many of the therapists preferred psychodynamic approaches. (We discuss more about implementation barriers in Chapters 7 and 8).
>
> <u>Measure selected</u>: The student presented the PHQ9 as a quick measure for assessing risk and evaluating progress to see, whatever the approach chosen, whether depression resolved, or at least was reduced, at the end of the treatment period.

This example demonstrates how systematic reviews cover an area of knowledge in an in-depth way to set the context for your own study without necessarily having to find, summarize, and critically appraise individual studies, a labor-intensive and time-consuming process. Of course, your ability to use systematic reviews will depend on their availability in your topic area. In the next section, we discuss the variety of systematic reviews.

VARIATIONS OF SYSTEMATIC REVIEWS

Aside from systematic reviews/meta-analyses, other kinds of reviews have also developed. The most basic of these is the literature review, which you have likely already completed yourself (maybe you have called them *research papers*). These have no research question, preset plan, or methodology, although they represent an attempt to synthesize findings of studies in narrative.

Because reviews appear on similar or overlapping topics, there is now a type of study called an *overview of reviews* (the name the Cochrane Collaboration uses), *umbrella reviews* (the Joanna Briggs Institute nomenclature), meta-reviews, and reviews of reviews (Hunt et al., 2018). The purpose of overviews of systematic reviews, or umbrella reviews, as they are called, is to systematically retrieve, critically appraise, and synthesize the results of multiple systematic reviews on a topic. Overviews can examine explanations for discrepant results and conclusions, mapping the available evidence, and identifying gaps in the literature (Hunt et al., 2018). An example is Fordham et al. (2021), who performed an overview of CBT for a variety of different clinical conditions; another is an overview of systematic reviews for youth anxiety treatment (Bennett et al., 2016).

Evidence maps and *scoping reviews* are other types of reviews. They are similar in that they involve a systematic search of a broad field to identify the volume, nature, and characteristics of the primary research, including a range of research designs and methods, as well as gaps in knowledge and needed research (Arksey & O'Malley, 2005, as cited in Pham et al., 2014; Miake-Lye et al., 2016). Evidence maps are distinguished by presenting results in a user-friendly format, such as a visual figure/graph or searchable database (Miake-Lye et al., 2016). A comprehensive example is the mapping of interventions for homelessness (see https://www.homelessnessimpact.org/gap-maps). Much latitude exists around definitions and formats of scoping reviews and evidence maps, and more standardization is being called for.

To distinguish itself from the systematic review, the scoping review has a broader purpose than a systematic review and typically has a more expansive inclusion criteria for studies. Scoping reviews may help provide context for a chosen topic area. As an example, "A Scoping Review of Contemporary Social Work Practice with Veterans" presents the "scope" of the scholarship in this area, so the reader gets a sense of what is already known and where to focus more narrowly.

A *systematic review* aims to comprehensively locate and synthesize the research that bears on a particular question. It uses organized, transparent, and replicable procedures at each step in the process. Systematic reviews may vary as to how they synthesize evidence. At the top of the pyramid is the use of a quantitative synthesis method, meta-analysis. Another way to synthesize evidence is through descriptive means in narrative and tables. In that sense, it is similar to the literature review. Another means is if the studies only involve qualitative studies (Chapter 6). In that case, findings of the original studies are synthesized qualitatively.

A final type of review is the rapid review, which is an abbreviated systematic review, perhaps focusing on only the published literature, a certain time frame (e.g., last 10 years), or one country. It is usually done in response to stakeholders that need evidence fairly quickly to make a decision. Reviews on rapid reviews have noted that there is considerable latitude around methods (Hamel et al., 2020; Harker & Kleijnen, 2012). Common shortcuts involved only one person doing screening, extraction, and quality appraisal. We have covered the variety of reviews, including literature reviews, systematic reviews, scoping reviews, rapid reviews, and umbrella reviews, as you will likely uncover them as you search for systematic reviews on your topic. They may also help you answer PICO questions, as well as provided needed context. In the resources section below, there are links to tables and figures that explain the differences between the variety of reviews.

WHAT IF THERE ARE MULTIPLE SYSTEMATIC REVIEWS?

One final question we will address here is about what to do when there are multiple systematic reviews on a topic. Since the decision would depend on a number of factors, there are no hard and fast rules, but here are some guidelines to consider.

1. As mentioned, systematic reviews registered with Cochrane, the Campbell Collaboration, and the Joanna Briggs Institute are guaranteed to be of high quality. Having a review registered on PROSPERO means that a preset plan was developed.
2. A systematic review without a meta-analysis automatically downgrades its quality; however, it still might provide useful information in that the authors have collected and described a great deal of studies on your topic of interest.

3. You have learned how to critically appraise systematic reviews, so all things being equal, you would trust the results more from a high-quality review since the authors have worked hard to avoid bias.

The following case by Brian White is used to illustrate how one may handle multiple systematic reviews.

Sheila is a 50-year-old, African American female, who currently lives alone in an apartment in a mid-Atlantic urban area. She has little social support and lives on public assistance. She often has a depressed mood most of the day and has difficulty sleeping most nights because she often worries about death. Sheila makes statements, such as, "I don't feel like being around anyone," "I always want to be by myself," "I don't want to be bothered," and "I feel sad all the time." Sheila has been diagnosed with generalized anxiety disorder and major depressive disorder and is to receive therapy once a week through an outpatient center. Sheila considers herself a Christian and attends a Baptist church every Sunday. She reports, "I read my Bible, and pray every night that God will keep me safe."

PICO: The student formulated the following PICO question: Does religiously/spiritually oriented psychotherapy improve outcomes in adults suffering from clinical anxiety and depression?

Search and Appraisal: The student found that there were no Cochrane, Campbell, or Joanna Briggs Institute studies on this topic. In PubMed, Embase, and Scopus, he found four systematic reviews that might answer this question. (We won't provide all the summary and critical appraisal tables here because of the numbers of reviews, but he pulled out the salient points.)

The first was called *A Systematic Review of the Effects of Religion: Accommodative Psychotherapy for Depression and Anxiety* (Paukert et al., 2011). This study did not have a meta-analysis so the student put it on hold and moved to the second one, *Religious and Spiritual Interventions in Mental Health Care: A Systematic Review and Meta-Analysis of Randomized Controlled Clinical Trials* (Gonclaves et al., 2015). The issue with this study, which limited its applicability to the problem at hand, was that it considered any study that tested a religious and/or spiritual intervention with any kind of problem, including physical disease, or in healthy individuals. Therefore, this study seemed to have limited relevance for a person who was suffering from clinical depression and anxiety.

The third study was entitled *Faith-Adapted Psychological Therapies for Depression and Anxiety: Systematic Review and Meta-analysis* (Anderson et al., 2015). The inclusion criteria for this review was that primary studies had to be faith-adapted psychological therapies for clinically diagnosed depression and anxiety. When looking at only the Christian-oriented psychological treatments (his client was Christian), there were only 2 studies but, taken together, they were more effective than control groups (no treatment, waiting list, or treatment as usual) at a statistically significant effect. The four studies that compared Christian-oriented psychological treatment against standard CBT also found a statistically significant effect. For anxiety, the authors weren't able to pool results in meta-analysis, but their overall conclusion was "that faith-adapted CBT appears to be effective (i.e. superior to control conditions), and there is some possible suggestion that it may be superior to standard CBT in the treatment of depression and anxiety." A major limitation to these findings was that all of the studies had a high risk of bias, which tempers the results. The authors also did not perform an overall meta-analysis of the faith-adapted studies, which comprised Christian, Muslim, and spiritual, but rather divided the studies up by type of control group and the three categories.

Finally, a fourth systematic review was located, *Religion and Spirituality* (Worthington et al., 2011). These authors considered the studies together, and found that religious and spiritual psychotherapies produced greater improvement in clients than those in no-treatment control groups on both psychological (.45) and spiritual outcomes (.51) at posttest, and were maintained at a smaller effect at follow-up. Religious and spiritual psychotherapies also showed greater improvement in clients than those in alternate psychotherapies on both psychological ($d = .26$) and spiritual outcomes (.41) at both posttest and at follow-up.

Taking the results of Worthington et al. (2011) and Anderson et al. (2015), the student believed he had enough tentative support to proceed with a religiously adapted psychotherapy for Sheila. We continue discussing this case in Chapter 9, but for now we want to emphasize with the increased number of reviews being published, it may mean that multiple reviews might be available on your topic. This example and the guidelines we offered show how to examine the reviews for their relevance and salience to your topic, their quality, and how the results tie in to your own PICO question.

CONCLUSION

Systematic reviews, along with meta-analysis, and variations of reviews, have been the subject of this chapter. Rigorous summaries and syntheses of existing bodies of knowledge can inform our PICO questions. Therefore, students need a clear understanding of how to find, read, and apply the results of reviews to their PICO question. As this chapter has argued, reviews are emerging as an even more salient way to approach the EBP process than are simply single RCTs while reducing the burden on individual, time-strapped practitioners to undergo this laborious search, read, and appraisal process themselves.

FURTHER RESOURCES

CRITICAL APPRAISAL TOOLS

1. Center of Evidence-Based Medicine: https://www.cebm.net/wp-content/uploads/2019/01/Systematic-Review.pdf
2. Assessment of Multiple Systematic Review (AMSTAR): https://amstar.ca/Amstar_Checklist.php
3. Joanna Briggs Checklists: https://jbi.global/critical-appraisal-tools

TABLES AND FIGURES THAT EXPLAIN THE VARIETY OF REVIEWS

Kysh, Lynn (2013): Difference between a systematic review and a literature review. [figshare]. http://dx.doi.org/10.6084/m9.figshare.766364

https://www.google.com/search?client=safari&rls=en&q=figures+comparing+types+of+reviews&ie=UTF-8&oe=UTF-8

FOR YOUR PRACTICE

ACTIVITY #1:

In Chapter 4, you already located a randomized, controlled trial that fit your PICO question. If it is testing an intervention study using a standardized measure, compute an effect size at posttest and at follow-up (if the latter is applicable):
Study name here:
Outcome of interest:
Time period: (posttest or a specified follow-up period):
Mean for experimental group for the outcome measure chosen:
Mean for the control group for the outcome measure chosen:
Standard deviation of the mean of the control group outcome measure:
Effect size:
What does this effect size mean?

ACTIVITY #2:

Select an RCT that answers your PICO question and uses an outcome that is measured in frequency counts. Compute an odds ratio at posttest and at follow-up (if the latter is applicable):
Study Name here:
Outcome of interest:
Time period: (posttest or a specified follow-up period):
Number of events of interest that occurred in the experimental group:
Total number of participants in the experimental group for that time period:
Number of events of interest that occurred in the control group:
Total number of participants in the control group for that time period.
Divide the total number of events by the total number of participants in the experimental group by the number of events by the total number of participants in the control group.
What is the OR:
What do the authors say it means?

ACTIVITY #3: SUMMARY OF A SYSTEMATIC REVIEW

Locate a systematic review that answers one of your PICO questions. Complete the summary as you've been taught in this chapter.

Author and Purpose	Inclusion Criteria	Results

ACTIVITY #4: COMPLETE A CRITICAL APPRAISAL OF A SYSTEMATIC REVIEW

Using the Joanna Briggs Checklist, complete an appraisal for the study that you summarized.

Items in Joanna Briggs Checklist for Systematic Reviews and Research Syntheses

1. Was the purpose clearly stated?
2. Was the search strategy appropriate?
    a. Did the authors use several, relevant academic data bases?
    b. Did a librarian assist in formulating search terms and strings?
3. Were the sources and resources used to search for studies adequate (i.e., Were there two researchers working independently to screen articles, documenting the process?)
4. Was a PRISMA[1] figure used to show how many studies were screened and eliminated at each stage of the search and screening process to arrive at a final number?
5. Were there methods to minimize errors in data extraction? (i.e., were there at least two independent researchers doing data extraction?):
6. How was the quality of the individual studies ascertained?
    a. Was a particular tool used? What variables were examined?
    b. Was critical appraisal conducted by two or more reviewers independently?
7. Did they do meta-analysis to combine studies?
    If no meta-analysis, what was the stated reason?
    If not, what was the method or system for combining or categorizing studies?
8. Was the likelihood of publication bias assessed?
    Did the researchers include unpublished studies in their inclusion criteria?
    Did the researchers use statistical methods for addressing publication bias? What did they report?

---

1. PRISMA stands for Preferred Reporting Items for Systematic Reviews and Meta-Analyses, which is a set of standards and items for reporting in systematic reviews and meta-analyses.

9. Did the authors present policy and/or practice implications that were supported by the results of the study?
10. Were the specific directives for new research appropriate?

REFERENCES

Anderson, N., Heywood-Everett, S., Siddiqi, N., Wright, J., Meredith, J., & Mcmillan, D. (2015). Faith-adapted psychological therapies for depression and anxiety: Systematic review and meta-analysis. *Journal of Affective Disorders, 176C*, 183–196. https://doi.org/10.1016/j.jad.2015.01.019

Anie, K. A., Green, J., & Anie, K. A. (2015). Psychological therapies for sickle cell disease and pain. *Cochrane Database of Systematic Reviews, 2015*(5), CD001916–CD001916. https://doi.org/10.1002/14651858.CD001916.pub3

Bennett, K., Manassis, K., Duda, S., Bagnell, A., Bernstein, G. A., Garland, E. J., Miller, L. D., Newton, A., Thabane, L., & Wilansky, P. (2016). Treating child and adolescent anxiety effectively: Overview of systematic reviews. *Clinical Psychology Review, 50*, 80–94. https://doi.org/10.1016/j.cpr.2016.09.006.

Chow, K. M., Chan, J. C., Choi, K. K., & Chan, C. W. (2016). Effects of psychoeducation interventions to improve sexual functioning, quality of life, and psychological outcomes in gynecological cancer patients. *Cancer Nursing, 39*(1), 20–31.

Cohen, J. (1969). *Statistical power analysis for the behavioral sciences*. Academic Press.

Cohen, J. (1988). *Statistical power analysis for the behavioral sciences* (2nd ed.). Lawrence Erlbaum Associates.

Cuijpers, P., Cristea, I. A., Ebert, D. D., Koot, H. M., Auerbach, R. P., Bruffaerts, R., & Kessler, R. C. (2016). Psychological treatment of depression in college students: A meta-analysis. *Depression and Anxiety, 33*(5), 400–414. https://doi.org/10.1002/da.22461

Fordham, B., Sugavanam, T., Edwards, K., Stallard, P., Howard, R., Das Nair, R., . . . Lamb, S. (2021). The evidence for cognitive behavioural therapy in any condition, population or context: A meta-review of systematic reviews and panoramic meta-analysis. *Psychological Medicine, 51*(1), 21–29. https://doi.org/10.1017/S0033291720005292

Gonçalves, J., Lucchetti, G., Menezes, P., & Vallada, H. (2015). Religious and spiritual interventions in mental health care: A systematic review and meta-analysis of randomized controlled clinical trials. *Psychological Medicine, 45*(14), 2937–2949. https://doi.org/10.1017/S0033291715001166

Hamel, C., Michaud, A., Thuku, M., Affengruber, L., Skidmore, B., Nussbaumer-Streit, B., Stevens, A., & Garritty, C. (2020). Few evaluative studies exist examining rapid review methodology across stages of conduct: A systematic scoping review. *Journal of Clinical Epidemiology, 126*, 131–140. https://doi.org/10.1016/j.jclinepi.2020.06.027

Harker, J., & Kleijnen, J. (2012). What is a rapid review? A methodological exploration of rapid reviews in health technology assessments. *International Journal of Evidence-Based Healthcare, 10*(4), 397–410. https://doi.org/10.1111/j.1744-1609.2012.00290.x

Hunt, H., Pollock, A., Campbell, P., Estcourt, L., & Brunton, G. (2018). An introduction to overviews of reviews: Planning a relevant research question and objective for an overview. *Systematic Reviews, 7*(1), 39. https://doi.org/10.1186/s13643-018-0695-8

Ibrahim, A. K., Kelly, S. J., Adams, C. E., & Glazebrook, C. (2013). A systematic review of studies of depression prevalence in university students. *Journal of Psychiatric Research, 47*(3), 391–400. https://doi.org/10.1016/j.jpsychires.2012.11.015

Lejuez, C. W., Hopko, D. R., Acierno, R., Daughters, S. B., & Pagoto, S. L. (2011). Ten year revision of the brief behavioral activation treatment for depression: Revised treatment manual. *Behavior Modification, 35*(2), 111–161. https://doi.org/10.1177/0145445510390929

Miake-Lye, I. M., Hempel, S., Shanman, R., & Shekelle, P. G. (2016). What is an evidence map? A systematic review of published evidence maps and their definitions, methods, and products. *Systematic Reviews, 5*, 28. https://doi.org/10.1186/s13643-016-0204-x

Paukert, A. L., Phillips, L. L., Cully, J. A., Romero, C., & Stanley, M. A. (2011). Systematic review of the effects of religion-accommodative psychotherapy for depression and anxiety. *Journal of Contemporary Psychotherapy, 41*, 99–108. https://doi.org.proxy.library.upenn.edu/10.1007/s10879-010-9154-0

Pham, M. T., Rajić, A., Greig, J. D., Sargeant, J. M., Papadopoulos, A., & McEwen, S. A. (2014). A scoping review of scoping reviews: Advancing the approach and enhancing the consistency. *Research Synthesis Methods, 5*, 371–385. https://doi.org/10.1002/jrsm.1123

Schmucker, M., & Lösel, F. (2017). Sexual offender treatment for reducing recidivism among convicted sex offenders: A systematic review and meta-analysis. *Campbell Systematic Reviews, 13*, 1–75. https://doi.org/10.4073/csr.2017.8

Valdebenito, S., Eisner, M., Farrington, D. P., Ttofi, M. M., & Sutherland, A. (2018). School-based interventions for reducing disciplinary school exclusion: A systematic review. *Campbell Systematic Reviews, 14*(1), 1–216. https://doi.org/10.4073/csr.2018.1

Worthington, E. L., Jr., Hook, J. N., Davis, D. E., & McDaniel, M. A. (2011). Religion and spirituality. *Journal of Clinical Psychology, 67*, 204–214. https://doi.org.proxy.library.upenn.edu/10.1002/jclp.20760

Young, J. F., Jones, J. D., Sbrilli, M. D., Benas, J. S., Spiro, C. N., Haimm, C. A., Gallop, R., Mufson, L., & Gillham, J. E. (2019). Long-term effects from a school-based trial comparing interpersonal psychotherapy-adolescent skills training to group counseling. *Journal of Clinical Child & Adolescent Psychology, 48*(sup1), S362–S370. https://doi.org/10.1080/15374416.2018.1479965.

CHAPTER 6

QUALITATIVE RESEARCH AND THE EBP PROCESS

With Holly Bell

> *Maya is a student at a field placement where trauma-focused cognitive-behavioral therapy (TF-CBT) was implemented for youth who had undergone trauma, most commonly sexual abuse. This public clinic serves self-referred families and those whom the courts have mandated. Maya reported that the licensed clinicians at the agency struggle to implement the TF-CBT protocol with the youth they saw in this community-based setting. One of their concerns involved engagement of parents/caregivers in treatment; the other, which overlapped, was the lack of homework completion among youth. Parents have to encourage and reinforce their children's completion of out-of-session tasks. Maya's interest was piqued, and she developed the following PICO questions: (1) How can practitioners engage caregivers in TF-CBT?? (2) How can providers increase the uptake of homework in TF-CBT?*

QUALITATIVE RESEARCH

This chapter describes qualitative research and its place in the evidence-based practice (EBP) process. We define qualitative research as "any kind of research that produces findings not arrived at using statistical procedures or other means of quantification" (Strauss & Corbin, 1998, p. 11). In other words, language and narrative is the subject for analysis. Qualitative research has also been defined at its most basic level as asking "open questions about phenomena as they occur in context rather than setting out to test predetermined hypotheses"

(Carter & Little, 2007). Qualitative research involves an *inductive* approach that moves from specific observations to broader generalizations and theories. In contrast, much of quantitative research is deductive—a top-down approach—in that there are theories and hypotheses to be tested.

The foundation textbook used in your first-year MSW or BSW course likely explained qualitative research from the perspective of how to undertake this type of inquiry. However, in the EBP process, qualitative research may be used to answer the following PICO question: What is the "lived experience" (experiences, life events, perspectives, attitudes) of a particular problem from the viewpoint of someone who has experienced it? Recall that the EBP process involves the best available evidence integrated with client characteristics and the practice setting. This question addresses the "client perspective" on the acceptability of a particular approach and experiences trying to cope and manage the problem. Some qualitative studies, even if not about a specific intervention, may still have direct implications for service delivery. For example, in a qualitative research synthesis, parents of children with developmental disabilities reported having difficulty navigating the social service care system and getting the help they needed (Corcoran, 2016). An implication is that any intervention with parents taking care of children with these disabilities would need education and advocacy on accessing key services, so trying to get help does not end up being another stressor.

CHARACTERISTICS OF QUALITATIVE RESEARCH

Qualitative research is used when exploring new topics about which little is known, seeking to understand the subjective meaning that individuals assign to situations, behaviors, or beliefs (Padgett, 2017). Social workers generally find the characteristics of qualitative research compatible with clinical work and its methods (Padgett, 2017). In "practice wisdom," one generalizes how to approach certain problems and clients from previous experience. Both social work and qualitative research rely on interviewing people about their perspectives. Social workers are interested in the lived experiences of people, taking into account their context and the meaning they make out of life challenges. Often, qualitative researchers tend to have more personal relations with the research participants who open up their lives—giving time and sharing intimate stories and personal information with interviewers. We are also trained in cultural sensitivity and routinely do cross-cultural work. We examine our positionality in relation to people with whom we work and our biases to engage in reflexivity, that is, explicit self-aware analysis of one's role as the primary analytic tool. Moreover, we are versed in the ethics and standards of the profession, such as confidentiality and professional boundaries, challenges that may arise in qualitative research when participants disclose sensitive, illegal, or painful information and material.

While qualitative research may feel like a better fit for social workers, knowing how to apply qualitative research to a practice situation, particularly when multiple studies on a topic can't be easily compared or aggregated, can be frustrating. Practitioners who have only had a cursory introduction to qualitative methods in a research course that focused heavily on quantitative methods may be bewildered by the diversity of qualitative methods and intimidated by how to read, understand, and use such data, not to mention how to judge the quality of the study they are reading. This chapter is designed to help you know how to read qualitative studies to glean the information you need to inform practice.

WHAT KIND OF EVIDENCE DOES QUALITATIVE RESEARCH PRODUCE?

One of the most challenging differences between qualitative and quantitative research is epistemology, or how we know what we know. Quantitative research proceeds from the idea that there is an objective world that is knowable through the scientific method, by testing hypotheses, eliminating bias in data collection and analysis, and determining general population trends by extrapolating results from a random sample. Qualitative research not only departs from this positivist perspective but is grounded in diverse and often unfamiliar ways of knowing (Hartman, 1990).

Another challenge in understanding qualitative research is its diverse disciplinary roots. Authors and researchers from various fields may use different terms and categorize the various epistemologies and methodologies in different ways. We see this in a brief review of textbooks used in research methods courses in social work and their discussion of epistemologies. For example, Hilton, Fawson, Sullivan, and DeJong et al. (2019) discuss only two. They address positivism, which holds that there is an objective reality that exists independent of people's perceptions of it. The positivist perspective is that scientists can use objective techniques to discover aspects of it, the basis of quantitative research. The other epistemology explored in Hilton et al. (2019) is subjectivism/interpretivism, which focuses on the subjective and personal meanings that people attach to themselves, to what they do, and to the world around them, the domain of much of qualitative research (p. 258). To these, Rubin and Babbie (2016) add an *empowerment paradigm*, which seeks to make social change, and Yegidis et al. (2017) contribute *postpositivism*, a sort of "positivism lite," which acknowledges an objective reality but is concerned with how the researcher's values, biases, and background knowledge impact access to that reality; *pragmatism*, which focuses on the practical uses of research in real-life situations; and *phenomenology*, which studies the subjective experience of the individual of a particular phenomenon (p. 127). Two other epistemologies that you may see discussed in the research are the *critical paradigm*, which focuses on power dynamics with the goal of not just understanding a situation but also changing it; and *postmodern/poststructural perspectives*, which deconstruct, problematize, and question the basic assumptions of cultural discourses or conversations (Merriam & Tisdale, 2015). One example of the latter is Park et al.'s (2020) analysis and critique of the concept of resilience in social work literature.

Despite the focus in recent years on distinguishing the epistemological undergirding of qualitative research both within qualitative methods and from quantitative methods, most published qualitative studies remain agnostic or don't state their epistemological stance (Padgett, 2017, p. 8). With this in mind, you may ask yourself, "Why do I need to know this stuff? I'm a social worker, not a philosopher." At its heart, the question of what constitutes "evidence" in "evidence-based practice" IS a question of epistemology. It is why, for example, most researchers working today would consider a survey, an experiment, and a case study—but not a horoscope—as "evidence" (Braun & Clarke, 2013). Epistemology comes into the picture when we consider the relationship of the researcher to participants, how to judge a study's quality and the strategies used to make a study rigorous, how researchers represent themselves and the participants in the final write-up, and what claims the researcher makes for the study (Carter & Little, 2007). As a reader, you do not have to be an expert in these complex issues, but you should keep these ideas in mind and be aware of the researcher's assumptions, whether stated explicitly or not.

In the subjective world in which most qualitative research is conducted, the researcher's role is critical. To manage this subjectivity, qualitative researchers practice reflexivity, which Probst (2015) defines this way:

> Reflexivity is an important tool that enables the researcher to stay engaged in critical self-awareness throughout the research process. It is the embodiment of an epistemology in which the knower is always present, a way of looking that gazes outward at what is taking place while sustaining an inward gaze at the looker. More than just a vehicle for honesty or management of the research experience, reflexivity offers a means for using self-knowledge to inform and enhance the research endeavor. (p. 46)

Qualitative researchers reflect on who they are (insider or outsider to the topic and sample population), what they know, and how this provides insight or barriers to what the data are saying in memos, with colleagues and mentors, and in the final write-up. It is a way of managing, rather than eliminating, what quantitative researchers call "bias."

METHODOLOGIES

Unlike quantitative research, which developed from the natural sciences, qualitative research has its roots in many disciplines, contributing to a number of disparate methodologies that fall under its umbrella. Padgett (2017) names six approaches or methodologies you will most likely find in social work journals: ethnography, grounded theory, case study analysis, narrative approaches, phenomenological analysis, and action and community engaged research. Ethnography originated from anthropology to learn about and document a culture's story using participant observation and interviews. Phenomenology has deep philosophical roots involving the nature of reality and knowledge but, at its most basic level, centers on people's lived experience of a phenomenon, such as grief or coming out (Neubauer et al., 2019). Grounded theory, focusing on developing new theories for understanding a phenomenon, arose from sociology (Strauss & Corbin, 1998). Case studies examine a real-life, contemporary bounded system or systems over time through detailed in-depth data collection, generally from multiple data types (sometimes including both qualitative and quantitative data) (Atkinson, 2002; Stake, 1995; Yin, 2017). While there is some overlap with ethnography, the case in a case study can be an individual, an organization, an event, or some other bounded phenomenon. Narrative approaches focus on the stories that people tell about themselves, with some purpose in mind, to a specific audience (Riesman, 2008). Analysis can focus on what was told, how it was told, or how the story fits into larger social discourses, such as disability. Participatory action research (PAR), a particular type of action and community engaged research, is committed to empowering participants in communities to be more equal partners in the research process for the purpose not just of understanding a social problem but also changing it (Baum et al., 2006; Rubin & Babbie, 2016). A popular method in public health, it appeals to social workers because of its focus on social change. Like case study research, PAR may use both qualitative and quantitative measures.

Many otherwise high-quality and useful studies do not identify themselves within any particular methodology. If your searching leads you into the territory of other disciplines, you may encounter many other approaches or, even more confusing, the same approach called by a different name by another author or in another discipline (for example, narrative and life story interviews). Some good resources for gaining a basic understanding of the variety and terminology of qualitative research methodologies are the *SAGE Encyclopedia of Qualitative Research Methods* (Givens, 2008) and the *SAGE Dictionary of Qualitative Inquiry* (Schwandt, 2015).

METHODS

The most-used method for qualitative research in social work involves individual interviews in which the interviewer develops a comprehensive picture of people's background, attitudes, and actions in their terms (Staller, 2013). Further, individual interviews seek to understand and describe the meanings of central themes in the life of participants. Another standard method of data collection is focus group interviewing. Focus groups involve a collection of unrelated individuals who are recruited because they share key characteristics with the target population, have knowledge pertinent to the focus group topic, and have the time to participate (Krueger & Casey, 2014). The researcher then leads a group discussion where opinions and opinions are expressed on a specific topic for 1 to 2 hours. The interactions between group members may reveal additional information regarding the topic than might emerge in a one-on-one interview. Data can be captured using a video or digital recording device or writing copious notes. In addition to individual and focus group interviews, qualitative researchers also use data from other sources, including social media, videos, observations of events, and archival documents, such as legal briefs or case records (Padgett, 2017).

DATA COLLECTION

Unlike quantitative measurement (see Chapter 7), measures used for qualitative research are not standardized. Most often, they are semistructured, meaning that questions are listed, as well as follow-up prompts to elicit further information, that is asked of all participants, but interviewers can feel free to follow up on novel information presented by participants.

Semistructured interviews or any interview schedule chosen by qualitative researchers are generally created for that particular study. However, they can also be adapted from other researchers' qualitative work with permission.

Participant observation may be conducted with prolonged time in the field. It generally follows a similarly exploratory and open-ended approach, becoming more structured as the researcher gains familiarity with the site. Hilton et al. (2019) describe the steps of participant observation. Once the researcher has selected the setting, he or she must find a way to gain access, through gatekeepers in the settings (such as agency directors). Then they must develop rapport with people in the setting, establishing a role so that they can "disappear" to some extent in the setting. This involves deciding the extent to which the researcher will observe or participate. They then go about systematically observing and recording their observations and casual conversations in field notes. This can be combined with formal interviews with key informants. When variables in a setting can be measured quantitatively, researchers may use coding schemes to measure and record observations.

Archival documents, such as court records, case files, legal and medical records, newspaper articles, and, increasingly, online data, can all be data sources for qualitative studies. They are often easier to access than individual interviews, but the researcher has less control over the content, so they are often used to supplement interview data (Padgett, 2017).

SAMPLING

Sampling is one of the key places where epistemology makes a noticeable difference (Staller, 2021). As the goals of qualitative research are different, the sampling strategies are also different. In quantitative research, random selection and representativeness are important because they help the researcher generalize characteristics from a study sample to a larger population. The purpose of qualitative research is not to generalize in this statistical sense, but to understand and interpret the phenomenon's meaning for the study participants. This way, researchers may learn things that can be transferred or applied to similar situations, but this is not the focus. In fact, qualitative research is often the method of choice when it would not be possible to draw a random sample because the population is small, stigmatized, or otherwise hard to access (Padgett, 2017). Rather than using random sampling, sampling in qualitative research is purposive—that is, the sample is drawn from people who are most likely to have the answers to the questions the researcher is interested in. Patton (2002) lists over a dozen different types of sampling strategies, from homogeneous sampling (choosing participants who are as similar to one another as possible) to maximum variation sampling (choosing participants who are different from one another) to deviant case sampling (looking for participants who exhibit the most extreme form of a phenomenon). Among the most commonly used strategies are convenience, snowball, and theoretical sampling. As the name implies, convenience sampling involves sampling those who are available and easiest to capture. On the other extreme, snowball sampling is used to locate participants who might be stigmatized, hidden, or otherwise challenging to recruit. In this method of sampling, once a member of the population is located and is willing to be part of the study, the researcher requests that they let others in the community know about the research. They are provided with researcher contact information if potential participants should want to learn more. Theoretical sampling involves choosing subsequent participants or data sources based on what the researcher understands about the previously collected data. Originally developed by grounded theory researchers, theoretical sampling now has migrated to other approaches.

Sample sizes in qualitative studies tend to be small. How sample size is determined is flexible and not wholly predetermined and there are few fixed rules (Staller, 2021). In general, a good sample for a qualitative study needs to be appropriate to the research question and the aims of the study and provide an adequate amount of data to understand the topic and answer the research questions fully. Sample size may depend on methodology, discipline, population, resources, topic, and the richness of the data being collected. Often data collection ends at the point of saturation (another term developed by grounded theorists but now in wider usage) when additional data do not result in new information (Staller, 2021).

While the discussion thus far has concerned sampling participants for interviews, researchers also have to decide what and how much to collect when using other data sources. For example, which online chat group focuses most precisely on the topic of interest and how many posts to collect; how many observations of an event or at a particular site; how many newspaper articles about a new policy or how many case records from an agency will provide enough information to answer the research question? When reading a qualitative study, practitioners should consider what they know about the diversity of their population of interest and ask themselves if they think the study sample seems adequate in terms of size and characteristics and whether the findings from this sample might be transferable to the clients they are working with.

DATA ANALYSIS

Analysis in qualitative research involves a focus on narratives and language. Although some researchers conduct analysis directly on audio and video recordings or other visual data, in most situations, data must be transformed into text. Individual and focus group interviews must be recorded and transcribed. Observations must be written up in field notes. Although the different methodologies have unique strategies and foci, qualitative analysis generally involves breaking down the original data into units of text—a word, a phrase, an idea, a whole narrative or discourse—and then categorizing these units into themes. Coding, as this process is generally called, can be conducted by a single researcher or with a team of researchers. Today, most qualitative researchers use data analysis software such as NVivo, ATLAS.ti, or HyperRESEARCH to manage the large volume of material a qualitative study generates (Padgett, 2017).

Padgett (2017) further outlines some of the common aspects of qualitative data analysis: immersion in the data by reading and rereading numerous times; going deep into individual data sources as well as looking for patterns across the data; paying attention to the context in which the data were collected; and linking data to theory and prior research. This generally involves both inductive and deductive processes (p. 179).

Results are not usually provided numerically as they are in quantitative research but are discussed in narrative as themes labeled, described, and illustrated with quotes from the data. The quotes are a way to illustrate themes and connect the reader to the voice of the participants. They provide the evidence for the points the researcher is trying to make and should "ring true" for the practitioner to be useful.

ANALYSIS OF A QUALITATIVE STUDY

In this section, we detail how to understand, analyze, and summarize a qualitative study, as well as how to appraise its quality. Generally, you will find a qualitative study more readable than quantitative research. The methods are similar to clinical interviewing and the results might make more sense to you, written in narrative rather than numbers derived from statistical analyses.

Qualitative studies can follow the same outline as quantitative studies as they both involve empirical research. The qualitative study starts with background information on the problem and a literature review, building an argument for the research question in the particular study. The methods section data collection includes a description of the sample, measures, and data analysis with presented results, followed by a discussion. This section summarizes the study findings, relates them to previous literature, and offers implications for further research and practice. The limitations of the study are also generally addressed.

SUMMARIZING QUALITATIVE STUDIES

Here we offer a template of a summary that we have evolved throughout the years. Understand that there are different ways to summarize a qualitative study, and authors offer various versions, but most contain similar elements. After the template, we present an example of a qualitative study that was used to inform the PICO question introduced earlier: *How can we improve homework compliance in youth and families undergoing TF-CBT?* (See Table 6.1.)

> Author and purpose: Qualitative research is generally exploratory, so hypotheses are not provided. The purpose usually relates to an in-depth understanding of a subject or experience. Occasionally, *sensitizing frameworks* or theory is used in qualitative research upfront. However, theory can also be incorporated at any stage of the research process as data indicate what might be important (Padgett, 2017).
>
> Sampling: The sampling method will generally involve convenience, purposive, snowball sampling, or some combination. This column is also a place to report some basic aggregate information about the sample, such as socioeconomic status (SES), ethnicity/race, etc.
>
> Data Collection/Instrumentation: Data collection methods usually involve a semistructured interview schedule that is used to guide individual interviews or focus groups.

TABLE 6.1 Example Summary of Qualitative Study

Authors and Purpose	Sampling	Data Collection/ Instrumentation	Data Analysis	Themes
Bunnell et al. (2021) Exploring barriers to homework completion in trainers' and families' views, as well as potential mobile health solutions.	Trainers were contacted (unknown number) and 21 agreed to be interviewed (convenience sample) 12 families who had undergone at least 4 sessions of TF-CBT Caregivers generally white females ($n = 12$) and youth ($n = 12$)	Semistructured interview guided individual interviews	NVivo qualitative analysis software using common and then focused coding.	Provider perspectives: (1) provider barriers: clinicians didn't know how to engage families in presenting homework, understanding rationale, individualizing, and following up. (2) patient-level barriers: families saw therapy as only when they were present in therapy, they consistently "forgot." (3) Task-level barriers using word "homework" because of negative connotations (4) Environmental barriers families have busy and chaotic lives Family perspectives (1) homework triggering (2) forgetting/not understanding Task level Youth find tasks boring. Environmental Busy families Therapist didn't reinforce

Qualitative Research and the EBP Process • 87

Data Analysis: Because BSW and MSW students will have had less exposure to the myriad qualitative research data analytic methods, the student should briefly relate what the authors describe here. At its most basic level, data analysis involves categorizing data into themes.

Results: This section involves listing the themes the authors report in the results or findings section of their paper. In the paper, you will also read illustrative quotes.

CRITICAL APPRAISAL OF QUALITATIVE STUDIES

Even though qualitative research is not generally based in a positivist epistemology that describes an objective reality, the focus on the subjective does not mean that "anything goes." Qualitative researchers are concerned about the quality of their work and how to judge it. However, this discussion is complicated by the overall goal of qualitative research itself, the diversity of methodologies, and the diversity of epistemologies that undergird them (Padgett, 2017).

Lincoln and Guba (1985) first coined the phrase "trustworthiness" as an alternative to the concepts of reliability, validity, and generalizability that provide the basis for assessing quality in positivist (quantitative) research. Trustworthiness has four components:

1. credibility: do the data adequately portray the experiences of the participants?
2. transferability: can these findings be "transferred" to other groups and settings?
3. dependability: does the researcher document the research process so that it accounts for the changes reported?
4. confirmability: does the researcher thoroughly support findings with the data?

As qualitative research has expanded beyond the postpositive stance of Lincoln and Guba, new ways to think about assessing quality have emerged. Padgett (2017) mentions two: *ecological validity* (Shadish et al., 2002), in which a study has validity because it is conducted in a naturalistic rather than experimental situation, and *evidentiary adequacy* (Erickson, 1985; Morrow & Smith, 1995), which draws its value and quality from extended time in the field and the richness and diversity of evidence presented.

Padgett (2017) addresses some of the critical weaknesses of qualitative research. She cites three barriers to trustworthiness: reactivity (how the researcher changes the setting by their presence), researcher bias, and participant bias. She also presents six strategies that are common in the literature (within a "contemporary positivist" framework) for ensuring trustworthiness: prolonged engagement in the setting; maintaining an audit trail of field notes, decisions, and data; peer debriefing; negative case analysis (searching for cases to disprove emerging findings); member checking (presenting findings to participants for their feedback); and triangulation of data sources, researchers, and theory. Not all strategies are appropriate for all methodologies, and the concept of "bias" that Padgett uses here clearly signals a more postpositivist epistemology that not all methodologies subscribe to. However, studies that mention using one or more of these strategies may give the practitioner more confidence in the study's trustworthiness.

There is also diversity in the skill with which researchers use a particular method. There is considerable controversy about what constitutes grounded theory, and many studies that call themselves grounded theory, for example, are not producing theory. However, they may still be strong studies that provide valuable information. There are some approaches, like discourse analysis and narrative analysis, for which there is little guidance about the methodology and, therefore little guidance about how to judge if it's used "correctly." We should note that the idea that there is one right way to conduct research is an epistemological assumption that some methodologies do not share.

However, practitioners can use common sense when reading qualitative studies, the same kind of common sense (and benign skepticism) you might use when assessing a story told by a friend or a client. Rather than asking, "Is this a good study?" a better question is, "Does this study provide clear and useful information that can help me better serve my clients"? Expanding on the ideas of Lietz and Zayas (2010) and Shek et al. (2005), we suggest that the transparency with which the research is written—with concepts and methods explained in nontechnical language, assumptions, and reflexivity made clear, extensive description of context and quotes from participants, and explicit discussion of strategies to enhance quality—is more important to practitioners than assessing the quality of the research against some outside standard. That responsibility appropriately belongs to the peer reviewers of the journal where the article was published, not the practitioner who wants to use the findings to inform their work with clients.

Several critical appraisal tools are available to assess qualitative studies' adherence to quality standards for carrying out qualitative research. Because most of these assume knowledge beyond what you would have for the MSW level, we only took some of the basic elements of the Critical Assessment Tool for Qualitative Research (Joanna Briggs Institute, 2017). In the following section, we provide a template with brief notes on the particular quality criterion and how it might relate to your thinking as a practitioner, using the example of Bunnell et al. (2021). (See Table 6.2).

HOW THE QUALITATIVE STUDY INFORMS THE CASE

From the earlier discussion of epistemology, you can see that the factors used to assess the utility of quantitative studies to address PICO questions, particularly impact and rigor of the study, are positivist in nature and don't fit the subjectivist/interpretivist frame of qualitative research. Therefore, we focus more here on transferability in examining the Bunnell et al. (2021) study and the PICO question, *How can providers increase the uptake of homework in TF-CBT?* Bunnell et al. (2021) gathered perspectives from both youth and parents perspectives, as well as expert providers/trainers. The majority of the family participants were white in Bunnell et al. (2021), and Maya's agency had more diverse representation among referred families, perhaps making the findings less transferable. However, Maya was able to glean information from the study that answered the PICO question with specific suggestions that she and her colleagues at the agency could use to *increase the uptake of homework in TF-CBT*.

First, she learned that providers should (1) avoid the word "homework" due to its negative connotations; instead they could rely on descriptions like *practice* or *self-care*. Second,

TABLE 6.2 Template of Critical Appraisal and Sample

Critical Assessment Tool Criteria	Questions to Ask as a Practitioner	Practitioner Notes
Is the theory perspective and research method well aligned?	Are the methods explained in a way that makes sense for you as a practitioner? Are concepts and methods defined and explained in a way that make sense to you?	The authors describe the approach as "constructivist grounded theory," and semistructured interviews were conducted.
Does the research method align well with the research question?	Given the question that the researcher is asking, does their approach for gathering the data make sense to you?	The semistructured interviews aligned with the research question, although the theoretical approach was to develop new theory (i.e., grounded theory). No evidence that new theory was created beyond thematic analysis.
Have the methods used for data collection been described in enough detail?	For example, what interview questions were asked? How were research participants recruited?	Yes.
What methods did the researcher use to analyze the data, and what quality control measures were used?	Does the researcher detail how the analysis was done? Do they tie these procedures to their stated methodology?	Methods to analyze data: (1) Initial and secondary coding passes were conducted to identify themes (2) Focused coding was then used to "ensure that data were coded completely with minimal redundancy (Miles & Huberman, 1994)." Quality control: (1) first author came up with themes (2) reviewed by an expert in qualitative research (second author) and an expert in CBT homework (fourth author) "Divergent perspectives on theme descriptions ($n = 2$) and classifications ($n = 1$) were compared until agreement was reached" (p. 276).
Are the results credible?	Does the story the researcher is telling "ring true?" If you are reading about a social problem or client group with which you have some experience, does what the author says about the group seem plausible?	While the results are credible, no new theories were generated (i.e., grounded theory). Indeed, the authors made a statement that: "The results of this study aligned well with existing literature, providing additional support for these recommendations." (p. 284)

90 • EVIDENCE-BASED PRACTICE PROCESS IN SOCIAL WORK

Is there a statement locating the researcher culturally or theoretically? Are theories explained in a way that makes sense?	Although the study was based on constructivist grounded theory, which was said to make use of "the researcher's prior knowledge and influence in the process," there was no explicit statements about location of researchers.
Was the relation between the researcher and participant explicit? Is the researcher explicit about their relationship to the study and research participants and how their position impacts the research? Are they "insiders" or "outsiders" to the research?	Unclear; the relationship between the researcher and participant was not explicitly stated in the article. The authors acknowledged, "interviews were coded by the first author, and there is potential for variability in coding that was not accounted for (i.e., the same themes might have been classified in different ways)" (p. 284). However, the fact that themes were reviewed and any discrepancies were discussed with the second and fourth authors was seen as a way to overcome this limitation.
Are participants and their voices adequately represented? Is there enough detail from the data (for example, the words of participants, description of setting and context) included in the findings to give you confidence about the overall claims the researcher is making?	The authors admit to not looking for strengths necessarily: "With respect to interview questions and results, they tended to focus on barriers and challenges and provided less of an opportunity for trainers and family members to share factors that may have led to successes with homework assignments." (p. 284)
Evidence of ethical approval by an appropriate body? A statement on the ethical approval process followed should be in the report	Yes; Institutional Review Board at the Medical University of South Carolina
Do the conclusions drawn in the research report flow from the analysis, or interpretation, of the data? Again, does the story the researcher is telling "ring true?" Does the discussion section consider other possible interpretations and limitations of these conclusions?	Yes; conclusions flow from the analysis to the interpretation of the data collected.

Qualitative Research and the EBP Process • 91

providers should offer psychoeducation on the role of homework in the treatment and be able to individualize it to client circumstances. Finally, barriers to homework should be addressed rather than ignoring or minimizing them. In sum, the Bunnell et al. (2021) study was instrumental in answering this "how" practice-based question.

QUALITATIVE RESEARCH SYNTHESIS

In Chapter 5, we covered systematic reviews of quantitative research and meta-analysis. A comparable process to *meta-analysis* exists for *qualitative* research, referred to as *metasynthesis* or *qualitative research synthesis*. This methodology is designed to systematically review and integrate results of primary qualitative studies that have been conducted on a particular topic using qualitative methods (Finfgeld, 2003; Sandelowski, 2006). Metasynthesis can build knowledge in a particular area of study by drawing on all the relevant qualitative studies at once, offering, at the very least, a summary of these findings (*aggregating* the results), with the possibility of new interpretations of findings (*interpretive* data analytic approaches) (Aguirre & Bolton, 2014; Drisko, 2020). Thus, the knowledge on a given subject may become more substantive than if only individual studies were examined (Finfgeld, 2003). The nursing field is most known for this type of study, so health-related interdisciplinary topics of interest to social work might be most represented there.

The EBP process, as described throughout this book, involves three concepts: (1) research evidence (answering "how" PICO questions and those on lived experience); (2) practitioner context when studies plumb for practitioner perspectives; and (3) consumer experiences, characteristics, and preferences. Qualitative research and its synthesis can offer "a means of giving consumers a voice in the decision-making process through the documentation of their experiences, preferences and priorities" (Aromataris & Munn, 2017, 2.2). Therefore, it can potentially contribute to all three of the facets of EBP.

As an MSW student, it is important to know how to locate qualitative research syntheses: use search terms involving your topic *and* "qualitative research synthesis" or "metasynthesis." Similarly, it is important to develop the ability to read and summarize key points of the study. To that end, we rely on the same template presented in Chapter 5 and apply it to a metasynthesis on the delivery of TF-CBT (Neelakantan et al., 2019). (See Table 6.3.) Because a metasynthesis sums up a body of knowledge and is a major research undertaking, one might not be available on your topic. Additionally, and as discussed, qualitative research has a signature role in studying emerging and sensitive phenomena that may not have received previous research attention. Almost by definition, therefore, when at least several qualitative studies exist on a certain phenomenon, it is time to shift to new questions that will advance the research.

Some of the same critical appraisal issues exist for meta-synthesis as they do for qualitative studies; an MSW student wouldn't be able to evaluate whether methods were appropriately followed without a thorough foundation in qualitative research. Therefore, we present a truncated version of some quality appraisal indicators drawn from Johanna Briggs that you should be able to identify in a particular study. (See Table 6.4.)

TABLE 6.3 Summary of Systematic Review/Metasynthesis Example

Author and Purpose

Neelakantan et al. (2019)
Purpose: to review "qualitative evidence on youth and caregivers' experiences of TF-CBT to better understand user perspectives on process and outcomes of treatment" (p. 877).

Inclusion Criteria

Qualitative studies of youth 19 and younger and their caregivers who had undergone TF-CBT.

Results

Total N of studies: 8 from 7 countries

I. Engagement:
1. Clients didn't know what to expect in the therapy, not sure if they were going to connect with therapist, and fear of having to share personal history.
2. saw therapy as a safe space for support and coping
3. felt reassured when provider gave credentials and experience, and said they were used to hearing a lot of stories and details.
4. aided by provider expertise, confidentiality, and pacing.
5. therapeutic alliance important to development.

II. Treatment components
1. CBT coping techniques were helpful
2. Exposure: youth felt negative affect and anxiety at prospect of exposure, youth found benefits to being able to tolerate cues and memories. Exposure was better with "relaxation exercises while constructing the trauma narrative; drawings and physical reenactments; empathy and kindness on part of therapist; clear psychoeducation; and sensitive pacing." Exposure was hindered by feeling pressured to talk and lack of acknowledgment of distress.
3. caregivers appreciated their time with the therapist, which increased caregivers' understanding about how to support their children

Caregiver involvement impeded by
Initial reluctance of child to go to treatment; initial lack of sufficient information about how to be helpful to child; and concrete barriers, such as fitting in treatment with employment and taking care of other children.

III. Therapeutic outcomes
Youth and families reported a range of positive outcomes from being involved in TF-CBT.

TABLE 6.4 Critical Appraisal for Qualitative Research Synthesis and Application to Neelakantan et al. (2019)

Study	Search strategy appropriate?	Were there two independent reviewers to conduct all three: *screening* and search of studies, *data extraction*, and *critical appraisal* of individual studies?	What were the variables examined in critical appraisal of primary studies?
	At least *two databases searched, an academic librarian* should be consulted, there should be some *attempt to find the gray literature* and not just rely on the published studies, there should be *no date parameters*, and a *figure describing the search* process should be displayed to understand the number of studies that ultimately made it into the final sample.	For the purposes of reliability, two people independently should fulfill *each* of these tasks.	
Neelakantan et al. (2019)	Multiple databases and the gray literature was searched with no date parameters to limit studies possible. A figure illustrated the search process. The only limitation was that an academic librarian wasn't named.	Only one person was involved in search, data extraction, and quality appraisal.	Critical Appraisal Skills Program and standards from the National Institute for Health and Care Excellence

HOW THE QUALITATIVE RESEARCH SYNTHESIS INFORMS THE CASE

The PICO question was: *What are the facilitators and barriers to the successful application of the treatment?* Overall, the student found that the participants in the study were similar to the age group at her agency, youth, 17 and under, who had been traumatized. Youth in the study reported valuing the therapeutic space they experienced as safe and comforting. They enjoyed the individual attention and empathy they received. Caregivers also appreciated the sessions and saw benefits for their relationship with their child. Themes further elucidated youth and caregiver receptivity to TF-CBT, what they found particularly helpful, and suggestions for improving responsiveness.

These were the study's implications that answered the PICO question on how to improve the delivery of TF-CBT. First, families needed more psychoeducation: (1) to describe the rationale for the treatment method, particularly exposure; (2) to address the importance of caregivers being involved in their children's treatment; and (3) to explain how each session is structured so clients have clear expectations. The second implication involved the technique of exposure. The client should be prepared in advance with coping techniques in place to anticipate some possible short-lived distress. Exposure must be delivered with sensitive pacing, and practitioners should devise individualized and creative ways to process the trauma narrative/hierarchy.

SUMMARY

This chapter covered the role of qualitative research in the EBP process. We began with a brief review of qualitative inquiry since many students get little exposure to it in their curriculum. In the EPB process, qualitative research can either answer a PICO directly or can contribute to information about client or provider preferences. The in-depth information offered in qualitative research can answer "how," as in "How can providers help youth who are taking part in TF-CBT?," or "lived experience" questions. An example using an empirically supported treatment for treatment who have gone through trauma, TF-CBT, was threaded through the chapter to show the role this type of inquiry can play in the EBP process.

FOR YOUR PRACTICE

ACTIVITY #1: MULTIPLE-CHOICE QUESTIONS

1. What PICO question does this article inform? Contessa et al. (2023) conducted a qualitative study with a large sample which found that participants expressed a range of trauma-related experiences after their suicide loss with many symptoms persistent and lasting for months.

A. What is an effective intervention for people who have lost a family member to suicide on trauma symptoms?
   B. What is the lived experience of relatives of people who have died by suicide?
   C. What type of scale is useful in assessment of trauma in people who have lost a relative through suicide?
   D. How prevalent is PTSD among people whose relatives have died by suicide?
2. Which of the following is a qualitative study?
   A. Antoniou, P., Cooper, M., Tempier, A., & Holliday, C. (2017). Helpful aspects of pluralistic therapy for depression. *Counseling &. Psychotherapy Research, 17*, 137–147. https://doi.org.proxy.library.upenn.edu/10.1002/capr.12116

   This is the description of the method: "Thirty-nine clients received psychological treatment in a multi-site study exploring alternative interventions to standardized 'evidence-based' approaches. Eighteen consented to a face-to-face or telephone change interview at the end of their treatment. Change interviews aim to elicit clients' perspectives regarding changes that they noticed during, and after therapy and also the possible causes of these changes. Their descriptions were transcribed and analyzed thematically using explicit coding of themes which were audited by the research team" (p. 137).
   B. Lundgren, L., Amodeo, M., Cohen, A., Chassler, D., & Horowitz, A. (2011). Modifications of evidence-based practices in community-based addiction treatment organizations: A qualitative research study. *Addictive Behaviors, 36*(6), 630–635. https://doi.org/10.1016/j.addbeh.2011.01.003
   C. Lengnick-Hall, R., Fenwick, K., Hurlburt, M. S., Green, A., Askew, R. A., & Aarons, G. A. (2019). Let's talk about adaptation! How individuals discuss adaptation during evidence-based practice implementation. *Journal of Children's Services, 14*(4), 266–277. https://doi.org/10.1108/JCS-05-2018-0010.

   Method: "This study qualitatively examines 127 meeting notes to understand how implementers and researchers talk about adaptation during the implementation of SafeCare, an ESI aimed at reducing child maltreatment and neglect" (p. 266).
   D. All of the above.
   E. None of the above.
3. Which is a common method of data collection in qualitative research?
   A. Standardized measures.
   B. Semistructured questionnaire.
   C. Functional analysis
   D. Rating scales
4. How is qualitative data analyzed?
   A. Testing hypotheses for statistical significance.
   B. Looking at multiple observations and seeing how one can categorize them into representative themes.
   C. Chi square
   D. None of the above.

ACTIVITY #2:

In small groups, using the templates provided, summarize a qualitative study that informs your PICO and conduct a quality appraisal of the study. How do the findings inform your practice-based question?

REFERENCES

Aguirre, R. T., & Bolton, K. W. (2014). Qualitative interpretive meta-synthesis in social work research: Uncharted territory. *Journal of Social Work, 14*(3), 279–294.

Aromataris, E., & Munn, Z. (Eds.). (2020). JBI Manual for Evidence Synthesis. JBI 2020. Available from https://synthesismanual.jbi.global. https://doi.org/10.46658/JBIMES-20-01

Atkinson, J. (2002, June 6–8). *Four steps to analyze data from a case study method* [Conference Session]. ACIS 2002. http://aisel.aisnet.org/acis2002/38

Baum, F., MacDougall, C., & Smith, D. (2006). Participatory action research. *Journal of Epidemiology and Community Health, 60*(10), 854–857.

Braun, V., & Clarke, V. (2013). *Successful qualitative research: A practical guide for beginners*. Sage.

Bunnell, B. E., Nemeth, L. S., Lenert, L. A., Kazantzis, N., Deblinger, E., Higgins, K. A., & Ruggiero, K. J. (2021). Barriers associated with the implementation of homework in youth mental health treatment and potential mobile health solutions. *Cognitive Therapy and Research, 45*(2), 272–286. https://doi.org/10.1007/s10608-020-10090-8

Carter, S. M., & Little, M. (2007). Justifying knowledge, justifying method, taking action: Epistemologies, methodologies, and methods in qualitative research. *Qualitative Health Research, 17*(10), 1316–1328.

Corcoran, J. (2016). *Living with mental disorder: Insights from qualitative research*. Routledge.

Contessa, J. C., Padoan, C. S., Silva, J. L. G. da, & Magalhães, P. V. S. (2023). A qualitative study on traumatic experiences of suicide survivors. *OMEGA Journal of Death and Dying, 87*(3), 730–744. https://doi-org.proxy.library.upenn.edu/10.1177/00302228211024486

Drisko, J. (2020). Qualitative research synthesis: An appreciative and critical introduction. *Qualitative Social Work, 19*(4), 736–753. https://doi.org/10.1177/1473325019848808

Erickson, F. (1985). Qualitative methods in research on teaching. In M. D. Wittrock (Ed.), *Handbook of research on teaching* (3rd ed., pp. 119–161). Macmillan.

Finfgeld, D. L. (2003). Metasynthesis: The state of the art—so far. *Qualitative Health Research, 13*(7), 893–904.

Given, L. M. (Ed.). (2008). *The Sage encyclopedia of qualitative research methods*. Sage.

Hilton, T. P., Fawson, P. R., Sullivan, T. J., & DeJong, C. R. (2019). *Applied social research: A tool for the human services*. Springer.

Joanna Briggs Institute. (2017). *Critical appraisal checklist for qualitative research*. Retrieved from https://jbi.global/sites/default/files/2019-05/JBI_Critical_Appraisal-Checklist_for_Qualitative_Research2017_0.pdf

Krueger, R., & Casey, M. A. (2014). *Focus groups: A practical guide for applied research* (5th ed.). Sage.

Hartman, A. (1990). Many ways of knowing. *Social Work, 35*(1), 3–4.

Lietz, C. A., & Zayas, L. E. (2010). Evaluating qualitative research for social work practitioners. *Advances in Social Work, 11*(2), 188–202.

Lincoln, Y., & Guba, E. (1985). *Naturalistic inquiry*. Sage.

Merriam, S. B., & Tisdell, E. J. (2015). *Qualitative research: A guide to design and implementation*. Wiley.

Miles, M. B., & Huberman, A. M. (1994). *Qualitative data analysis: An expanded sourcebook* (2nd ed). Sage Publications, Inc.

Morrow, S. L., & Smith, M. L. (1995). Constructions of survival and coping by women who have survived childhood sexual abuse. *Journal of Counseling Psychology, 42*(1), 24–33.

Neelakantan, L., Hetrick, S., & Michelson, D. (2019). Users' experiences of trauma-focused cognitive behavioural therapy for children and adolescents: A systematic review and metasynthesis of qualitative research. *European Child and Adolescent Psychiatry, 28*(7), 877–897. https://doi.org/10.1007/s00787-018-1150-z

Neubauer, B. E., Witkop, C. T., & Varpio, L. (2019). How phenomenology can help us learn from the experiences of others. *Perspectives on Medical Education, 8*(2), 90–97.

Padgett, D. (2017). *Qualitative methods in social work research* (3rd ed.). Sage.

Park, Y., Crath, R., & Jeffery, D. (2020). Disciplining the risky subject: A discourse analysis of the concept of resilience in social work literature. *Journal of Social Work, 20*(2), 152–172.

Patton, M. Q. (2002). *Qualitative research and evaluation methods*. Sage.

Probst, B. (2015). The eye regards itself: Benefits and challenges of reflexivity in qualitative social work research. *Social Work Research, 39*(1), 37–48.

Riessman, C. K. (2008). *Narrative methods for the human sciences*. Sage.

Rubin, A., & Babbie, E. (2016). *Research methods for social work* (9th ed.). Brooks/Cole, Cengage Learning.

Sandelowski, M. (2006). "Meta-jeopardy": The crisis of representation in qualitative metasynthesis. *Nursing Outlook, 54*(1), 10–16.

Schwandt, T. (2015). *The SAGE dictionary of qualitative inquiry* (4th ed.). Sage.

Shadish, W. R., Cook, T. D., & Campbell, D. T. (2002). *Experimental and quasi-experimental designs for generalized causal inference*. Houghton, Mifflin and Company.

Shek, D. T., Tang, V. M., & Han, X. Y. (2005). Evaluation of evaluation studies using qualitative research methods in the social work literature (1990–2003): Evidence that constitutes a wake-up call. *Research on Social Work Practice, 15*(3), 180–194.

Stake, R. E. (1995). *The art of case study research*. Sage.

Staller, K. M. (2013). Epistemological boot camp: The politics of science and what every qualitative researcher needs to know to survive in the academy. *Qualitative Social Work, 12*(4), 395–413.

Staller, K. M. (2021). Big enough? Sampling in qualitative inquiry. *Qualitative Social Work, 20*(4), 897–904.

Strauss, A., & Corbin, J. (1998). *Basics of qualitative research techniques*. Sage.

Yegidis, B. L., Weinbach, R. W., & Myers, L. L. (2017). *Research methods for social workers*. Pearson.

Yin, R. K. (2017). *Case study research and applications* (6th ed.). Sage.

SECTION III
IMPLEMENTING THE EVIDENCE

CHAPTER 7

INTRODUCTION TO IMPLEMENTATION SCIENCE

With Sean E. Snyder and Courtney Benjamin Wolk

Social work education, training, and practice are guided by the main tenets of ecological systems theory (Bronfenbrenner, 1979, 1989). We know that multiple and inter-related systems simultaneously influence psychosocial outcomes among the clients we work with or advocate for. To review, the clients' individual characteristics, needs, abilities, and immediate personal networks are underscored at the microsystem level. The *mesosystem* considers the agencies, organizations, and community/neighborhood contexts that influence or shape the nature and quality of our clients' abilities and personal networks. How and under what conditions organizations and communities can deliver effective services and promote well-being is contingent on the *exosystem* factors (funding, court system, policies, and governmental reform). Finally, the *macrosystem* considers the client's unique set of personal experiences (e.g., culture, values, social norms, and religious beliefs), and how they provide a lens through which to interpret future experiences. In short, context matters!

Now, consider these interlocking contexts as a social worker or clinician. Thus far, this book has underscored how to use data collected from an ecological assessment (Step 1, or "INPUT" stage) to delineate a well-formed question (e.g., PICO question; Step 2). The PICO question is then used to identify search terms for evidence (Step 3). You then critique or critically appraise the evidence (Step 4, or "PROCESS" stage) and select and implement the intervention or evidence-based treatment that would be most effective and culturally applicable for your client (Step 5, or "OUTPUT" stage), and monitor progress (Step 6) (Rubin & Bellamy, 2012). In essence, the book thus far has focused on micro practice—or how to use evidence to engage in the helping process effectively. What

---

Antonio R. Garcia, Sean E. Snyder, Courtney Benjamin Wolk, and Jacqueline Corcoran, In: *Evidence-Based Practice Process in Social Work*. Edited by: Antonio R. Garcia and Jacqueline Corcoran, Oxford University Press. © Oxford University Press 2024.
DOI: 10.1093/oso/9780197579848.003.0007

happens, however, if the meso-, exo-, and macrosystems are not equipped to support the implementation of your treatment plan? Do you have the resources and capacity to engage in the evidence-based practice (EBP) process? Are the interventions purported to benefit clients available, accessible, and applicable? What if an agency mandates that you implement an empirically supported intervention (ESI) or refer a client to engage in an ESI, irrespective of whether the ESI is perfectly aligned with what your client may need or what the evidence is guiding you to implement? We grapple with these perplexing questions in the last section of this book, highlighting what conditions at the meso and exo levels are needed to effectively engage in Step 5 of the EBP process.

The proceeding chapters focus heavily on information that may be more useful or applicable for social workers who are passionate about leading teams or directing organizations and creating the conditions necessary for clinicians, staff, and stakeholders to implement an ESI. Like social workers and other direct service providers, leaders need support to create optimal contexts that are necessary for them to engage in Step 5 of the EBP process. Without question, leadership is key. Limited efforts are devoted to educating supervisors on best strategies to engage staff and caseworkers in the implementation process, so our hope is to fill that critical gap in knowledge.

In addition to the mounting expectations to support staff and meet deliverables as an agency, leaders will feel top-down pressures from policymakers, payers, or other key macro-stakeholders. Funding is contingent on submitting "evidence," demonstrating that what they are doing, as an agency, is effective in meeting clients' needs and addressing their issues of concern. Take, for example, the Family First Prevention Services Act (FFPSA). The federal law, passed on February 9, 2018, as part of the Bipartisan Budget Act, reforms the federal child welfare financing streams (Title IV-E and Title IV-B of the Social Security Act) by allowing federal reimbursement for evidence-based mental health services, substance use treatment, and in-home parenting skills training to prevent children from entering foster care (Torres & Mathur, 2018). The law requires that to be eligible for funding, states may only use interventions that have proven to be effective in rigorously designed studies and includes provisions for establishing the Title IV-E Prevention Services Clearinghouse (the Clearinghouse) to determine which programs meet the inclusionary threshold as outlined by the Administration for Children and Families (ACF) (Wilson et al., 2019). For some states, leaders respond to these mandates by opting to commission an independent technical review for the ESI they would prefer to implement, hoping that ACF will issue a temporary evidence rating until such time that the Clearinghouse completes their lengthy evidence review (Garcia, Pecora, et al., 2020). Dr. Garcia and colleagues recently completed an independent review for Iowa and Utah, whose leaders believed that SafeCare would best meet the needs of their population. These leaders selected SafeCare, given that it targets multiple risk factors for abuse and neglect by enhancing positive parent–infant/child interactions, promoting a safer home environment and appropriate supervision, reducing risk for unintentional injury, and encouraging systematic parental health decision-making for parents of children 5 years old or younger. A "big draw" or an appealing characteristic for leaders is that SafeCare providers work with families in their homes. It took our independent review team over 6 months to complete a review and to ultimately recommend a "Well-Supported" rating for ACF consideration.

In addition to selecting ESIs and commissioning independent reviews, leaders are confronted with the challenges of motivating staff to undo or "de-implement" old practices and embrace innovation. How do leaders in Iowa and Utah convince and educate their staff to refer their clients to SafeCare? While leaders in these two states are just now actively learning how to implement ESIs, case studies reflecting various systems of care summarized below may inform their efforts (as well as your initiatives) by shedding light on (1) barriers leaders and stakeholders grapple with during the implementation process, and (2) innovative strategies to mitigate barriers.

While leaders and administrators may find these last few chapters helpful, we also do not want to discount the utility of this information for direct service providers or clinicians. While our students and the clinicians we collaborate with are dedicated to adhering to the EBP process, numerous factors hinder their ability to follow suit. As a clinician, what do you do if you cannot access scholarly databases to search for relevant and impactful evidence? What should you do if the evidence does not align with your target population? Said another way, what do you do if the clients you service are not represented in research studies? As we engage in the EBP process, how do we balance social justice and pay tribute to the rich and expansive experiences of an increasingly diverse target population while also acknowledging and mitigating the contexts that hinder implementation of an ESI or treatment plan?

We draw on case studies and various research projects in the following two chapters to illustrate the types of barriers you may experience during the ESI implementation process and what strategies scholars, leaders, and clinicians use to address those barriers. We hope to offer you a framework and tools to shrink the divide between the best available evidence and the effective use of evidence in real-world practice contexts.

IMPLEMENTATION SCIENCE FRAMEWORKS, MODELS, AND STRATEGIES

Students often cite numerous barriers that may prevent them from engaging in Step 5 of the EBP process. To begin, an ESI may not be available and too costly for community clinicians to implement. Additionally, resources and organizational capacities often need to be optimized to achieve implementation (Aarons et al., 2011; Aarons & Palinkas, 2007; Palinkas & Aarons, 2009). Lack of transformational leadership (Aarons et al., 2015; Aarons & Sommerfeld, 2012; Powell et al., 2017), staff turnover, high caseloads, lack of acceptability or "buy-in" for the ESI by workers and leaders, and organizational incapacity and resistance to change impede efforts to fully engage in the implementation process (Aarons et al., 2009; Moullin, et al., 2019; Palinkas et al., 2017; Palinkas, 2018). The field of implementation science (e.g., Bauer et al., 2015; Eccles & Mittman, 2006) aims to elucidate our understanding of barriers and facilitators to ESI implementation success and offers potential solutions. In implementation science, attending to context is paramount. There are a number of implementation frameworks (Nilsen, 2015; Proctor et al., 2009), some of which we will discuss in these chapters, such as the consolidated framework for implementation research or CFIR (Damschroder et al., 2009), which points to determinants of implementation, and the exploration preparation implementation and sustainment (EPIS) framework, which specifies implementation processes (Aarons et al., 2011). Implementation strategies are the "methods or techniques used to enhance the adoption, implementation, and sustainability of a clinical program or practice" (Powell et al., 2015). Powell and colleagues (2015) have specified 73 implementation strategies within healthcare, such as those related to training, consultation, incentives, and policies. Implementation scientists focus their attention on the impact of their implementation strategies on outcomes such as the fidelity with which an ESI is delivered by community providers, the reach of the ESI to the target population in the community, and whether the organization can sustain the ESI. The interested reader is referred to the work of Proctor and colleagues (2011) for a description of the eight established implementation outcomes and a discussion of how they differ from traditional client and service outcomes. While we don't expect you to become implementation scientists in your efforts to bring ESIs to the settings in which you work, we share this brief description of the field because it guides much of our own work and thinking in these chapters. We will discuss some of these implementation science concepts in more detail in the subsequent chapters.

During Dr. Garcia's practice, he did not possess the language to articulate the science undergirding the optimal contexts or settings that are required to implement his service plans. To date, we still do not have a clear understanding of how to grapple with the evolving inner and outer settings or contexts that influence whether an ESI is implemented to fidelity. There is a good reason for this—translating research into practice is a complex process that involves: (1) disseminating the information to stakeholders, including social workers and clinicians, (2) adopting the program and successfully implementing it, and (3) sustaining the optimal conditions to deliver the ESI over time.

Implementation science provides us a platform to question and examine the systematic processes, activities, and resources to integrate effective interventions into practice settings (Rabin et al., 2008). Implementation experts aim to bridge the divides between the generation of the best available research evidence and the use of that evidence in real-world practice (Palinkas, 2018). The lingering question is what exactly are the contextual factors that matter the most, how do they affect implementation activities at various stages, and in what ways do they influence outcomes? We offer a brief overview of commonly cited implementation science frameworks and models to help you gain some familiarity with this fairly new field of study. We acknowledge discussion about models and frameworks is often "dry," leaving many of our students questioning how to apply them to their own practice. Drawing from real-life case studies and research projects, we will illustrate how frameworks, particularly CFIR (Damschroeder et al., 2009), could be used to (1) inform the implementation of the best available evidence and (2) identify and mitigate barriers to apply the EBP process.

It is important to define our terms within implementation science and practice, as these constructs serve us in different ways. Nilsen (2015) offers a summary of these key terms: implementation process models, implementation frameworks, and change theories. Implementation process models outline the steps of putting the research into practice (Nilsen, 2015); the EPIS model (Aarons et al., 2011) is a commonly used process model. Implementation frameworks are the descriptive architecture of contexts for implementation;

for instance, they can help us to map out organizational features, client/patient characteristics, or aspects of the ESI itself. Lastly, implementation efforts need to have a theory of change behind them—why do people and organizations change?

For the purposes of illustrating how implementation science informs implementation practice, we will focus on implementation frameworks, and specifically CFIR (Damschroder et al., 2009), as these can help us to understand key barriers and facilitators to implementation. For more on implementation process models like EPIS, consult the work of Aarons and colleagues (2011; https://episframework.com/). Many frameworks have been proposed in implementation science, and we have already mentioned two of the more commonly used ones, CFIR and EPIS.

The CFIR (Damschroder et al., 2009), now one of the most cited implementation science frameworks, represents a culmination of 19 published theories, models, and frameworks from 1992–2008 that were used to translate research findings into practice, particularly within the healthcare sector. Diffusion of innovations theory delineates three factors, all of which are core tenets of CFIR, that influence the implementation process: (1) inner and outer contextual factors or settings; (2) perceptions that people, government, and organizations have about the ESI; and (3) characteristics of the people who adopt or fail to adopt the program (Dearing & Cox, 2018; Moullin et al., 2019; Palinkas, 2018; Proctor et al., 2011). Damschroder and colleagues (2009)—the original creators of CFIR—combined certain constructs across theories, including diffusion of innovations theory, and separated and added others to derive the following five critical domains: (1) intervention characteristics, (2) inner setting, (3) outer setting, (4) implementation process, and (5) the characteristics of individuals involved.

Within each domain, they delineate several potential factors that may affect implementation success. As noted by Damschroder et al. (2009), CFIR barriers related to *Intervention Characteristics* are delineated as follows: (1) intervention source, (2) evidence strength and quality, (3) relative advantage, (4) adaptability, (5) trailability, (6) complexity, (7) design quality and packaging, and (8) costs. The *Characteristics of the Individuals Involved* domain includes: (1) knowledge and beliefs about the intervention, (2) self-efficacy, (3) individual stage of change, and (4) individual identification with the organization. The *Inner Setting* refers to features of the implementing organization to consider when gearing up to or attempting to implement a particular intervention, or arguably, the EPB process in general, include the following: (1) structural characteristics; (2) networks and communications; (3) intraorganizational cultural exchanges; (4) culture; (5) implementation climate, which is impacted by (a) tension for change, (b) compatibility, and (c) relative priority; (6) organizational incentives and awards; and (7) goals and feedback. The *Outer Setting* refers to the environment external to the organization (i.e., the sociopolitical context). Outer Setting factors include the following: (1) patient needs and resources, (2) cosmopolitanism, (3) peer pressure, (4) external policies and incentives, and (5) interorganizational cultural exchanges. *Implementation Process* factors include: (1) planning a sequence of events required to implement an ESI; (2) engaging an implementation team inclusive of (a) key opinion leaders, (b) formally appointed internal implementation leaders, (c) champions, (d) key stakeholders, (e) external change agents, and (f) patients/consumers; (3) executing the implementation plan; and (4) reflecting and evaluating the progress and quality of the implementation process.

In the forthcoming two case studies (based on real-life implementation cases), we illustrate how the CFIR could be used to pinpoint the types of barriers you might experience across some of these domains. In the first case, you will see the influence of an underresourced agency and the impacts that context had on implementation of an ESI, with follow-up commentary on a more ideal implementation scenario. In the second case, you will see what implementation looks like within optimal conditions and draw on the lessons learned for your future implementation practice.

CASE SCENARIO: RESPONDING TO NEGLIGENT TREATMENT AND INTERPERSONAL VIOLENCE IN SUBOPTIMAL IMPLEMENTATION CONDITIONS

Dr. Garcia revisits a case he was assigned to as a Child Protective Services (CPS) worker, who was responsible for investigating the alleged incidents of child maltreatment, and if needed, providing services to reduce odds of children being placed in foster care. He received a referral from a concerned neighbor, alleging four children (ages 2, 4, 5, and 7) were neglected and exposed to ongoing intimate partner violence in the home. There were concerns about the children's lack of medical attention and poor school attendance, parental problems such as substance abuse, drug dealing, criminal history, and quality of living issues such as filthy home conditions and no food in the home. CPS records show prior history of two referrals alleging the same concerns. The mother is 24 years of age and is Mexican American, and the father is 28 years of age and identifies as African American.

Despite Dr. Garcia's best efforts to adhere to the EBP process to prevent family disruption, the children still ended up in foster care. There are numerous plausible reasons as to why this occurred: lack of family motivation to change, historical or system-induced trauma for the family, barriers to access treatment, or lack of quality services that align with the family's needs, strengths, and cultural values. While all these reasons are plausible, he still wondered how much of the overarching reason had to do with organizational and contextual incapacity to adhere to Step 5 of EBP process—that is, to "apply" or implement the case plan as intended. In this case example, how Dr. Garcia applied the EBP process for the 5- and 7-year-old children and when he had to modify plans to grapple with suboptimal implementation conditions and contexts that were out of his control are discussed. We find that many students and seasoned providers face similar obstacles, and may not know the most effective way to mitigate them.

STEP 1: ASSESSMENT

The agency had mandated the use of "family assessments," much like what we refer to as a biopsychosocial assessment. During Dr. Garcia's interview with the mother in Washington state, she openly reported that the father physically assaulted her several times over the past 5 years and that his behavior has escalated during the past 2 years. At the initial home visit, she reported to Dr. Garcia that he had moved out of the home. He noticed there was very little food in the home and that the children's immunizations were not up to date. The mother is unemployed and receives public assistance. The mother underscores her love for her children. While the mother's parents were born and raised in Mexico, they later immigrated to Southern California before she was born. During her childhood, she observed her father "beat her mother to a pulp." When she was around 8 years old, her father left the home, and her mother took on the sole responsibility of raising her. To this day, her mother is supportive and encourages her.

The mother disclosed that she has a drug addiction (drug of choice is methamphetamines), having started using drugs when she lived in Southern California during her early 20s. Before moving to Washington state, she reportedly completed outpatient substance abuse treatment. She admitted her relapse is partly a consequence of relocating and losing contact with her sponsor from Southern California.

During the interview with the 7-year-old girl at school, she appeared shy and withdrawn. She did report that mom and dad fight a lot, and that her mother gets "owies" on her face and legs. She did not disclose child physical abuse. During the interview with the 5-year-old, he appeared restless and had a difficult time remaining attentive. Despite his distractions, he also disclosed that mother and father fight a lot, and that they both "smoke pot" every day. The school counselor reported that the 7-year-old is usually withdrawn, appears depressed, and isolates herself from her peers while the 5-year-old is disruptive, "fidgety," and has difficulty staying focused.

STEP 2: DEVELOP WELL-FORMED QUESTIONS

Based on Dr. Garcia's assessment, he formulated the following question to guide his work: What are the most effective interventions for Latinx children between the ages of 5 and 7 who (1) are exposed to interpersonal violence and parent substance abuse, and (2) exhibit symptoms of internalizing/externalizing disorders?

STEP 3: SEARCH FOR EVIDENCE—"INPUT" PROCESS

At the time (as a recently hired MSW social worker), Dr. Garcia did not have access to university-based search tools, and he was not privy to evidence-based clearinghouse websites at the time. Online search tools like the CEBC website were not even available until the last year he was employed as a CPS worker in 2006. All he had at his disposal was an outdated list of community-based services, as well as Homebuilders, that we could refer = clients to.

STEP 4: CRITICALLY APPRAISE EVIDENCE— "PROCESS STAGE"

Truth be told, he did not have the intra and interorganizational resources to critically appraise the "standard" case plan. He heard anecdotally from his supervisor and colleagues that Homebuilders is effective or impactful, namely that it is a family preservation program that typically reduces risk factors that otherwise if left unaddressed would lead to children being placed in foster care. It was not feasible to determine the validity, given that in that moment in time, he was not privy to researchers or clinicians who (1) conducted a research design strong enough to conclude Homebuilders is effective, and (2) tested the effectiveness of Homebuilders among Latina mothers who struggle to maintain sobriety.

STEP 5: SELECT AND IMPLEMENT THE EVIDENCE—"OUTPUT STAGE"

Out of convenience and availability, he referred the mother and her children to Homebuilders. The mother agreed to random urinalysis, outpatient substance abuse treatment by a local provider, and attendance at a domestic violence support group. Homebuilders agreed to transport the mother to her appointments, conduct home visits, offer in-home parenting education, and serve as a liaison for connecting the children to daycare and mental health assessment and services, if warranted, for her children.

STEP 6: MONITOR CLIENT PROGRESS—EVALUATION STAGE

At the 2-month follow-up, the service provider from Homebuilders reported that the mother was not in compliance with the service plan. She often was not home for scheduled home visits with Homebuilders. The CPS Hotline received additional reports, alleging same concerns, noting that the father was back in the home. Dr. Garcia filed a Dependency Petition, a legal document outlining previous efforts to reduce risk factors and why the children remain at risk of harm, along with a pick-up order to remove the children from the home. Upon entering the home at the time with law enforcement, the door was open, but no one was there. Based on the conditions of the home (broken furniture, windows, shattered glass, no food), and the mother's current emotional/behavioral state, he concluded risk of harm to the children had not been reduced.

CASE SCENARIO #1: ALTERNATIVE CASE PLANNING

To this day, Dr. Garcia wonders if he could have done more to prevent the children from being placed in foster care. In this next section, while acknowledging Steps 1 and 2 are not modifiable, the optimal or "gold standard" ESI selection process for steps 3–6 are explained below.

STEP 3: SEARCH FOR EVIDENCE—"INPUT" PROCESS

As reviewed in previous chapters, we now have access to multiple sources of information (or inputs), including exhaustive university-based search tools and evidence-based clearinghouse websites, including the California Evidence-Based Clearinghouse (CEBC) website.

STEP 4: CRITICALLY APPRAISE EVIDENCE—"PROCESS STAGE"

A recent study Dr. Garcia published with his colleagues reviewed all the interventions from the California Evidence-Based Clearinghouse (CEBC) designed to improve parenting practices and promote positive child behavioral outcomes (Garcia et al., 2019). They identified four evidence-based parenting interventions from the CEBC deemed "well-supported" by at least one RCT or quasi-experimental research study *and* achieved a diversity threshold in which at least 40% of the study samples included children and families of color. They include parent-child interaction therapy (PCIT), trauma-focused cognitive behavioral therapy (TF-CBT), Level 4 Triple P (Pathways Positive Parenting Program) or TripleP, and multisystemic therapy (MST). Please refer to Garcia et al. (2019) for a brief description of each ESI, a summation of key findings from each study that meets the aforementioned inclusion criteria, and a description of the sample for each study. In sum, these interventions address child disruptive behaviors; attention-deficit/hyperactivity disorder, posttraumatic stress disorder, and depression symptoms; parenting stress; and poor school functioning.

Of those four interventions, while PCIT (ages 2–7), TF-CBT (ages 3–18), and TripleP (ages 0–16) are age-appropriate, TF-CBT is geared toward addressing children's externalizing and internalizing behaviors that develop because of repeated trauma exposures. As well, parents can also see improvement in their mental health (Holt et al., 2014). Looking at Homebuilders, the emphasis is on addressing crises and improving family functioning. While at least one RCT supports the intervention, the evidence is based primarily on the experiences of White samples (Wood et al., 1988—72% White; Fraser et al., 1996—82.7% White; Walton, 1998—82.7% White). To that end, there is sound rationale for questioning Homebuilders' adaptability, evidence strength, and intervention source. Hearing client testimonials or stories from those who represent racially diverse backgrounds and graduated from Homebuilders or reviewing reports highlighting outcomes for children/families who completed the intervention could be useful.

STEP 5: SELECT AND APPLY THE EVIDENCE—"OUTPUT STAGE"

While Dr. Garcia would select TF-CBT based on his critical appraisal of publicly available evidence, many child welfare agencies are not equipped to refer clients to TF-CBT, due to costs (see the intervention characteristics domain of CFIR), lack of networking with external agencies to train staff to deliver TF-CBT (outer setting of CFIR), or caseworker's lack of knowledge or self-efficacy as to when and how to refer clients to an ESI (individuals involved of CFIR). Countless other CFIR factors may derail implementation. In his case, the agency was not ready or prepared to implement TF-CBT due to favoring "services as usual" and not prioritizing efforts to engage in innovation (inner setting), and there was a lack of opinion leaders and program champions who could build momentum and disseminate information or motivate staff (implementation process). As noted, Dr. Garcia observed CFIR barriers within the five domains. As a clinician, you can pinpoint precisely why you might struggle to engage in Step 5 of the EBP process. Even if Dr. Garcia follows the EBP process, he may not be able to apply the evidence, leaving him no choice but to revert to services as usual.

In this case, Dr. Garcia would still advocate for his clients, by first sharing his conclusions. Next, he would consult with his supervisor and request to collectively search for a locally trained TF-CBT clinician to refer clients with similar circumstances. Even if Dr. Garcia may need to resort to what is available—in this case, Homebuilders, he can at least do his part to advocate for the next client at the agency who could benefit from TF-CBT. Does Dr. Garcia think implementing TF-CBT would have prevented the children from entering foster care? We have no data to address this question with certainty, albeit it appears both the mother and father needed to focus on their sobriety. The optimal plan would be for the children to engage in TF-CBT in their foster care placement setting.

STEP 6: MONITOR CLIENT PROGRESS—EVALUATION STAGE

To examine whether externalizing and internalizing symptoms decrease, Dr. Garcia recommends the foster parents complete the Strengths and Difficulties Questionnaire ([SDQ], Goodman, 1997). The SDQ is a 25-item questionnaire that assesses parent perceptions of the degree of strengths and difficulties children experience across five domains: Emotional Symptoms (5 items), Conduct Problems (5 items), Hyperactivity (5 items), Peer Problems (5 items), and Prosocial Behaviors (5 items). Each item is rated on a 3-point Likert scale, with responses ranging from 0 Not True to 2 Certainly True. The total problem scores sum the scores for the four difficulty scales. The SDQ has demonstrated adequate psychometric properties (mean subscale Cronbach's alpha = .73) (Goodman, 1997).

CASE SCENARIO #2: THE EFFECTIVENESS AND APPLICABILITY OF EVIDENCE-BASED PARENTING IN OPTIMAL CONDITIONS

In the following case, the implementation climate, defined by Powell and colleagues (2017) as employees' shared perception that innovation is expected, supported, and rewarded in the organization was optimized for innovation. In 2015, Dr. Garcia and colleagues (2019)) had a rare opportunity to prospectively examine the implementation process as two child welfare agencies in the Mid-Atlantic received funding to implement TripleP. Funding, transformational leadership, and efforts to train, educate, and motivate caseworkers were underway. Despite these encouraging contextual factors at the onset, one of our MSW students in training hit a roadblock with a case she was assigned to. We present the case herein to provide context.

> *Elisa is a 28-year-old, monolingual Spanish-speaking single mother of four children who are at high risk for removal by the state Department of Children and Families (DCFS) for abuse and neglect. Elisa fled her home in Puerto Rico 2 years ago to escape an abusive relationship she was in after the father of her youngest child was murdered. She has 7-year-old fraternal twins, a 3-year-old daughter, and a 2-year-old son. The family lived in a homeless shelter until 2 months ago, when their time in the shelter ran out. She was able to find an apartment but spends her entire cash assistance allotment on rent each month and cannot pay for other necessities. Elisa's oldest son was diagnosed with PTSD after reporting flashbacks due to violence he witnessed in Puerto Rico and his experience in the shelter. Her oldest daughter is parentified; her 3-year-old daughter refuses to follow her mother's directions, often leaving the house without permission; and her 2-year-old son is nonverbal. The child welfare agency first became involved due to a report from the oldest children's school that Elisa is extremely overwhelmed and unable to meet the mental health needs of her children. Elisa does not believe in psychotropic medication and refuses to follow the psychiatrist's recommendation for her oldest son. She frequently leaves the children at home with various caregivers to run errands. Multiple people come and go from her home at will. She relies on threats and physical discipline to gain compliance from the children and reports their behavior is almost always out of control. The family has no furniture, toys, blankets, very few clothes, and personal items, and struggles to have enough food. Elisa already feels that the child welfare caseworker is judging her parenting capabilities.*

STEP 1: QUESTION FORMULATION

Which in-home intervention is more effective in (1) improving monolingual Spanish-speaking mothers' parenting behaviors and capacities and (2) reducing their children's externalizing and internalizing behaviors—TripleP or MST? The student selected MST as the comparison, given that it was the other available ESI available at her agency.

STEP 2: BIOPSYCHOSOCIAL ASSESSMENT

See information above.

STEPS 3 AND 4: EVIDENCE SEARCH AND APPRAISAL

The student initially reviewed information about MST and TripleP from the CEBC website. The CEBC website provides a list of peer-reviewed studies specific to each ESI. While the student found several articles supporting the use of TripleP to teach parenting skills and promote positive child functioning (DeGraff et al., 2008a, 2008b; Sanders et al., 2014), she did not find any peer-reviewed articles that examined the effectiveness of TripleP with monolingual Spanish-speaking mothers. After reviewing the CEBC, the student concluded that MST is not appropriate, given the age range of the children involved in the case.

STEP 5: SELECTING AND IMPLEMENTING THE INTERVENTION

While the TripleP program provides materials in Spanish, no studies support the efficacy for implementing it among monolingual Spanish-speaking mothers. Neither she nor any of her agency colleagues speak Spanish. Thus, she referred her client to a "traditional" parenting class for Spanish-speaking clients that had not been evaluated. This is a clear case of when the Individuals Involved are not equipped to implement the ESI for a specific population and when the evidence in and of itself does not support it. In this case, what would you do? This case exemplifies the need to communicate and collaborate with leaders and stakeholders to hire and train bilingual service providers. Oftentimes, advocacy is required to ensure that the implementation process will apply to diverse populations.

APPLYING CFIR TO SCIENCE AND REAL-WORLD PRACTICE

The case examples above illustrate the complexity of aligning the needs and strengths of clients with an optimal case plan that incorporates the best available evidence (the intervention source) and considers providers' and stakeholders' knowledge, beliefs, and skillsets (characteristics of the individuals involved). We also highlighted the importance of optimizing the inner and outer settings or contexts to engage in Step 5 of the EBP process. In the next chapter, we delve deeper into how to mitigate CFIR barriers by drawing on lessons learned from implementation research studies.

FOR YOUR PRACTICE

ACTIVITY #1: EXAM QUESTIONS

1. Select the best answer that reflects what implementation science is.
    A. Implementation science involves identifying the most effective processes and activities needed to implement an EBP.

    B. Implementation science experts aim to bridge the gap between evolving research evidence and the use of evidence into real-world practice.
    C. Both A and B.
    D. Implementation efforts do not need to have a theory of change.

2. Select the best answer distinguishing the differences between the implementation process models and an implementation framework.
    A. Implementation process models outline the steps of putting the research into practice, whereas an implementation framework refers to the descriptive architecture of contexts for implementation.
    B. The exploration preparation implementation and sustainment (EPIS) model is a framework.
    C. The consolidated framework for implementation research is a process model.
    D. Implementation process models can help us to map out organizational features, client/patient characteristics, or aspects of the ESI itself.

3. Which one of these responses do not reflect a domain of the CFIR?
    A. Intervention characteristics and implementation process
    B. Inner and outer setting
    C. Directions on how to put research into practice
    D. Characteristics of individuals involved

4. Implementation process factors include all the following except:
    A. Planning a sequence of events required to implement an ESI.
    B. Engaging an implementation team and executing the implementation plan.
    C. Evaluating the progress of the implementation process.
    D. Developing a theory for how to achieve implementation.

5. True or False: The inner setting involves considering patient or client characteristics, whereas the outer setting involves networks and communication.

ACTIVITY #2: INTERVIEW AN AGENCY DIRECTOR

Interview a supervisor or agency director who is in the process of implementing an evidence-based intervention. Inquire about why the intervention was selected and the types of barriers they have grappled with, and how they addressed them.

ACTIVITY #3: CONDUCT A SELF-ASSESSMENT

There are many validated, freely available measures of implementation constructs that you and/or your organization may wish to use to examine capacity for implementation, inform implementation planning, and support self-reflection. We especially like the ones available here: https://www.implementationleadership.com/measures.

REFERENCES

Aarons, G. A., Ehrhart, M. G., Farahnak, L. R., & Hurlburt, M. S. (2015). Leadership and organizational change for implementation (LOCI): A randomized mixed method pilot study of a leadership and organization development intervention for evidence-based practice implementation. *Implementation Science, 10*(1), 11.

Aarons, G. A., Hurlburt, M., & Horwitz, S. M. (2011). Advancing a conceptual model of evidence-based practice implementation in public service sectors. *Administration and Policy in Mental Health, 38*(1), 4–23. https://doi.org/10.1007/s10488-010-0327-7

Aarons, G. A., & Palinkas, L. A. (2007). Implementation of evidence-based practice in child welfare: Service provider perspectives. *Administration and Policy in Mental Health and Mental Health Services Research, 34*(4), 411–419.

Aarons, G. A., & Sommerfeld, D. H. (2012). Leadership, innovation climate, and attitudes toward evidence-based practice during a statewide implementation. *Journal of the American Academy of Child and Adolescent Psychiatry, 51*(4), 423–431.

Aarons, G. A., Wells, R. S., Zagursky, K., Fettes, D. L., & Palinkas, L. A. (2009). Implementing evidence-based practice in community mental health agencies: A multiple stakeholder analysis. *American Journal of Public Health, 99*(11), 2087–2095.

Bauer, M. S., Damschroder, L., Hagedorn, H., Smith, J., & Kilbourne, A. M. (2015). An introduction to implementation science for the non-specialist. *BMC Psychology, 3*(1), 32. https://doi.org/10.1186/s40359-015-0089-9.

Bronfenbrenner, U. (1979). *The ecology of human development*. Harvard University Press.

Bronfenbrenner, U. (1989). Ecological systems theory. *Annals of Child Development, 6*, 187–249.

Damschroder, L. J., Aron, D. C., Keith, R. E., Kirch, S. R., Alexander, J. A., & Lowery, J. C. (2009). Fostering implementation of health services research findings into practice: A consolidated framework for advancing implementation science. *Implementation Science, 4*, 50. https://doi.org/10.1186/1748-5908-4-50.

Dearing, J. W., & Cox, J. G. (2018). Diffusion of innovations theory, principles, and practice. *Health Affairs, 37*(2), 183–190. https://doi.org/10.1377/hlthaff.2017.1104.

DeGraff, I., Speetjens, P., Smit, F., De Wolff, M., & Tavecchio, L. (2008a). Effectiveness of the Triple P Positive Parenting Program on parenting: A meta-analysis. *Family Relations, 57*, 553–566. https://journals.sagepub.com/doi/10.1177/0145445508317134

DeGraff, I., Speetjens, P., Smit, F., De Wolff, M., & Tavecchio, L. (2008b). Effectiveness of the Triple P Positive Parenting Program on behavioral problems in children. *Behavior Modification, 32*, 714–735. https://doi.org/10.1177/0145445508317134

Eccles, M. P., & Mittman, B. S. (2006). Welcome to Implementation Science. *Implementation Science, 1*, 1–3;). https://doi.org/10.1186/1748-5908-1-1

Fraser, M. W., Walton, E., Lewis, R. E., Pecora, P. J., & Walton, W. K. (1996). An experiment in family reunification: Correlates of outcomes at one-year follow-up. *Children and Youth Services Review, 18*(4/5), 335–361.

Garcia, A. R., DeNard, C., Morones, S., & Eldeeb, N. (2019). Mitigating barriers to implementing evidence-based interventions: Lessons learned from scholars and agency directors. *Children and Youth Services Review, 100*, 313–331.

Garcia, A. R., Myers, C., Morones, S., Ohene, S., & Kim, M. (2020). "It starts from the top": Caseworkers, leaders, and TripleP providers' perceptions of implementation processes and contexts. *Human Service Organizations: Management, Leadership, and Governance, 44*(3), 266–293. https://doi.org/10.1080/23303131.2020.1755759.

Garcia, A. R., Pecora, P. J., Schnell, A. H., Burnson, C., & Harris, C. (2020). Technical reviewing for the Family First Prevention Services Act: Strategies and recommendations. *Children and Youth Services Review, 119*, 105597. https://doi.org/10.1016/j.childyouth.2020.105597

Goodman, R. (1997). The Strengths and Difficulties Questionnaire: A research note. *Journal of Child Psychology and Psychiatry, 38*, 581–586. https://www.sdqinfo.org/py/sdqinfo/b3.py?language=Englishqz(USA)

Holt, T., Jensen, T. K., & Wentzel-Larsen, T. (2014). The change and the mediating role of parental emotional reactions and depression in the treatment of traumatized youth: Results from a randomized controlled study. *Child and Adolescent Psychiatry and Mental Health, 8*, 11. https://doi.org/10.1186/1753-2000-8-11

Moullin, J. C., Dickson, K. S., Stadnick, N. A., Rabin, B., & Aarons, G. A. (2019). Systematic review of the exploration, preparation, implementation, sustainment (EPIS) framework. *Implementation Science, 14*(1), 1–16. https://doi.org/10.1186/s13012-018-0842-6.

Nilsen, P. (2015). Making sense of implementation theories, models and frameworks. *Implementation Science, 10*, 53–66; https://doi.org/10.1186/s13012-015-0242-0

Palinkas, L. A. (2018). *Achieving implementation and exchange: The science of delivering evidence-based practices to at-risk youth*. Policy Press.

Palinkas, L. A., & Aarons, G. A. (2009). A view from the top: Executive and management challenges in a statewide implementation of an evidence-based practice to reduce child neglect. *International Journal of Child Health and Human Development, 2*(1), 47–55.

Palinkas, L. A., He, A. S., Choy-Brown, M., & Hertel, A. L. (2017). Operationalizing social work science through research–practice partnerships: Lessons from implementation science. *Research on Social Work Practice, 27*(2), 181–188. https://doi.org/10.1177/1049731516666329

Powell, B. J., Mandell, D. S., Hadley, T. R., Rubin, R. M., Evans, A. C., Hurford, M. O., & Beidas, R. S. (2017). Are general and strategic measures of organizational context and leadership associated with knowledge and attitudes toward evidence-based practices in public behavioral health settings? A cross-sectional observational study. *Implementation Science, 12*(1), 64.

Powell, B. J., Waltz, T. J., Chinman, M. J., Damschroder, L. J., Smith, J. L., Matthieu, M. M., . . . Kirchner, J. E. (2015). A refined compilation of implementation strategies: Results from the Expert Recommendations for Implementing Change (ERIC) project. *Implementation Science, 10*(1), 21. https://doi.org/10.1186/s13012-015-0209-1

Proctor, E. K., Landsverk, J., Aarons, G., Chambers, D., Glisson, C., & Mittman, B. (2009). Implementation research in mental health services: An emerging science with conceptual, methodological, and training challenges. *Administration and Policy in Mental Health, 36*(1), 24–34. https://doi.org/10.1007/s10488-008-0197-4

Proctor, E., Silmere, H., Raghavan, R., Hovmand, P., Aarons, G., Bunger, A., et al. (2011). Outcomes for implementation research: Conceptual distinctions, measurement challenges, and research agenda. *Administration and Policy in Mental Health, 38*, 65–76.

Rabin, B. A., Brownson, R. C., Haire-Joshu, D., Kreuter, M. W., & Weaver, N. L. (2008). A glossary for dissemination and implementation research in health. *Journal of Public Health Management and Practice, 14*(2), 117–123. https://doi.org/10.1097/01.PHH.0000311888.06252.bb

Rubin, A., & Bellamy, J. (2012). Steps in the EBP process. In *Practitioner's guide to using evidence based practice* (pp. 19–36). Wiley & Sons.

Sanders, M. R., Kirby, J. N., Tellegen, C. L., & Day, J. J. (2014). The Triple P-Positive Parenting Program: A systematic review and meta-analysis of a multi-level system of parenting support. *Clinical Psychology Review, 34*(4), 337–357. https://doi.org/10.1016/j.cpr.2014.04.003.

Torres, K., & Mathur, R. (2018). *Fact sheet: Family first prevention services act*. First Focus Campaign for Children.

Walton, E. (1998). In-home family focused reunification: A six-year follow-up of a successful experiment. *Social Work Research, 22*(4), 205–214.

Wilson, S. J., Price, C. S., Kerns, S. E. U., Dastrup, S. D., & Brown, S. R. (2019). *Title IV-E prevention services clearinghouse handbook of standards and procedures, version 1. 0, OPRE Report # 2019-56*. Office of Planning, Research, and Evaluation, Administration for Children and Families, U.S. Department of Health and Human Services.

Wood, S., Barton, K., & Schroeder, C. (1988). In-home treatment of abusive families: Cost and placement at one year. *Psychotherapy, 25*(3), 409–414.

CHAPTER 8

IDENTIFYING AND ADDRESSING COMMON BARRIERS TO APPLYING THE EBP PROCESS

With Courtney Benjamin Wolk and Sean E. Snyder

In this chapter, we delve into several research projects that examined the implementation of empirically supported interventions (ESIs) across different service sectors (e.g., child welfare, behavioral health, schools). Rather than cite barriers to implementation that may emerge within each of the five domains of the consolidated framework for implementation research (CFIR) (Damschroder et al., 2009), we will rely on the framework as a template for aligning specific strategies to address each barrier. While we find that students, clinicians, and leaders grasp the barriers, just talking about barriers can leave one feeling hopeless about how they will ever surmount them. Fortunately, implementation science includes numerous methods or "implementation strategies" to implement ESIs in the context of such barriers (Waltz et al., 2019). Next, we expand upon the CFIR framework and describe practical strategies or recommendations to address barriers, drawing on the implementation science literature and lessons we have learned from relevant implementation science research studies or projects.

IMPLEMENTATION SCIENCE PROJECT EXAMPLE #1: WALTZ AND COLLEAGUES (2019)—MULTIPLE SYSTEMS

As part of a 2019 study published by Waltz and colleagues (2019), implementation researchers and practitioners ($n = 169$) matched implementation strategies to address 39 potential barriers based on CFIR construct definitions. The participants in Waltz and colleagues included participants from varied systems. About a third (34.3%) of the participants were employed or affiliated with the US Veterans Health Administration. They ranked up to seven implementation strategies that would best address each barrier. During the data collection process, the participants could select strategies for the barrier or skip to another barrier. We present the descriptions of each barrier and the strategies the participants selected to address them for each of the five CFIR domains. These strategies were derived from the CFIR website: https://cfirguide.org/choosing-strategies/. The website includes a hyperlink to download the selection tool (an Excel sheet with macros). Once downloaded, you can select relevant barriers, and the tool will generate different strategies to address them. For simplicity, Waltz and colleagues specified the strategies endorsed by the majority (50%+ or referred to herein as level 1 strategies) of the participants, as well as those endorsed by 20%–49% (level 2 strategies) of participants. These "levels" are specified in Table 8.1 (a–e). We offer a review of key findings and themes related to their findings below.

CFIR DOMAIN: INTERVENTION CHARACTERISTICS

Only two implementation strategies across all eight of these characteristics reached level 1 status: (1) access new funding to mitigate costs related to implementation, and (2) promote adaptability to meet local needs. Interestingly, 20%–49% of the implementation experts from the Waltz study identified common "level 2" strategies to mitigate barriers across most or all the intervention characteristics: (1) capture and share local knowledge, (2) conduct educational meetings, (3) identify and prepare champions, (4) inform local opinion leaders, and (5) assess for readiness and identify barriers and facilitators, to name a few. Thus, instilling these strategies may offer maximum impact depending on your needs within the agency.

CFIR DOMAIN: CHARACTERISTICS OF INDIVIDUALS INVOLVED

Implementation experts from Waltz and colleagues' (2019) study highlighted common strategies to mitigate barriers related specifically to stakeholders involved in the implementation process. Some of these barriers included negative attitudes toward innovation, lacking self-efficacy or enthusiasm, and a low level of commitment to the organization. Level 1 and/or 2 strategies to mitigate these barriers include conducting educational

TABLE 8.1A Intervention Characteristics from the Consolidated Framework for Implementation Research; CFIR

Intervention Characteristics	Barrier Description	Strategies to Address Barriers Across Multiple Systems (Waltz, Powell, et al., 2019)(1)*	Strategies to Address Barriers in Child Welfare Contexts (Garcia et al., 2019, 2020) (2)	Strategies to Address Barriers in School Contexts	Strategies to Address Barriers in Behavioral Health and Juvenile Justice Contexts
Intervention Source	Stakeholders have a negative perception of the innovation because of the entity that developed it and/or where it was developed.	*1. Build acoalition. 2. Capture and share local knowledge. 3. Conduct educational meetings. 4. Identify and prepare champions. 5. Inform local opinion leaders. 6. Obtain and use patients/consumers and family feedback. 7. Promote adaptability. 8. Use advisory boards and work groups. 9. Visit other sites.*	1. Supervisors need strategies to motivate staff to embrace innovation and to feel motivated to refer clients to the EBP. This might entail providing caseworkers and staff opportunities to observe an EBP session to assess applicability (caseworkers/supervisors). 2. Ensure program champions convey a clear message about the EBP and the implementation blueprint, namely when/how to make referrals (caseworkers/supervisors).	1. Gather and share evidence from other similar schools or districts that have implemented the intervention. 2. Visit other schools to see the EBP in action. 3. Use an advisory board to explore the intervention's potential and consider alternatives	Integration strategy-Education/modeling to increase optimism, beliefs about consequences, social/professional role and identity (e.g., working with detention staff move toward trauma-informed work, away from punitive perspective)
Evidence Strength and Quality	Stakeholders have a negative perception of the quality and validity of evidence supporting the intervention.	*1. Capture and share local knowledge. 2. Conduct educational meetings. 3. Conduct educational outreach visits. 4. Conduct local consensus discussions. 5. Develop academic partnerships. 6. Develop educational materials. 7. Distribute educational materials. 8. Identify and prepare early adopters. 9. Identify and prepare champions. 10. Inform local opinion leaders.*	1. Develop and sustain practice-research partnerships (scholars). 2. Develop trainings that showcase how the EBP is delivered (caseworkers/supervisors).	1. Provide education about how the effectiveness of the intervention has been evaluated in the school context previously. 2. Champions and key opinion leaders from within the district share personal experiences or those of early adopters in using the EBP. 3. Develop research-practice partnerships with local academic institutions.	1. Provide education and training for the direct service staff supervising the young people

(continued)

TABLE 8.1A Continued

Intervention Characteristics	Barrier Description	Strategies to Address Barriers Across Multiple Systems (Waltz, Powell, et al., 2019)(1)*	Strategies to Address Barriers in Child Welfare Contexts (Garcia et al., 2019, 2020) (2)	Strategies to Address Barriers in School Contexts	Strategies to Address Barriers in Behavioral Health and Juvenile Justice Contexts
Relative Advantage	Stakeholders do not see the advantage of implementing the innovation compared to an alternative solution or keeping things the same.	1. *Alter incentive/allowance structures.* 2. *Assess for readiness and identify barriers and facilitators.* 3. Conduct cyclical small tests of change. 4. *Conduct educational meetings.* 5. Conduct local consensus discussions. 6. *Conduct local needs assessment.* 7. Identify and prepare champions. 8. Increase demand. 9. Inform local opinion leaders. 10. Promote adaptability. 11. Visit other sites.	Provide caseworkers and staff with decreased workload or responsibilities if they are expected to learn about a new EBP (caseworkers/supervisors).	1. Conduct professional development meetings with school personnel to educate them about the intervention and discuss how it compares to other innovations. 2. Adapt the intervention to promote alignment with other educational initiatives (e.g., PBIS: https://psycnet.apa.org/record/2009-05713-002)	Education, modeling, persuasion about belief about consequences and potential loss aversion; tie toward goals of the program; reinforcement of learning through "pop-in" consultation with program therapists on site at the detention center
Adaptability	Stakeholders do not believe that the innovation can be sufficiently adapted, tailored, or reinvented to meet local needs.	**1. Promote adaptability.** 2. Assess for readiness and identify barriers and facilitators. 3. Capture and share local knowledge. 4. Conduct cyclical small tests of change. 5. Conduct local consensus discussions. 6. Conduct local needs assessment. 7. Create a learning collaborative. 8. Facilitate relay of clinical data to providers. 9. Identify and prepare champions. 10. Identify early adopters. 11. Tailor strategies.	1. Dialogue with supervisors and CEOs about effective approaches to disseminate information about EBPs (directors). 2. Encourage exchanges of thoughts, beliefs, and knowledge about EBPs during staff meetings (directors). 3. Adapt case studies in manualized interventions (such as TripleP) to better align with the experiences of the target population (caseworkers/supervisors).	1. Implement the EBP on a smaller scale first, then assess the need to further adapt before rolling out to additional classrooms or schools. 2. Initial implementers from within the district share their experience with implementation to other prospective implementers. 3. Conduct focus groups or interviews with key stakeholders to understand barriers and use this data to inform tailoring	

Trialability	Stakeholders believe they cannot test the innovation on a smaller scale within the organization or undo implementation if needed.	*1. Assess for readiness and identify barriers and facilitators. 2. Capture and share local knowledge. 3. Conduct cyclical small tests of change. 4. Facilitation. 5. Inform local opinion leaders. 6. Model and stimulate change. 7. Promote adaptability. 8. Stage implementation scale-up. 9. Tailor strategies. 10. Use an implementation advisor.*	No recommendations provided.	1. Support stakeholders in trialing the intervention before scale up; pilot the innovation with support from an external expert.	1. Use of persuasion by leadership to set expectations
Complexity	Stakeholders believe that the innovation is complex based on their perception of duration, scope, radicalness, disruptiveness, centrality, and/or intricacy and number of steps needed to implement.	*1. Assess for readiness and identify barriers and facilitators. 2. Capture and share local knowledge. 3. Conduct cyclical small tests of change. 4. Conduct ongoing training. 5. Create a learning collaborative. 6. Develop a formal implementation blueprint. 7. Facilitation. 8. Identify and prepare champions. 9. Identify early adopters. 10. Model and stimulate change. 11. Organize clinician implementation team meetings. 12. Promote adaptability. 13. Provide ongoing consultation. 14. Stage implementation scale-up. 15. Tailor strategies.*	1. Ensure stakeholders are knowledgeable of when it is appropriate to implement an EBP. 2. This entails making sure caseworkers are aware of the EBP, and know about the referral process. Caseworkers may need to staff a few cases with directors or experts to gain more knowledge of when and how to make referrals to an EBP (caseworkers/supervisors).	1. Provide training and consultation to support implementers as they develop knowledge and skills needed to implement the innovation. 2. Leverage existing implementation teams to support novice implementers. 3. Build an implementation network within the district for ongoing peer support	Promote adaptability—tailor to the context of education level, consider "active ingredients" of intervention; partner with frontline staff to use their language and culture to familiarize new/complex concepts

(*continued*)

TABLE 8.1A Continued

Intervention Characteristics	Barrier Description	Strategies to Address Barriers Across Multiple Systems (Waltz, Powell, et al., 2019)(1)*	Strategies to Address Barriers in Child Welfare Contexts (Garcia et al., 2019, 2020) (2)	Strategies to Address Barriers in School Contexts	Strategies to Address Barriers in Behavioral Health and Juvenile Justice Contexts
Design quality and packaging	Stakeholders believe the innovation is poor quality based on the way it is bundled, presented, and/or assembled.	1. Conduct educational meetings. 2. Conduct local consensus discussions. 3. Develop and implement tools for quality monitoring. 4. Develop educational materials. 5. Obtain and use patients/consumers and family feedback. 6. Promote adaptability. 7. Purposely reexamine the implementation.	1. Recruit program champions within the agency. 2. Ensure program champions convey a clear message about the EBP and the implementation blueprint. 3. Negative attitudes are likely to shift if they observe EBP sessions. They need to know that the EBP "works" for their clients (caseworkers/supervisors).	1. Revamp program materials when possible to include school/district branding and increase attractiveness and usability for end users. 2. Gather and share local implementation data to increase confidence in the innovation	1. Design for implementation—leadership needs to know the implementers know what they are doing, consider 2. Audit/feedback to increase participation in delivery of implementation strategies
Cost	Stakeholders believe the innovation costs and/or the costs to implement (including investment, supply, and opportunity costs) are too high.	1. **Access new funding.** 2. Alter incentive/allowance structure. 3. Alter patient/consumer fees. 4. Develop resource-sharing agreements. 5. Fund and contract for clinical innovation. 6. Involve executive boards. 7. Make billing easier. 8. Model and stimulate change. 9. Place innovation on fee for service list/formularies. 10. Use other payment schemes.	1. Implement "train the trainer" models to cut down on expenditures. 2. Share resources (e.g., trainers, training protocol, program champions, funding mechanisms, billing procedures) with colleagues/peers employed in other systems (scholars/directors).	1. Apply for grants to offset costs, 2. Advocate to payers/funders to support the EBP (e.g., through insurance reimbursement).	Cost-benefit analysis—consider how the innovation can increase staff competency, help with emotional regulation, reduce sick time/turnover or reducing other occupational safety issues (e.g., return on investment)

*Note: Strategies in bold text denote major endorsement (i.e., ≥50%) by participants (level 1). Italicized text represents strategies endorsed by 20%–49% of participants (level 2).

1. Strategies identified by implementation researchers and practitioners from varied systems. About a third (34.3%) of the participants were employed or affiliated with the US Veterans Health Administration.

2. Strategies identified by child welfare caseworkers and supervisors during the implementation of TripleP (Garcia et al., 2020), and by child welfare scholars and agency directors during the implementation of MST, PCIT, TripleP, and TF-CBT (Garcia et al., 2019).

TABLE 8.1B Inner Contextual Factors from the Consolidated Framework for Implementation Research; CFIR

Inner Context Factors	Barrier Description	Strategies to Address Barriers Across Multiple Systems (Waltz, Byron, et al., 2019)(1)*	Strategies to Address Barriers in Child Welfare Contexts (Garcia et al., 2019, 2020) (2)	Strategies to Address Barriers in School Contexts	Strategies to Address Barriers in Other Behavioral Health and Juvenile Justice Contexts
Structural Characteristics	The social architecture, age, maturity, and size of an organization hinder implementation	1. *Assess for readiness and identify barriers and facilitators.* 2. Build a coalition. 3. Capture and share local knowledge. 4. Change physical structure and equipment. 5. Conduct cyclical small tests of change. 6. Identify and prepare champions. 7. Identify early adopters. 8. Promote adaptability. 9. Promote network weaving.	In light of turnover, new hires need to be trained about the new EBP on an ongoing basis. Thus, training protocol and how to disseminate knowledge needs to change to accommodate the influx of new hires. Trainings about a new EBP, for example, should be incorporated into new personnel training and associated agency manuals (caseworkers/supervisors).	1. Assess for readiness on a school-by-school (principal-by-principal) basis. 2. Leverage key opinion leaders within the school/district and those with long-standing institutional knowledge and experience implementing innovations within the district. 3. Develop a plan to address turnover.	Include training for new hires and then ongoing training (required 40 hours per year per state regulations)
Networks and communications	The organization has poor quality or nonproductive social networks and/or ineffective formal and informal communications.	**1. Promote network weaving. 2. Organize clinician implementation team meetings.** 3. Build a coalition. 4. Capture and share local knowledge. 5. Centralize technical assistance. 6. Conduct local consensus discussions. 7. Create a learning collaborative. 8. Facilitation. 9. Inform local opinion leaders.	1. Agency workers need to cultivate relationships with trained clinicians (directors).	1. Build a network or learning collaborative to support implementation. 2. Develop a plan for communication about the innovation. 3. Leverage existing implementation teams or technical assistance coaches when possible	Identify champions on each shift to ensure continuity of communication across "tours" or shifts.

(continued)

TABLE 8.1B Continued

Inner Context Factors	Barrier Description	Strategies to Address Barriers Across Multiple Systems (Waltz, Byron, et al., 2019)(1)*	Strategies to Address Barriers in Child Welfare Contexts (Garcia et al., 2019, 2020) (2)	Strategies to Address Barriers in School Contexts	Strategies to Address Barriers in Other Behavioral Health and Juvenile Justice Contexts
*Intraorganizational cultural exchanges (Note: Not a CFIR construct, added by Garcia et al., 2019, 2020).	Limited opportunities to engage in debate and discussion about the implementation process (D)		1. Send brief and sporadic emails to staff about EBPs that encourage further debate and discussion (directors). 2. Dialogue with supervisors and CEOs about effective approaches to disseminate information about EBPs (directors). 3. Encourage exchanges of thoughts, beliefs, and knowledge about EBPs during staff meetings (directors/scholars).	1. Principals and champions encourage discussion about the innovation during routine staff meetings	1. Use formal communication channels (staff meetings, supervisory sessions); consider 2. Environmental restructuring (e.g., staff common areas, bulletin boards, use QR codes to link to more information)
Culture	Cultural norms, values, and basic assumptions of the organization hinder implementation.	1. **Identify and prepare champions.** 2. Assess for readiness and identify barriers and facilitators. 3. Capture and share local knowledge. 4. Conduct educational meetings. 5. Conduct local consensus discussions. 6. Conduct local needs assessment. 7. Create a learning collaborative. 8. Facilitation. 9. Promote adaptability. 10. Recruit, designate, and train for leadership. 11. Tailor strategies. 12. Use advisory boards and workgroups. 13. Inform local opinion leaders.	1. Embrace and model a culture of knowledge exchange and debate (scholars/directors/caseworkers/supervisors). 2. Instill a culture of referring to an EBP. This entails making sure caseworkers are aware of the EBP, and know about the referral process. Caseworkers may need to staff a few cases with directors or experts to gain more knowledge of when and how to make referrals to an EBP (caseworkers/supervisors).	1. Engage and educate leadership and leverage champions to convey that implementation is expected and valued	Ensure EBP is part of new staff orientation, use champions to ensure sustainability and buffer against previous culture.

Implementation Climate	There is little capacity for change, low receptivity, and no expectation that the use of the innovation will be rewarded, supported, or expected.	**1. Assess for readiness and identify barriers and facilitators.** 2. Alter incentive/allowance structures. 3. Conduct local needs assessment. 4. Facilitation. 5. Identify and prepare champions. 6. Identify early adopters. 7. Recruit, designate, and train for leadership.	1. Recruit and retain program champions (scholars/directors). 2. Share client success stories with staff (directors). 3. Provide staff opportunities to observe EBP sessions (caseworkers/supervisors).	1. Implement the EBP first in schools that are more open or enthusiastic about the EBP, then share their experience with other prospective schools to generate enthusiasm. 2. Leverage district-level policies and mandates to support and reward implementation
1. tension for change	Stakeholders do not see the current situation as intolerable or do not believe they need to implement the innovation.	1. Assess for readiness and identify barriers and facilitators. 2. Alter incentive/allowance structures. 3. Conduct local consensus discussions. 4. Conduct local needs assessment. 5. Facilitate relay of clinical data to providers. 6. Identify and prepare champions. 7. Inform local opinion leaders. 8. Involve patients/consumers and family members	1. Ensure stakeholders are knowledgeable of when it is appropriate to implement an EBP. 2. This entails making sure caseworkers are aware of the EBP, and know about the referral process. Caseworkers may need to staff a few cases with directors or experts to gain more knowledge of when and how to make referrals to an EBP (caseworkers/supervisors).	1. Collect and disseminate data about current gaps or inadequacies in care for students. 2. Prepare and support motivated stakeholders, including families, to advocate the EBP be offered.	Key messaging about beliefs about consequences and beliefs about capabilities
2. compatibility	The innovation does not fit well with existing workflows nor with the meaning and values attached to the innovation, nor does it align well with stakeholders' own needs and/or it heightens the risk for stakeholders.	1. Assess for readiness and identify barriers and facilitators. 2. Build a coalition. 3. Conduct cyclical small tests of change. 4. Conduct local consensus discussions. 5. Conduct local needs assessment. 6. Facilitation. 7. Identify and prepare champions. 9. Promote adaptability. 10. Tailor strategies.	Shifting attitudes ensue after staff recognize or observe that EBPs are effective in addressing issues of concern (directors). This entails providing caseworkers opportunities to observe EBP sessions to assess practicality and applicability (caseworkers/supervisors).	1. Adapt and tailor the innovation to fit within existing workflows and structures. 2. Educate and advocate for how the EBP aligns with district priorities and supports educational activities	Adapt and tailor using local language, invite feedback and auditing (Plan Do Study Act strategy)

(continued)

TABLE 8.1B Continued

Inner Context Factors	Barrier Description	Strategies to Address Barriers Across Multiple Systems (Waltz, Byron, et al., 2019)(1)*	Strategies to Address Barriers in Child Welfare Contexts (Garcia et al., 2019, 2020) (2)	Strategies to Address Barriers in School Contexts	Strategies to Address Barriers in Other Behavioral Health and Juvenile Justice Contexts
	Perception that the EBP does not align with cultural values or not applicable to diverse target population (scholars and directors).		1. Modify (a) case exemplars in evidence-based treatment manuals to align or reflect the lived experiences of the target population, (b) the program to reflect inclusion of different types of caregivers, (c) the name of the program to sound more educational rather than therapeutic, and (d) the language, images, and handouts to reflect the target population (scholars and directors). 2. Share client success stories with staff (directors).	1. During training, use case examples, vignettes, and video clips that reflect the cultural diversity of district students and staff. 2. Develop plans to ensure equity in EBP implementation. 3. Adapt the innovation to be culturally responsive and appropriate.	Consider previous adaptations; distill common elements and use iterative strategies to infuse EBP with local culture and language.
3. relative priority	Stakeholders perceive that the implementation of the innovation takes a backseat to other initiatives or activities.	*1. Alter incentive/allowance structures. 2. Assess for readiness and identify barriers and facilitators. 3. Conduct local consensus discussions. 4. Conduct local needs assessment. 5. Increase demand. 6. Mandate change.*	1. Leaders need to mandate EBP implementation (scholars).	1. Leadership should help implementers prioritize the EBP in light of competing demands. 2. Principals and leaders convey the importance of implementation through policy mandates or incentives	Consider incentives and reinforcement strategies

	Lack of support to balance crises and extra demands of implementing EBPs (S&D)		1. Ensure clear protocols and procedures for crisis management are in place and that implementers have adequate support. 2. Ensure adequate EBP prep time, which may mean release from or a decrease in other professional responsibilities
4. organizational incentives and rewards	There are no tangible (e.g., goal-sharing awards, performance reviews, promotions, salary raises) or less tangible (e.g., increased stature or respect) incentives in place for implementing the innovation.	**1. Alter incentive/allowance structures.** 2. Audit and provide feedback. 3. Develop and implement tools for quality monitoring. 4. Fund and contract for clinical innovation. 5. Identify and prepare champions. 6. Recruit, designate, and train for leadership. 7. Use other payment schemes. 8. Access new funding.	Incentivize caseworkers to get trained to deliver an EBP, or make referrals (caseworkers).	1. District level incentives (e.g., financial or otherwise). 2. Principals share successes during staff meetings	1. Use financial incentives, paying attention to policies set forth by direct service staff unions in collective bargaining agreements
5. goals and feedback	Goals are not clearly communicated or acted on, nor do stakeholders receive feedback that is aligned with goals.	**1. Audit and provide feedback.** 2. Conduct educational meetings. 3. Develop a formal implementation blueprint. 4. Develop and implement tools for quality monitoring. 5. Develop and organize quality monitoring systems. 6. Facilitate relay of clinical data to providers. 7. Organize clinician implementation team meetings.	Provide caseworkers, supervisors, and staff with updates on the implementation process (scholars/directors).	1. Collect and analyze data about student improvement and implementation outcomes and share this data back with implementers in a user-friendly format. 2. Support implementers who are struggling in improving their use of the EBP through consultation or mentoring.	Plan Do Study Act is an iterative feedback strategy where changes are tested to see what works.

(continued)

TABLE 8.1B Continued

Inner Context Factors	Barrier Description	Strategies to Address Barriers Across Multiple Systems (Waltz, Byron, et al., 2019)(1)*	Strategies to Address Barriers in Child Welfare Contexts (Garcia et al., 2019, 2020) (2)	Strategies to Address Barriers in School Contexts	Strategies to Address Barriers in Other Behavioral Health and Juvenile Justice Contexts
6. learning climate	The organization has a climate where (a) leaders do not express their own fallibility or need for stakeholders' assistance or input; (b) stakeholders do not feel that they are essential, valued, and knowledgeable partners in the implementation process; (c) stakeholders do not feel psychologically safe to try new methods; and (d) there is not sufficient time and space for reflective thinking or evaluation	**1. Facilitation.** 2. Alter incentive/allowance structures. 3. Conduct local consensus discussions. 4. Identify and prepare champions. 5. Promote adaptability. 6. Recruit, designate, and train for leadership. 7. Organize clinician implementation team meetings.	1. Educate caseworkers on research design and importance of evaluation (scholars). 2. Recruit and retain program champions.	1. Provide ongoing support to implementers, tailored to each school. 2. Promote the sharing of successes and failures at regular meetings. 3. Champions or those with longer tenure in the school model sharing challenging cases and asking for input.	Organizational readiness work, work on preimplementation education and messaging.

	Directors are unaware, at times, of when and how best to disseminate information about EBPs to staff (directors). Locating and synthesizing research is not feasible; and staff meetings and traditional trainings and informational handouts about a new EBP are ineffective dissemination strategies (caseworkers/supervisors).	Share client success stories with staff (directors). Provide staff opportunities to observe EBP sessions (caseworkers/supervisors).	1. Share success stories at school and district meetings. 2. Engage academic collaborators or EBP experts to support the distillation and dissemination of evidence.
Implementation Readiness	There are few tangible and immediate indicators of organizational readiness and commitment to implement the innovation.	**1. Assess for readiness and identify barriers and facilitators.** 2. Alter incentive/allowance structures. 3. Build a coalition. 4. Conduct educational meetings. 5. Conduct local consensus discussions. 6. Conduct local needs assessment. 7. Obtain formal commitments.	1. Ensure stakeholders are knowledgeable of when it is appropriate to implement an EBP. 2. This entails making sure caseworkers are aware of the EBP, and know about the referral process. Caseworkers may need to staff a few cases with directors or experts to gain more knowledge of when and how to make referrals to an EBP (caseworkers/supervisors). 3. Recruit and retain program champions.	1. Utilize existing district data and informational meetings with key stakeholders to understand readiness, leveraging existing meetings when possible. 2. Assemble or leverage existing implementation teams to support schools in getting ready for implementation. 3. Conduct informational meetings and educational sessions to generate enthusiasm and obtain commitments. Readiness assessment—focus groups if possible, drop in sessions to accommodate staff schedules.

(continued)

TABLE 8.1B Continued

Inner Context Factors	Barrier Description	Strategies to Address Barriers Across Multiple Systems (Waltz, Byron, et al., 2019)(1)*	Strategies to Address Barriers in Child Welfare Contexts (Garcia et al., 2019, 2020) (2)	Strategies to Address Barriers in School Contexts	Strategies to Address Barriers in Other Behavioral Health and Juvenile Justice Contexts
1. leadership engagement	Key organizational leaders or managers do not exhibit commitment and are not involved, nor are they held accountable for the implementation of the innovation	1. Alter incentive/allowance structures. 2. Conduct local consensus discussions. 3. Develop a formal implementation blueprint. 4. Develop disincentives. 5. Identify and prepare champions. 6. Increase demand. 7. Involve executive boards. 8. Obtain formal commitments. 9. Recruit, designate, and train for leadership.	Leaders need to mandate EBP implementation (scholars) and convey to staff, caseworkers, and clinicians that the selected EBP is effective and will meet the needs of the target population (caseworkers/supervisors).	1. District leaders mandate EBP implementation. 2. District leaders incentivize principals to implement the EBP in their school. 3. Work with parents and families to advocate that the EBP be offered.	
2. available resources	Resources (e.g., money, physical space, dedicated time) are insufficient to support the implementation of the innovation.	1. Access new funding. 2. Alter patient/consumer fees. 3. Capture and share local knowledge. 4. Change physical structure and equipment. 5. Develop resource-sharing agreements. 6. Fund and contract for clinical innovation. 7. Make billings easier. 8. Use other payment schemes.	1. Implement "train the trainer" models to cut down on expenditures. 2. Share resources (e.g., trainers, training protocol, program champions, funding mechanisms, billing procedures) with colleagues/ peers employed in other systems (scholars/directors).	1. Apply for grants to offset costs, 2. Advocate to payers/funders to support the EBP (e.g., through insurance reimbursement). 3. Adapt the EBP to make it more feasible to implement in low resource context. 4. Share resources across schools/ implementers when possible	If possible, consider capitation model/ value-based payment arrangements to overcome fee for service limitations.

| 3. access to information and knowledge | Stakeholders do not have adequate access to digestible information and knowledge about the innovation nor how to incorporate it into work tasks. | **1. Conduct educational meetings. 2. Develop educational materials. 3. Distribute educational materials.** 4. Capture and share local knowledge. 5. Conduct educational outreach visits. 6. Conduct ongoing training. 7. Create a learning collaborative. 8. Identify and prepare champions. 9. Provide local technical assistance. 10. Shadow other experts. | Ensure there are internal experts available for staff. Caseworkers may need to staff a few cases with directors or experts to gain more knowledge of when and how to make referrals to an EBP (caseworkers/ supervisors). | 1. Discuss implementation challenges and successes at school and district meetings. 2. Engage academic collaborators or EBP experts to support the distillation and dissemination of evidence. | Listening in sessions, have staff discuss challenges with community-academic partner. |

1. Strategies identified by implementation researchers and practitioners from varied systems. About a third (34.3%) of the participants were employed or affiliated with the US Veterans Health Administration.
*Note: Strategies in bold text denote major endorsement (i.e., ≥50%) by participants. Italicized text represents strategies endorsed by 20%–49% of participants.
2. Strategies identified by child welfare caseworkers and supervisors during the implementation of TripleP (Garcia et al., 2020), and by child welfare scholars and agency directors during the implementation of MST, PCIT, TripleP, and TF-CBT (Garcia et al., 2019).

meetings, assessing for readiness and identifying barriers and facilitators, identifying and preparing champions, conducting local needs assessments, and altering incentive/allowance structures.

CFIR DOMAIN: INNER SETTING OR CONTEXT

Waltz and colleagues (2019) illuminated a few strategies across all seven inner context factors that meet criteria for level 1 status (i.e., 50%+ endorsement by implementation experts: (1) promote network weaving, (2) organize clinician implementation team meetings, (3) identify and prepare champions, (4) assess for readiness and identify barriers and facilitators, (5) alter incentive/allowance structures, (6) audit (i.e., review data) and provide feedback, (7) facilitation (i.e., an interactive problem-solving and support process; Ritchie et al., 2020), (8) access new funding, (9) conduct educational meetings, (10) develop educational materials, and (11) distribute educational materials. The experts also cited the need to develop a formal implementation blueprint, a level 2 strategy, a few times. For more in-depth descriptions of these various implementation strategies, see Powell and colleagues (2015).

CFIR DOMAIN: OUTER SETTING OR CONTEXT

Level 1 strategies were only identified for barriers related to patient needs and resources and cosmopolitanism: (1) conduct local needs assessment, (2) involve patients/consumers and family members, (3) obtain and use patients/consumers and family feedback, (4) promote network weaving, (5) develop academic partnerships, and (6) build a coalition. Commonly cited level 2 strategies included: (1) sing advisory boards and workgroups, (2) conducting educational outreach visits, and (3) developing resource-sharing agreements (Waltz et al., 2019).

CFIR DOMAIN: IMPLEMENTATION PROCESS

Unlike the previous CFIR domains, the informants who participated in the Waltz and colleagues (2019) study identified unique level 1 strategies to address implementation process barriers you may encounter. The informants suggested developing a formal implementation blueprint and conducting a local needs assessment during the planning phase. During the engagement phase, they recommend identifying and preparing champions. As for patients and consumers, they endorsed the following: (1) intervene with them to enhance uptake and adherence, (2) involve them and family members, and (3) prepare them to be active participants. Developing and implementing tools for quality monitoring auditing, and providing feedback should be prioritized during the reflection and evaluation stages. Apart from reflecting and evaluating, assessing for readiness, and identifying barriers and facilitators reached level 2 status for all the other phases of the implementation process.

TABLE 8.1C Outer Contextual Factors from the Consolidated Framework for Implementation Research; CFIR

Outer Context Factors	Barrier Description	Strategies to Address Barriers Across Multiple Systems (Waltz, Byron, et al., 2019)(1)*	Strategies to Address Barriers in Child Welfare Contexts (Garcia et al., 2019, 2020) (2)	Strategies to Address Barriers in School Contexts	Strategies to Address Barriers in Other Behavioral Health and Juvenile Justice Contexts
Patient needs and resources	Patient needs, including barriers and facilitators to meet those needs, are not accurately known and/or this information is not a high priority for the organization.	**1. Conduct local needs assessment. 2. Involve patients/consumers and family members. 3. Obtain and use patients/consumers and family feedback.** 4. Assess for readiness and identify barriers and facilitators. 5. Conduct local consensus discussions. 6. Intervene with patients/consumers to enhance uptake and adherence. 7. Prepare patients/consumers to be active participants. 8. Use advisory boards and workgroups.	Before the 1st session, clinicians should be trained to: (1) clarify the need for mental health treatment, (2) establish a foundation for a working relationship, (3) address stigmas, misconceptions, or negative attitudes about help-seeking, and (4) identify concrete barriers and provide resources to overcome those obstacles (scholars/directors).	1. Conduct focus groups with parents and students in the district to understand their needs, preferences, and priorities. 2. Develop implementation plans that address barriers and leverage facilitators to student and family engagement in the EBP. 3. Empower families to advocate for the EBP and to be informed about available mental health services.	Listening in sessions for youth about their preferences regarding services.
Cosmopolitanism	The organization is not well networked with external organizations.	**1. Promote network weaving. 2. Develop academic partnerships. 3. Build a coalition.** 4. Capture and share local knowledge. 5. Conduct educational outreach visits. 6. Create a learning collaborative. 7. Develop resource sharing agreements. 8. Involve executive boards. 9. Use advisory boards and workgroups. 10. Visit other sites.	Engage in interorganizational cultural exchanges. This involves the following: 1. Collaborate with agency and state leaders to identify solutions to barriers (scholars). 2. Deliver talks at local community centers and libraries to increase EBP awareness (scholars). 3. Other entities (courts/family law, CASA) need support and training on how best to de-emphasize traditional parenting services and consider uptake of innovation that is guided by science (caseworkers/supervisors).	1. Develop relationships with peer schools or districts. 2. Build research–practice partnerships with local academic institutions or EBP experts. 3. Develop connections and referral pathways with local payers, health systems, and clinicians.	Engage leaders cross-systems; academic partnerships can be a connector between systems to do education and training to have shared language and concepts across systems, e.g., trauma-informed care, CBT approaches to adolescents.

(continued)

TABLE 8.1C Continued

Outer Context Factors	Barrier Description	Strategies to Address Barriers Across Multiple Systems (Waltz, Byron, et al., 2019)(1)*	Strategies to Address Barriers in Child Welfare Contexts (Garcia et al., 2019, 2020)(2)	Strategies to Address Barriers in School Contexts	Strategies to Address Barriers in Other Behavioral Health and Juvenile Justice Contexts
Peer Pressure	There is little pressure to implement the innovation because other key peers or competing organizations have not already implemented the innovation, nor is the organization doing this in a bid for a competitive edge.	1. Alter incentive/allowance structures. 2. Conduct local consensus discussions. 3. Identify and prepare champions. 4. Identify early adopters. 5. Increase demand. 6. Inform local opinion leaders. 7. Involve executive boards. 8. Involve patients/consumers and family members.	No recommendations provided.		Target occupational stress—peers may not pressure others because they all recognize collective stress; "avoidance of conflict" so recognizing that there can be emotional regulation needs.
External policies and incentives	External policies, regulations (governmental or other central entity), mandates, recommendations or guidelines, pay-for-performance, collaborative, or public or benchmark reporting do not exist or they undermine efforts to implement the innovation.	1. Promote network weaving. 2. Develop academic partnerships. 3. Build a coalition. 4. Capture and share local knowledge. 5. Conduct educational outreach visits. 6. Create a learning collaborative. 7. Develop resource sharing agreements. 8. Involve executive boards. 9. Use advisory boards and workgroups. 10. Visit other sites.	Leaders need to mandate EBP implementation (scholars).	1. Advocate for policy changes at the state or national level. 2. Educate and empower families to advocate for change.	Be knowledgeable of policies, as end-users may cling to these policies as a barrier; harness knowledge of these policies in doing any training or educational work.
	Policies could be modified under direction of new leadership (scholars)		No recommendations provided.	1. Champions educate and advocate about the innovation to local leadership	

| *Interorganizational cultural exchanges (Note: Not a CFIR construct, added by Garcia et al., 2019, 2020). | 1. Lack of collaboration and communication between scholars, directors, and staff (scholars and directors). 2. Lack of awareness of EBPs among community stakeholders (scholars). | 1. Collaborate with agency and state leaders to identify solutions to barriers (scholars). 2. Deliver talks at local community centers and libraries to increase EBP awareness (scholars). 3. Other entities (courts/family law, CASA) need support and training on how best to de-emphasize traditional parenting services and consider uptake of innovation that is guided by science (caseworkers/supervisors). | More a thought here— be aware of outsider status, take time with readiness work, giving face time prior to doing the formal rollout. |

1. Strategies identified by implementation researchers and practitioners from varied systems. About a third (34.3%) of the participants were employed or affiliated with the US Veterans Health Administration. Italicized text represents strategies endorsed by 20%–49% of participants.
*Note: Strategies in bold text denote major endorsement (i.e., ≥50%) by participants.
2. Strategies identified by child welfare caseworkers and supervisors during the implementation of TripleP (Garcia et al., 2020), and by child welfare scholars and agency directors during the implementation of MST, PCIT, TripleP, and TF-CBT (Garcia et al., 2019).

TABLE 8.1D Individuals Involved—The Consolidated Framework for Implementation Research; CFIR

Factors Related to Individuals Involved	Barrier Description	Strategies to Address Barriers Across Multiple Systems (Waltz, Byron, et al., 2019)(1)*	Strategies to Address Barriers in Child Welfare Contexts (Garcia et al., 2019, 2020) (2)	Strategies to Address Barriers in School Contexts	Strategies to Address Barriers in Other Behavioral Health and Juvenile Justice Contexts
Knowledge and beliefs about the intervention	Stakeholders have negative attitudes toward the innovation, they place low value on implementing the innovation, and/or they are not familiar with facts, truths, and principles about the innovation.	1. **Conduct educational meetings.** 2. Assess for readiness and identify barriers and facilitators. 3. Capture and share local knowledge. 4. Develop educational materials. 5. Facilitation. 6. Identify early adopters. 7. Increase demand. 8. Inform local opinion leaders. 9. Stage implementation scale-up. 10. Conduct educational outreach visits. 11. Conduct local needs assessment. 12. Identify and prepare champions.	Scholars and directors need to (1) train staff on how to communicate with parents about EBPs, (2) increase face-to-face time in the agency and leave physical reminders for caseworkers to refer clients to the EBP, and (3) provide staff with quarterly newsletters about the EBP and the implementation process. Directors need to disseminate information by holding information booths during "EBP kick-off events," distributing brochures, engaging in 1:1 case consultations with caseworkers, and developing screening tools to help guide caseworkers in deciding which EBP to refer clients to. Negative attitudes are likely to shift if they observe EBP sessions. They need to know that the EBP "works" for their clients more so than what they review in a peer reviewed article or "what the statistics" say about a new EBP (directors, caseworkers/supervisors).	1. Use routine professional development meetings to provide education about the EBP, 2. Share local examples of the EBPs success with district students. 3. Leverage champions and key opinion leaders to generate enthusiasm and dispel misperceptions about the EBP.	Modeling is learning that occurs through observation and imitation; so doing role-plays and demonstrations of behaviors during training is modeling.

Self-efficacy	Stakeholders do not have confidence in their capabilities to execute courses of action to achieve implementation goals	1. Audit and provide feedback. 2. Conduct cyclical small tests of change. 3. Conduct educational outreach visits. 4. Conduct ongoing training. 5. Create a learning collaborative. 6. Facilitation. 7. Identify and prepare champions. 8. Make training dynamic. 9. Model and stimulate change. 10. Provide ongoing consultation. 11. Shadow other experts. 12. Provide local technical assistance.	Ensure stakeholders are knowledgeable of when it is appropriate to implement an EBP (caseworkers/supervisors). Scholars and directors need to (1) train staff on how to communicate with parents about EBPs, (2) increase face-to-face time in the agency and leave physical reminders for caseworkers to refer clients to the EBP, and (3) provide staff with quarterly newsletters about the EBPs (scholars/directors).	1. Provide education, training, and ongoing consultation in the EBP. 2. Develop partnerships with external or internal EBP experts and work to build EBP expertise within the district. 3. Leverage existing implementation or technical assistance teams to support implementers and monitor fidelity.
Individual stage of change	Stakeholders are not skilled or enthusiastic about using the innovation in a sustained way.	1. Alter incentive/allowance structures. 2. Conduct educational meetings. 3. Conduct educational outreach visits. 4. Conduct local consensus discussions. 5. Conduct ongoing training. 6. Create a learning collaborative. 7. Develop educational materials. 8. Identify and prepare champions. 9. Identify early adopters. 10. Inform local opinion leaders. 11. Make training dynamic. 12. Promote adaptability.	Scholars and directors need to (1) Train staff on how to communicate with parents about EBPs. (2) Increase face-to-face time in the agency and leave physical reminders for caseworkers to refer clients to the EBP. (3) Provide staff with quarterly newsletters about the EBP and implementation process (scholars/directors).	1. Build motivation to use the EBP through district-level policy mandates or incentives. 2. Principals can educate and encourage staff in their schools to use the EBP and reward/praise successes. 3. Promote the successes of early adopters district-wide.

(continued)

TABLE 8.1D Continued

Factors Related to Individuals Involved	Barrier Description	Strategies to Address Barriers Across Multiple Systems (Waltz, Byron, et al., 2019)(1)*	Strategies to Address Barriers in Child Welfare Contexts (Garcia et al., 2020) (2)	Strategies to Address Barriers in School Contexts	Strategies to Address Barriers in Other Behavioral Health and Juvenile Justice Contexts
	Stigma (scholars/directors)		Address the therapist as "coach" or "trainer" to destigmatize the process of receiving mental health treatment (scholars) and encourage therapists to work with clients to overcome stigma (directors).		
Individual identification with organization	Stakeholders are not satisfied with and have a low level of commitment to their organization.	1. Alter incentive/allowance structures. 2. Assess for readiness and identify barriers and facilitators. 3. Build a coalition. 4. Conduct local consensus discussions. 5. Conduct local needs assessment. 6. Identify and prepare champions. 7. Identify early adopters. 8. Organize clinician implementation team meetings. 9. Recruit, design, and train for leadership.	1. Supervisors need strategies to motivate staff to embrace innovation and to feel motivated to refer clients to the EBP. This might entail providing caseworkers and staff opportunities to observe an EBP session to assess applicability (caseworkers/supervisors). 2. Ensure program champions convey a clear message about the EBP and the implementation blueprint, namely when/how to make referrals (caseworkers/supervisors).	1. Explore ways to motivate and incentivize those who use the EBP. 2. Develop implementation teams that are supportive and psychologically safe spaces to discuss implementation challenges.	Consider occupational stressors, caseloads, restructuring the environment; what is staff use of benefits like EAP etc.

*Note: Strategies in bold text denote major endorsement (i.e., ≥50%) by participants. Italicized text represents strategies endorsed by 20%—49% of participants.

1. Strategies identified by implementation researchers and practitioners from varied systems. About a third (34.3%) of the participants were employed or affiliated with the US Veterans Health Administration.

2. Strategies identified by child welfare caseworkers and supervisors during the implementation of TripleP (Garcia et al., 2020), and by child welfare scholars and agency directors during the implementation of MST, PCIT, TripleP, and TF-CBT (Garcia et al., 2019).

TABLE 8.1E Implementation Process—The Consolidated Framework for Implementation Research; CFIR

Implementation Processes	Barrier Description	Strategies to Address Barriers Across Multiple Systems (Waltz, Byron, et al., 2019)(1)*	Strategies to Address Barriers in Child Welfare Contexts (Garcia et al., 2019, 2020) (2)	Strategies to Address Barriers in School Contexts	Strategies to Address Barriers in Other Behavioral Health and Juvenile Justice Contexts Strategies to Address Barriers in Other Behavioral Health and Juvenile Justice Contexts
Planning	A scheme or sequence of tasks necessary to implement the intervention has not been developed or the quality is poor.	**1. Develop a formal implementation blueprint. 2. Conduct local needs assessment.** 3. Assess for readiness and identify barriers and facilitators. 4. Conduct local consensus discussions. 5. Conduct ongoing training. 6. Develop and implement tools for quality monitoring. 7. Facilitation. 8. Identify and prepare champions.	Supervisors need confidence in their leaders ability to develop and implement a clear blueprint for implementing a new EBP. This roadmap should include strategies supervisors could rely on to motivate staff to embrace innovation and to feel motivated to refer clients to the EBP (caseworkers). Involve key actors, stakeholders, and frontline staff in the planning phase (scholars).	1. Develop a logic model of relevant inputs, activities, outputs and outcomes. 2. Assess barriers and facilitators and develop an implementation plan that accounts for barriers and leverages facilitators. 3. Engage and educate relevant stakeholders about the EBP.	Create the blueprint and be open with it, have time for open feedback during its development.
Engaging					
1. Opinion Leaders	Opinion leaders (individuals who have a formal or informal influence on the attitudes and beliefs of their colleagues with respect to implementing the intervention) are not involved or supportive.	**1. Inform local opinion leaders. 2. Identify and prepare champions.** 3. Build a coalition. 4. Conduct educational meetings. 5. Conduct local consensus discussions. 6. Identify early adopters. 7. Involve patients/consumers and family members. 8. Recruit, design, and train for leadership.		1. Determine who key opinion leaders are and educate and engage them to support implementation.	

(continued)

TABLE 8.1E Continued

Implementation Processes	Barrier Description	Strategies to Address Barriers Across Multiple Systems (Waltz, Byron, et al., 2019)(1)*	Strategies to Address Barriers in Child Welfare Contexts (Garcia et al., 2019, 2020) (2)	Strategies to Address Barriers in School Contexts	Strategies to Address Barriers in Other Behavioral Health and Juvenile Justice Contexts Strategies to Address Barriers in Other Behavioral Health and Juvenile Justice Contexts
2. Formally appointed internal implementation leaders	A skilled implementation leader (coordinator, project manager, or team leader), with the responsibility to lead the implementation of the innovation, has not been formally appointed or recognized within the organization.	1. **Identify and prepare champions.** 2. Assess for readiness and identify barriers and facilitators. 3. Develop a formal implementation blueprint. 4. Facilitate relay of clinical data to providers. 5. Identify early adopters. 6. Inform local opinion leaders. 7. Obtain formal commitments. 8. Organize clinician implementation team meetings. 9. Provide ongoing consultation. 10. Recruit, design, and train for leadership. 11. Use advisory boards. 12. Use an implementation advisor.	No recommendations provided.	1. Work with leadership to identify and appoint an implementation lead if one does not already exist.	Work with leaders to consider work task rebalancing to allow a staff to take on role of implementation leader.
3. Champions	Individuals acting as champions who support, market, or "drive-through" implementation in a way that helps to overcome indifference or resistance by key stakeholders are not involved or supportive.	1. **Identify and prepare champions.** 2. Build a coalition. 3. Conduct local consensus discussions. 4 Identify early adopters. 5. Inform local opinion leaders. 6. Organize clinician implementation team meetings. 7. Recruit, design, and train for leadership.	1. Supervisors need to engage in outreach, and recruit program champions within the agency (caseworkers/supervisors). 2. Ensure program champions convey a clear message about the EBP and the implementation blueprint, namely when/how to refer clients to the EBP. 3. Encourage champions who made referrals to provide testimonials as to how the EBP benefits clients (caseworkers/supervisors).	District leaders and school principals identify champions and support them to share successes and advocate for the innovation.	

4. Key stakeholders	*Multifaceted strategies to attract and involve key stakeholders in implementing or using the innovation (e.g., through social marketing, education, role modeling, training) are ineffective or nonexistent.*	**1. Identify and prepare champions.** 2. Assess for readiness and identify barriers and facilitators. 3. Build a coalition. 4. Conduct educational meetings. 5. Conduct local consensus discussions. 6. Conduct local needs assessment. 7. Create a learning collaborative. 8. Inform local opinion leaders. 9. Involve executive boards. 10. Use advisory boards and workgroups.	1. Supervisors need to engage in outreach (caseworkers/supervisors).	District leaders and school principals identify champions and support them to share successes and advocate for the innovation.
5. External change agents	Individuals from an outside entity formally facilitating decisions to help move implementation forward are not involved or supportive.	1. Build a coalition. 2. Create a learning collaborative. 3. Develop academic partnerships. 4. Facilitation. 5. Identify and prepare champions. 6. Inform local opinion leaders. 7. Involve executive boards. 8. Obtain formal commitments. 9. Use advisory boards and workgroups. 10. Use an implementation advisor.	No recommendations provided.	Develop an implementation team that includes stakeholders that are both internal and external to the school/district to ensure external collaborators are aware of organizational norms and priorities.

(continued)

TABLE 8.1E Continued

Implementation Processes	Barrier Description	Strategies to Address Barriers Across Multiple Systems (Waltz, Byron, et al., 2019)(1)*	Strategies to Address Barriers in Child Welfare Contexts (Garcia et al., 2019, 2020) (2)	Strategies to Address Barriers in School Contexts	Strategies to Address Barriers in Other Behavioral Health and Juvenile Justice Contexts Strategies to Address Barriers in Other Behavioral Health and Juvenile Justice Contexts
6. Patients/consumers	*Multifaceted strategies to attract and involve patients/customers in implementing or using the innovation (e.g., through social marketing, education, role modeling, training) are ineffective or nonexistent.*	1. Intervene with patients/consumers to enhance uptake and adherence. 2. Involve patients/consumers and family members. 3. Prepare patients or consumers to be active participants. 4. Alter patient/consumer fees. 5. Develop educational materials. 6. Identify and prepare champions. 7. Obtain and use patients/consumers and family feedback. 8. Use advisory boards and workgroups. 9. Use mass media.	1. Role-playing is critical. Clinicians and social workers need to know what to say when confronted with clients who are resistant and question the cultural and technical applicability of the EBP. 2. Consider disclosure. Opening up about experiences as a parent if relevant, may instill trust and encourage clients to share experiences. 3. Encourage parents to tell their own story. Instead of solely relying on case records or referral information, ask them directly what issues or challenges (with parenting) they grapple with. 4. Acknowledge it may take time for parents to realize some of their parenting strategies may reinforce children's misbehaviors (caseworkers/supervisors).	1. Conduct focus groups with parents and students in the district to understand their needs, preferences, and priorities. 2. Develop implementation plans that address barriers and leverage facilitators to student and family engagement in the EBP. 3. Empower families to advocate for the EBP and to be informed about available mental health services.	

Lack of initial client buy-in (scholars and directors).	Before the 1st session, clinicians should be trained to: (1) clarify the need for mental health treatment; (2) establish a foundation for a working relationship; (3) address stigmas, misconceptions, or negative attitudes about help-seeking; and (4) identify concrete barriers and provide resources to overcome those obstacles (scholars/directors).	1. Use motivational enhancement intervention strategies or rewards/token economies to motivate initial engagement.
Lack of client adherence due to parents own trauma and transiency (scholars and directors).	1. Provide motivational enhancement to counteract the mandated nature of involvement in the child welfare system. 2. Call caregivers to remind them about homework activities and future appointments. 3. Focus on family strengths and beliefs about parenting and mental health. 4. Parents need opportunities to develop bonds with other parents. 5. Caseworkers need to praise parents engagement in EBPs (scholars/directors).	1. Meet parents during school drop-off or pickup and facilitate engagement when parents may already be at the school. 2. Explore other levels or care or wrap around services that may be a better fit for families. 3. Use interventions with students, when appropriate, that do not require much caregiver engagement.

(continued)

TABLE 8.1E Continued

Implementation Processes	Barrier Description	Strategies to Address Barriers Across Multiple Systems (Waltz, Byron, et al., 2019)(1)*	Strategies to Address Barriers in Child Welfare Contexts (Garcia et al., 2019, 2020) (2)	Strategies to Address Barriers in School Contexts	Strategies to Address Barriers in Other Behavioral Health and Juvenile Justice Contexts Strategies to Address Barriers in Other Behavioral Health and Juvenile Justice Contexts
Executing	Implementation activities are not being done according to plan.	1. Assess for readiness and identify barriers and facilitators. 2. Conduct ongoing training. 3. Create a learning collaborative. 4. Develop a formal implementation blueprint. 5. Develop and implement tools for quality monitoring. 6. Develop and organize quality monitoring systems. 7. Facilitation. 8. Organize clinician implementation team meetings. 9. Provide local technical assistance. 10. Provide ongoing consultation. 11. Purposely reexamine the implementation. 12. Use and implementation advisor.	1. Assess organizational readiness for change (scholars/directors). 2. Develop an implementation plan and prepare to mitigate unforeseen implementation barriers as they occur (scholars/directors).	1. Use existing implementation or technical assistance teams in the district to support the execution of the implementation plan, or develop capacity for ongoing quality assurance if it does not already exist.	Technical assistance team that includes iterative strategies.

| Reflecting and evaluating | There is little or no quantitative and qualitative feedback about the progress and quality of implementation nor regular personal and team debriefing about progress and experience. | **1. Develop and implement tools for quality monitoring. 2. Audit and provide feedback.** 3. Capture and share local knowledge. 4. Develop and organize quality monitoring systems. 5. Facilitate relay of clinical data to providers. 6. Facilitation. 7. Obtain and use patients/consumers and family feedback. 8. Organize clinician implementation team meetings. 9. Purposely reexamine the implementation. 10. Use data experts. | 1. Provide caseworkers, supervisors, and staff with updates on the implementation process. 2. Provide staff with quarterly newsletters about the EBP and implementation process (scholars/directors). | 1. Use existing implementation or technical assistance teams in the district to support the execution of the implementation plan, or develop capacity for ongoing quality assurance if it does not already exist. 2. Develop formal and informal feedback systems. 3. Leverage existing meetings to briefly check in about implementation regularly. |

---

1. Strategies identified by implementation researchers and practitioners from varied systems. About a third (34.3%) of the participants were employed or affiliated with the US Veterans Health Administration.

Note: Strategies in bold text denote major endorsement (i.e., ≥50%) by participants. Italicised text represents strategies endorsed by 20%–49% of participants.

2. Strategies identified by child welfare caseworkers and supervisors during the implementation of TripleP (Garcia et al., 2020), and by child welfare scholars and agency directors during the implementation of MST, PCIT, TripleP, and TF-CBT (Garcia et al., 2019).

IMPLEMENTATION SCIENCE PROJECT EXAMPLE #2: GARCIA ET AL. (2019, 2020)—CHILD WELFARE CONTEXTS

To apply the CFIR to child welfare contexts, Dr. Garcia refers to qualitative studies he conducted with his colleagues (Garcia et al., 2019, 2020). Initially, for the 2019 study, they referred to the four ESIs referenced in Chapter 7: parent-child interaction therapy (PCIT), trauma-focused cognitive behavioral therapy (TF-CBT), Level 4 TripleP (Pathways Positive Parenting Program) or TripleP, and multisystemic therapy (MST). Scholars and agency leaders who implemented one of these ESIs in child welfare contexts and/or evaluated them were recruited to participate in a semistructured interview to identify implementation barriers and share how they mitigated them. While the study did not initially inquire about CFIR barriers, the implementation experts identified them during these in-depth interviews. Ultimately, 11 experts (7 scholars and 4 agency directors) shared recommendations and lessons about how they mitigated barriers (Garcia et al., 2019).

Around the same time, they also had an opportunity to learn about the experiences of child welfare providers implementing TripleP. Originating in 2015, the *Promoting and Empowering Positive Perceptions of Evidence-Based Parenting* (PEP2) study is a research-practice partnership born out of dedication to (1) prospectively explore the process of implementing TripleP in two child welfare agencies in the Mid-Atlantic, (2) develop an explanatory model linking how critical implementation activities and processes are interrelated to guide decision-making and (3) generate recommendations or strategies on how to address implementation barriers (Garcia et al., 2020). Altogether, child welfare workers or staff who can refer parents to TripleP ($n = 12$), their respective supervisors ($n = 4$), and TripleP clinicians who deliver the program ($n = 2$) participated in semistructured interviews that lasted between 30 and 80 minutes. For clarity herein, we then inferred which strategies they cited would most likely address each CFIR barrier.

CFIR DOMAIN: INTERVENTION CHARACTERISTICS

Unlike Waltz and colleagues (2019), Garcia and colleagues (2019, 2020) identified unique strategies that target each of the different CFIR barriers related to intervention characteristics: (1) ensure program champions convey a clear message about the ESI and the implementation blueprint, namely when/how to make referrals, (2) develop trainings that showcase how the ESI is delivered and/or observe an ESI session for staff to assess applicability, (3) adapt case studies in manualized interventions (in this case, TripleP) to better align with the experiences of the target population, and (4) allot time during staff meetings to exchange thoughts, beliefs, and knowledge about ESIs; thereby creating space to verbalize and challenge preconceived myths or negative perceptions about the EBP process. In sum, supervisors and caseworkers wanted to know, with confidence, that the ESI would meet the needs of their increasingly diverse target population. Providing them an opportunity to view what would happen during an ESI session if/when they refer their clients to the ESI would increase favorable impressions of innovation and how it is assembled.

CFIR DOMAIN: CHARACTERISTICS OF INDIVIDUALS INVOLVED

Garcia and colleagues' (2019, 2020) data illuminate the need for scholars and directors to (1) train staff on how to communicate with parents about ESIs, (2) increase face-to-face time in the agency and leave physical reminders for caseworkers to refer clients to the ESI, and (3) provide staff with quarterly newsletters about the ESI and the implementation process. Dr. Garcia recalls the dedication of agency directors to increase caseworker referrals and meet benchmarks for TripleP enrollment. Eventually, directors went "door-to-door," asking caseworkers to take the time to staff each of their cases. Collectively, they determined which families were eligible for TripleP, and the directors walked them through the referral process. While this process was time-consuming initially, it built momentum and cemented critical knowledge about the ESI and the referral process.

CFIR DOMAIN: INNER SETTING OR CONTEXT

Garcia and colleagues (2019, 2020) offer additional details for child welfare inner contexts. In his research, Dr. Garcia relies on the exploration preparation implementation and sustainment (EPIS) framework, given its specific applicability to child welfare and mental health contexts. Like CFIR, the framework outlines the inner and outer context factors for each of the four stages purported to impact service provision: (1) exploration (i.e., evaluate needs and identify potential solutions), (2) preparation (i.e., identify barriers and facilitators and conduct planning/outreach regarding the ESI), (3) implementation (i.e., ESI use is initiated with leadership and support for the ESI), and (4) sustainment (i.e., ESI continues to be delivered with ongoing quality assurance). To summarize, Aarons and colleagues' (2011) EPIS framework includes outer context factors, or experiences outside the agency, such as the sociopolitical context, leadership ties across systems, and intraorganizational networks. On the other hand, the inner context, resembling experiences within the agency, includes individual worker characteristics and attitudes toward ESIs, and organizational functioning, such as readiness for change, culture, and climate. For further review of the components of EPIS, please refer to Aarons and colleagues (2011) and Moulin and colleagues (2019). The website https://episframework.com/ also provides helpful resources. As noted in the previous chapter, the PEP2 study involved recruiting child welfare workers and supervisors to identify implementation barriers they had to grapple with while implementing TripleP and recommendations to address them. In preparation for the interviews, the study team relied on the EPIS framework to inform the questions asked of informants. Interviews revealed that agency directors relied on traditional strategies, including emails, brochures, sporadic 1:1 consultations, and staff meetings attended by the few workers who were not responding to crises, to disseminate knowledge to supervisors and caseworkers (Garcia et al., 2019).

Supervisors and caseworkers validated that these strategies were ineffective, with some reporting they did not know about TripleP and ESIs in general. Moreover, while others may have heard about TripleP in passing from a supervisor or colleague, they did not have adequate support to process how to rely on the information to inform practice (Garcia et al., 2020). These qualitative findings provided insight into why only 8% of caseworkers who participated in our study ($n = 130$) may have made a referral to TripleP (Myers et al., 2020). If they discussed TripleP with parents, the central messages about its benefits were poorly communicated, and common misunderstandings and negative assumptions about ESIs in general prevailed (e.g., lack of fit with client needs and acceptability, and concerns about feasibility and time to learn about new practices). Thus, it is evident that more efforts must be devoted to developing effective strategies to address broken communication channels and disseminate evidence to all key players to achieve implementation.

CULTURAL EXCHANGES: AN ADDITIONAL COMPONENT OF THE INNER SETTING

The communication breakdown compelled Dr. Garcia to add a unique characteristic to the inner setting or context—intraorganizational cultural exchanges. For implementation to succeed, simply receiving knowledge is insufficient. Instead, researchers and research users (e.g., child welfare workers) must share values and exchange knowledge of the evidence (Mitton et al., 2007; Nutley et al., 2007; Palinkas & Aarons, 2009). The exchange of knowledge, beliefs, and practices (referred to herein as "cultural exchanges") must then compel workers/stakeholders to process the information, evaluate its meaning, and determine whether and how they will decide to rely on the evidence in practice (Mitton et al., 2007; Palinkas et al., 2016). The question herein is whether the exchange led someone to modify their attitudes, perceptions, and/or practice behaviors.

Although the EPIS framed this PEP2 study, other strategies that may mitigate CFIR barriers were cited by informants. Considering turnover, a structural characteristic of child welfare agencies, new hires need to be trained about the new ESI on an ongoing basis. For example, training about a new ESI should be incorporated into new personnel training and associated agency manuals.

To promote compatibility, informants suggest modifying the following: (1) case exemplars in evidence-based treatment manuals to reflect the lived experiences of the target population, (2) the program to reflect inclusion of different types of caregivers, (3) the name of the program to sound more educational rather than therapeutic, and (4) the language, images, and handouts to reflect the target population.

Efforts should also be dedicated to instilling a culture of referring to the new ESI. This could entail incentivizing caseworkers to refer their clients to the ESI or, better yet, to get trained to deliver an ESI. Caseworkers may need to staff a few cases with leaders or internal experts to better understand when and how to refer their clients to the ESI. Sharing success stories of clients who graduated from the ESI and observing an ESI session are other strategies likely to promote the most advantageous learning climate. In turn, caseworkers may then feel intrinsically motivated to refer. Finally, program champions enhance the implementation climate by "selling the ESI" to their colleagues, highlighting the potential benefits of client engagement. These strategies work in tandem to also promote implementation readiness.

CFIR DOMAIN: OUTER SETTING OR CONTEXT

Garcia and colleagues (2019, 2020) underscore the importance of engaging in *interorganizational cultural exchanges*. While intraorganizational cultural exchanges focus on exchanges between colleagues *within* the agency (and thus are considered an internal contextual factor), interorganizational exchanges refer to exchanges caseworkers or other stakeholders engage in with colleagues outside of their agency. This process might involve a child welfare caseworker or an agency director engaging in dialogue with behavioral health providers to reach consensus about the details of a resource-sharing agreement. In relation to TripleP, the director of parenting services engaged in numerous conversations to establish a protocol for behavioral health leaders and providers to refer their clients to TripleP if they meet criteria and are at risk for child welfare involvement. This process involved networking, educational outreach, and developing resource-sharing agreements. Informants participating in Garcia and colleagues' (2019, 2020) studies also underscored the need to deliver talks at local community centers and libraries to increase ESI awareness. Other entities (courts/family law) also need support and training on how best to de-emphasize traditional parenting services and consider the uptake of innovation that is guided by science. Finally, they provided several recommendations for meeting client needs and increasing resources. Before the first session with clients, clinicians should be trained to (1) clarify the need for mental health treatment; (2) establish a foundation for a working relationship; (3) address stigmas, misconceptions, or negative attitudes about help-seeking; and (4) identify concrete barriers (e.g., lack of transportation or daycare) and provide resources to overcome those obstacles.

CFIR DOMAIN: IMPLEMENTATION PROCESS

Specific to the child welfare context (Garcia et al., 2019, 2020), agency leaders decided to implement TripleP due to (1) how flexible it is concerning how it is delivered (e.g., individual sessions or group format), and (2) established efficacy, with studies spanning over three decades showing that TripleP promotes positive child behaviors by enhancing the knowledge, skills, and confidence of parents in the general population (Sanders, 2012; Sanders et al., 2014). The conditions appeared optimal—agency directors received sufficient external funding to support training and implementation for two years. They developed screening protocols and referral forms during the planning phase. They gathered evidence from multiple sources (website clearinghouses, conferences, TripleP training sites, interorganizational collaboration with child welfare and mental health agencies, peer-reviewed publications, and academic researchers) to learn more about TripleP and how to best promote implementation (Garcia et al., 2019). Staff training and "kickoff events" were offered to increase awareness. However, only 8% out of the 130 caseworkers we surveyed made a referral to TripleP (Myers et al., 2020). After learning about these ineffective strategies and acknowledging that caseworkers still referred their clients to "traditional parenting classes," agency directors proposed a plan to increase referrals. It was not until agency directors staffed cases with caseworkers, educated them about which clients were eligible to participate in TripleP, and coached them on how to make referrals that referrals picked up. Soon thereafter, agency directors observed an uptick in parental engagement (i.e., completion of and satisfaction with TripleP). Thus, one of the key implementation drivers that may work for leaders is the 1:1 investment in time with workers.

At the same time, they recruited program champions to sustain cultural exchanges about TripleP and discuss the research evidence supporting the uptake of the intervention. As an administrative leader, one question you might ask is, "Who in your agency is motivated, educated, and prepared to 'pass down their knowledge' to colleagues and new hires in the agency?" We find that rather than scholars, "word of mouth" from colleagues, who attest, from their observations, that the ESI "works" and is culturally relevant, is most important for disseminating new information. To that end, as an "engagement" tactic, the directors recruited champions who made referrals and could provide their colleagues testimonials on how TripleP benefited the parents on their caseload. Thus, Garcia and colleagues' (2019, 2020) research validates Waltz and colleagues' (2019) finding related to the salience of "identifying and preparing champions" during the engagement phase. Garcia and colleagues add that key actors and stakeholders should also have a seat at the table during the initial planning phases, as they need to have "buy-in" about the changes that are about to ensue within the organization.

Informants in Garcia and colleagues' (2019, 2020) studies offered additional strategies to engage an optimal implementation team. Caseworkers noted that other organizations, courts, and child-serving systems need to be informed that a new ESI (versus referrals to services as usual) is prioritized. Leaders must allocate time to educate external providers about the benefits of the new ESI. Developing and delivering strategies to increase client or consumer active participation in the ESI is critical. Simply put, implementation fails if clients do not show up for treatment. Scholars, caseworkers, clinicians, and supervisors unveiled numerous effective strategies that they implemented:

1. Role-playing is critical. Clinicians and social workers need to know what to say when clients express reservations or ambivalence and question the cultural and technical applicability of the ESI.
2. Consider disclosure when appropriate. Opening up about experiences as a parent, if relevant, may instill trust and encourage clients to share experiences.
3. Encourage parents to tell their own stories. Instead of relying solely on case records or referral information, ask them what issues or challenges (with parenting) they grapple with.
4. Acknowledge that it may take time for parents to realize that some parenting strategies may reinforce children's misbehaviors.
5. Know in advance that parents may not adhere to treatment due to their trauma and transiency. In these cases, provide motivational enhancement to counteract the mandated nature of involvement in the child welfare system.
6. Call caregivers to remind them about homework activities and future appointments.
7. Focus on family strengths and beliefs about parenting and mental health.

8. Provide parents with opportunities to develop bonds with other parents.
9. Caseworkers should praise parents when they engage in an ESI.
10. As underscored in the previous chapter, clinicians should be trained to (a) clarify the need for mental health treatment; (b) establish a foundation for a working relationship; (c) address stigmas, misconceptions, or negative attitudes about help-seeking; and (d) identify concrete barriers and provide resources to overcome those obstacles.

Finally, informants suggested that leaders should provide caseworkers, supervisors, and staff with updates on the implementation process. This could entail distributing newsletters about the ESI and implementation process during the reflection and evaluation stage.

IMPLEMENTATION SCIENCE PROJECT EXAMPLE #3: SCHOOL MENTAL HEALTH CONTEXT ((C. WOLK ET AL., 2019)

Dr. Wolk's research program focuses on implementing mental health ESIs in nonspecialty mental health settings, including schools and primary care clinics. She also routinely consults with organizations seeking to implement ESIs or better integrate mental health services into their settings, leveraging implementation science methods and tools to help organizations succeed in implementing and sustaining ESIs. Dr. Wolk and her colleagues recently worked with local stakeholders to plan for the implementation of several new ESIs for an expanding school mental health program. They collaboratively examined contextual barriers and facilitators, guided by CFIR, and using EPIS to structure implementation planning, they identified candidate ESIs and prepared for implementation with long-term sustainment in mind.

There was a range of stakeholders involved in decisions around school mental health services in this project, including individuals representing the school district, the department of public health, and the Medicaid managed care payer for behavioral health services in the area. This group had already been meeting regularly to plan for changes to the school mental health service model. It had developed an initial logic model of relevant inputs, resources, outputs, and goals. Recognizing the complexity of the task at hand and seeking to use evidence to inform their decision-making, the group engaged the help of a team of academic collaborators. Moving forward, this group will be referred to as the school mental health (SMH) implementation team. This team assembled regularly for about a year to collaboratively develop a comprehensive implementation plan.

CFIR DOMAIN: OUTER SETTING

The SMH implementation team began meeting after the state announced upcoming changes to the requirements for publicly funded integrated mental health services, which key SMH stakeholders realized quickly would have implications for how the SMH services would need to be staffed and supervised, how community clinicians implementing services would need to be integrated within schools, and what clinical services would be reimbursed. This is an example of an external policy or incentive motivating implementation. Fortunately, this group of disparate stakeholders was already connected, shared a commitment to improving the mental health services students receive, and had existing community–academic partnerships (e.g., Pellecchia et al., 2018) they could leverage to support them in achieving their goals.

One of the first tasks the SMH implementation team undertook was to review existing services and administrative records and previously collected focus group data to understand the client's needs and resources. This was important to select ESIs for implementation that would meet the community's most pressing needs and identify where existing programs and services were not already adequately meeting those needs. This was an essential activity during the *Exploration Phase*. The group identified key clinical target areas for the student population in this district, namely trauma and disruptive behaviors in the classroom, to focus on during implementation planning. It was also important to the team that any ESIs selected had been tested previously with youth who matched the demographic profiles of district students, predominantly Black and lower socioeconomic status (SES) families.

CFIR DOMAIN: INNER SETTING

The SMH implementation team identified several strengths and potential barriers at the inner setting level that would require consideration during the *Preparation Phase* to ensure successful implementation and eventual sustainment. One major strength was the interest in and attention to use of ESIs by high-level leadership. Key administrative stakeholders had previously invested in and supported the implementation of mental health ESIs in school and nonschool contexts and had "bought in" to the importance of ESIs. While upper-level leadership was engaged and eager to facilitate ESI implementation, there was also the recognition that leaders at the next tier (e.g., school principals, agency directors) varied in their engagement and that implementation climate and readiness for ESIs varied greatly from school-to-school and agency-to-agency. The competing demands that these organizations contend with were acknowledged and appreciated, and the SMH implementation team recognized that any ESIs selected would need to be compatible with the SMH context. That is, ESIs would need to be delivered within the parameters of the school day (e.g., sessions needed to fit within a class period, which was shorter than a therapy hour) and by the personnel available (i.e., either therapists or behavioral consultants).

CFIR DOMAIN: INTERVENTION CHARACTERISTICS

As noted in the discussion of the outer setting, it was very important to the SMH implementation team that any ESIs selected for implementation have evidence to support their use with diverse urban youth, given that students in the district were predominantly Black. There was also a sizable Latinx student population in the district. An ESI that had only been tested with White, middle- to upper-SES youth, would not be sufficiently evidence-based for this population. To identify potential ESIs, Dr. Wolk and her academic colleagues used the PracticeWise database (https://www.practicewise.com/) to search for ESIs for school-aged youth presenting with traumatic stress reactions and disruptive behaviors, and to filter out ESIs that had not been tested for effectiveness with Black and/or Latinx youth. It was also crucial that any ESIs selected for implementation have added value above and beyond what was already being implemented, would fit the context as is or be adaptable to the particular context, be relatively low-cost, and not exceedingly complex for novice clinicians to learn to implement with training and an initial (e.g., 6-month) consultation period. With this information in mind, Dr. Wolk and her colleagues created a spreadsheet of potential ESIs, noting strengths and weaknesses in the critical domains, and then reviewed them with the larger SMH team. This process allowed them to eliminate interventions that would be infeasible or that were duplicative of existing interventions. For example, the Safety Planning Intervention (Stanley & Brown, 2012) was eliminated because the district already had a suicide crisis procedure that included safety planning elements. It also allowed them to identify interventions that would be most feasible to implement. One example was the Cognitive Behavioral Intervention for Trauma in Schools (CBITS; Stein et al., 2003) program; several stakeholders on the SMH team had already been involved with a CBITS pilot, which had been successful, and thus already had confidence in the intervention and established relationships with CBITS trainers.

CFIR DOMAIN: CHARACTERISTICS OF INDIVIDUALS INVOLVED

Based on the previous implementation experience of the SMH team members (e.g., Wolk et al., 2019), the group knew that the clinicians who would be implementing ESIs in the schools would vary greatly in their knowledge and preservice training in ESIs, their motivation to use ESIs, and their confidence, or self-efficacy to implement them. Given this, the team recognized that a robust training and consultation plan would need to be devised to support clinicians in learning and integrating ESIs into their practice. The team also recognized that clinicians would need time to develop skills in each ESI, and thus a rolling training plan was designed such that clinicians would be trained in at most one ESI per year.

CFIR DOMAIN: IMPLEMENTATION PROCESS

The SMH team focused their efforts on (1) the *Exploration and Preparation Phases* of EPIS, (2) planning for implementation (and long-term sustainment), and (3) engaging the relevant stakeholders to ensure adequate buy-in from leadership and frontline clinicians. At the end of their partnered planning work, the team identified three ESIs to be implemented over the next three years. The ESIs were CBITS, cognitive-behavioral therapy (CBT), and a model for clinician consultation to teachers to support them in addressing challenging behaviors in the classroom (Cappella et al., 2012). Expert trainers and consultants in each ESI were engaged, and a roll-out plan was derived in which each school-based clinicians would receive training in one ESI per year. The relevant stakeholders were engaged early and often in the planning process to ensure feasibility and arrange more practical implementation details, such as assuring clinicians would have adequate space to work in each school. Plans for ongoing monitoring and quality assurance were also developed collaboratively early on, with the partners agreeing on key metrics of success and methods for monitoring outcomes to inform iterative refinements to the implementation plan as the process unfolds. Due to the COVID-19 pandemic, the implementation start date had to be delayed, given that schools transitioned to remote learning and schools and clinicians transitioned to telehealth. However, the programs were able to be rolled out the following school year as students returned to in-person learning, and initial implementation outcome data are promising (Weiss et al., 2022).

IMPLEMENTATION SCIENCE PROJECT EXAMPLE #4: JUVENILE JUSTICE AND BEHAVIORAL HEALTH

The adage "it takes a village to raise a child" holds especially true for child systems of care, and the juvenile justice (JJ) system is no exception. Youth that have JJ system contact have higher rates of traumatic exposure and higher rates of PTSD than their non-JJ counterparts (Abram et al., 2015; Ford & Hawk, 2012; Modrowski & Kerig, 2019). Approximately 70% of these youth have a confirmed mental health diagnosis (Underwood & Washington, 2016), and oftentimes these youth need to rely on the JJ system for their mental healthcare.

JJ youth often have many touchpoints of care (Abram et al., 2015), and one point of care in which they are most vulnerable is juvenile detention. Let's turn our attention to this practice setting to see how implementation science helped bring in TF-CBT (Cohen et al., 2004; Cohen et al., 2012) and how its insights led to sustaining the effects of the intervention in a stressful environment. You will notice the implementation challenges were in the inner setting, despite the strengths and facilitators for implementation with the mental health agency.

CFIR DOMAIN: OUTER SETTING

How did the clinicians get into detention in the first place? Dr. Snyder's agency of reference is a community mental health center (CMHC). He and his colleagues subcontracted to provide services at the detention center as a result of a long-standing relationship with the city's department of behavioral health services and from its connection to many innovative initiatives in the city (Beidas et al., 2016). This highlights the CMHC's cosmopolitanism, which stems from long-standing relationship-building and maintenance. Before accepting the contract for services at the detention center, CMHC leadership considered the external policies and incentives needed to make services work and be sustainable. For example, the previous agency used a fee-for-service model, which may have been cost-efficient in the short-term. However, this payment modeling was not a good fit for providing services in detention. The detention setting is short-term and time-limited, with the service focus on safety assessment and brief intervention. In practice, many times detained youth may only require a mental health screening that could last 15–20 minutes, with risk assessments showing such youth to be at low risk for mental health problems in detention. In light of this service need, CMHC leadership advocated for a capitated payment model to provide the flexibility needed to meet the needs of these vulnerable youth.

CFIR DOMAIN: INNER SETTING

CMHC has a long history of retaining employees, which allows for greater knowledge retention and return on investment for any educational opportunities for its employees. However, Dr. Snyder's team was in a new setting and outside of their routine scope of practice. As subcontractors, the network and communication patterns had to mold to the operations of the detention center. The team also needed to uphold the detention center's primary mission of safety for the youth while adding therapeutic value to the milieu through its services. At times, the team found it challenging to balance ensuring safety and engaging in healing practices within the inner context.

The organizational culture at the CMHC valued EBPs and a trauma-informed approach. For the detention center, the culture was more diffuse, shifting toward the social welfare mandate and away from the punitive, correctional way of treating youngsters in the JJ system. Carryover of the "old way" from veteran employees came up against innovation attimes The Veteran employees had different life circumstances and were more risk averse with innovation because of loss aversion, which means that to learn something new, staff would have to give up some expertise that they previously owned. Regardless of the "clash of culture" with and within the detention center, there was a relatively high priority on an intervention to address trauma-related problems because youth presented with more problematic behaviors stemming from trauma responses.

CFIR DOMAIN: INTERVENTION CHARACTERISTICS

The intervention itself was seen as a need, and the intervention characteristics of TF-CBT itself may have been one of the inherently strong facilitators in the implementation process. TF-CBT has numerous trials to support its efficacy and effectiveness (Cohen et al., 2004; Cohen et al., 2012; de Arellano et al., 2014; Dorsey et al., 2017). The intervention was developed externally, but the CMHC provided much internal support and an organizational culture to support its implementation. The relative advantage to doing this was there had been no prior implementation of any EBP at the detention center, let alone one for trauma treatment. In summary, the treatment evidence was superior, its appropriateness was evident, and its need was paramount for the detention center.

After reading the outer context setting, you may have wondered, if detention is short-term, how could TF-CBT be appropriate, considering it is a 12- to 16-session protocol? Our team found that the average length of stay in detention was 20 days at the onset of the service contract, and it had ballooned to 30 days after some time, related to the difficulty of finding residential placements for youth needing that level of care. These youth needed care now and should not have to wait 60–90 days, languishing in detention with their uncomfortable symptomatology. To alleviate the initial worries of appropriateness, one of the developers of TF-CBT highlighted in consultation calls with newly trained clinicians that dropout is a common phenomenon in outpatient settings (de Haan et al., 2018) and the length of a treatment episode in detention would most likely mirror those rates given our length of stay data. Some dose of gradual exposure is better than no treatment! Lastly, TF-CBT was also very adaptable considering that it is modular and can have flexibility with fidelity. This speaks to the lack of complexity in delivering the intervention, and it is well understood that complexity is a CFIR construct.

CFIR DOMAIN: CHARACTERISTICS OF INDIVIDUALS INVOLVED

There was high buy-in for clinicians carrying out TF-CBT because of the knowledge and beliefs about the intervention. These favorable beliefs may have resulted from organizational culture for EBP delivery. Also in the training sequence for TF-CBT, preparatory work on the basics of child trauma, as well as the principles of its screening and assessment, was offered. A month or two after this workshop, a clinician could then take the intensive workshop with the master trainer to learn the intervention itself. Lastly, clinicians were required to attend monthly consultation calls with a master trainer in TF-CBT to solidify learning.

During the actual implementation of TF-CBT, having a defined treatment protocol helped clinicians feel confident in their abilities and knowledge of the EBP (Beidas & Kendall, 2010). For social workers or any other changemakers, it can be difficult to see the outcome of clinical work, so having a clinical feedback system through scheduled use of the Child PTSD Symptom Scale-5 (Foa et al., 2018) allowed the clinical team to know if the intervention was working. This feedback loop helped sustain implementation as even small doses of TF-CBT were helpful for youth (Snyder, 2018). Clinicians benefited from the aspects of training in TF-CBT, the workflow processes to support its use in clinical practice, and observing some positive effects of TF-CBT's delivery.

CFIR DOMAIN: IMPLEMENTATION PROCESS

After being awarded the contract for services, the clinical team did not immediately start implementing TF-CBT. Following the steps of EBP selection, Dr. Snyder and his team wanted to understand the population's culture and needs, Therefore, so the first year of services focused on providing trauma-*informed* services. The first years of the contract required rapid cycle prototyping, where the team defined a workflow, tested it for some time, made adjustments to the previous workflow, then tested the new workflow. Eventually, the team received consultation from academic partners to solidify a workflow that utilized evidence-based screening to determine level of need and then to match the youth to an EBP (see Rudd et al., 2020 for aspects of this process). Not every youth would be appropriate for TF-CBT, so the team needed to ensure our evidence-based psychosocial intervention coverage. Some youths may not have needed TF-CBT or our services at all and could stand to benefit from the supportive work of the frontline staff. This proved the most critical aspect of rolling out TF-CBT in the detention setting, creating a trauma-informed milieu.

Milieu refers to the social conditions of a place, and in a place that serves children, we consider the interactions of staff with youth as a therapeutic touchpoint. Dr. Snyder's team noticed that intervention in a therapy office could not be generalized to a punitive or non-trauma-informed environment. Organizational climate factors like burnout and frequent staff turnover can create a stressful milieu. Therefore, Dr. Snyder and his team developed training based on the principles of trauma theory and adolescent development to improve the milieu and to partner with frontline staff in our treatment of youth.

Much of the implementation strategies discussed focus on education and modeling (refer to social learning theory; Bandura & Walters, 1977) to affect factors related to organizational change, such as increasing optimism, changing beliefs about consequences of EBP use, and transforming social/professional roles and identity. These activities came in the form of training the clinicians in TF-CBT and frontline staff at the detention center. Another nested implementation strategy was tying the delivery of TF-CBT to the detention program's goals to help reinforce learning. Then, after establishing the connection of TF-CBT to the detention center goals, Dr. Snyder's team provides frontline staff pop-in consultations with on-site therapists to brainstorm ways to engage with problematic youth behavior on the floors. Partnering with frontline staff also helped promote adaptability, whereby they could have input with their language and culture to familiarize them with the concepts in TF-CBT. This links to the strategy of using localized knowledge. In order to make this training sustainable, trauma-informed care trainings were embedded in the new staff orientation process at the detention center. In summary, the implementation required a balancing act of training the subcontracted team in TF-CBT while doing organizational readiness and change activities to support its fit in the detention center context.

KEY THEMES ACROSS IMPLEMENTATION SCIENCE RESEARCH PROJECTS

Implementation science frameworks, like the CFIR and EPIS, have helped guide or frame an agenda that seeks to understand the contextual conditions necessary to achieve implementation and ensure clients receive the best available treatment. Remember that these frameworks are indeed only frameworks—they are not empirically validated. They should only be used as a tool to think about the potential factors that may influence your ability and capacity to engage in the EBP process fully. With each project, we illustrated how an implementation science framework could be used to guide your practice during Step 5 (Applying or Implementing) of the EBP process.

While findings across these four research projects need to be validated in other contexts with other EBPs, what we can discern herein, as also exemplified by the EPIS and CFIR, is that context matters—your ability to implement the EBP process is contingent on the inner and outer contexts you are embedded in. We can also conclude that more efforts must be devoted to preparing leaders and service providers to anticipate and address implementation barriers. These projects also underscore the value of preparing for implementation and eventual sustainment early on in the implementation process. The field of implementation science has identified by now that training clinicians in EBPs is not enough (Herschell et al., 2010); the implementation of EBPs is highly complex and multifaceted.

PRACTICAL TOOLS AND RESOURCES FOR AGENCY LEADERS/DIRECTORS

Considering the findings and lessons learned from the case studies highlighted in Chapters 7 and 8, you might ask yourself, as a director or administrator of a human services agency, what you may need to do to support your staff as they strive to promote implementation and ensure clients are provided ample opportunity to benefit from the EBP process.

- Rely on the EBP process and refer to process frameworks like EPIS or CFIR to guide you as you explore and select which EBP to implement in your organization.
- Recruit an implementation team to support you and offer their expertise and feedback. Stakeholders need to have buy-in! TripleP was selected due to need, its flexibility in delivery format, the evidence supporting the intervention, and adequate funding. However, some folks—namely supervisors and staff felt left out of the decision-making process.
- Assess whether your organization is prepared to engage in the implementation process. The CFIR observation tool (available at https://cfirguide.org/tools/tools-and-templates/) could be used to document areas in which your organization is thriving and limitations that need to be addressed.
- Administrators or leaders could use the Implementation Leadership Scale (ILS) (Aarons et al., 2014) to assess their subjective readiness to support staff during a new EBP rollout. They could also ask their staff to complete the ILS to gauge how they collectively feel about leaders' ability to engage in EBP implementation. Staff and leader versions of the ILS are available via the links at the bottom of this article: https://implementationscience.biomedcentral.com/articles/10.1186/1748-5908-9-45
- Select implementation strategies that are feasible and that leverage existing resources and relationships.
- Implement a quality assurance plan early, monitor implementation progress regularly, and adjust as needed.
- The Society for Implementation Research Collaboration (SIRC) maintains a database of online implementation resources at https://societyforimplementationresearchcollaboration.org/. One of our favorite sites for community stakeholders is UNC's National Implementation Research Network: https://nirn.fpg.unc.edu/ai-hub

FOR YOUR PRACTICE

ACTIVITY #1:

Rely on the EBP process to identify effective interventions for supporting reunification and appropriate for parents in the child welfare system who are addicted to methamphetamine. Identify 2–3 potential implementation barriers that could emerge and potential strategies to address them.

ACTIVITY #2:

Use the CFIR observation tool to assess whether your agency is prepared to implement an ESI or a novel intervention in your agency.

ACTIVITY #3:

If you are a supervisor, leader, or administrator contemplating or actively engaging in ESI implementation, ask your staff to complete the ILS. Report back to staff what is going well and what you are committed to do to address challenges.

ACTIVITY #4:

Identify at least two common implementation barriers and strategies to address them.

REFERENCES

Aarons, G. A., Ehrhart, M. G., & Farahnak, L. R. (2014). The implementation leadership scale (ILS): Development of a brief measure of unit level implementation leadership. *Implementation Science, 9,* 45–55. https://doi.org/10.1186/1748-5908-9-45

Aarons, G. A., Hurlburt, M., & Horwitz, S. M. (2011). Advancing a conceptual model of evidence-based practice implementation in public service sectors. *Administration and Policy in Mental Health, 38*(1), 4–23. https://doi.org/10.1007/s10488-010-0327-7

Abram, K. M., Zwecker, N. A., Welty, L. J., Hershfield, J. A., Dulcan, M. K., & Teplin, L. A. (2015). Comorbidity and continuity of psychiatric disorders in youth after detention: A prospective longitudinal study. *JAMA Psychiatry, 72*(1), 84–93. https://doi.org10.1001/jamapsychiatry.2014.1375

Bandura, A., & Walters, R. H. (1977). *Social learning theory* (Vol. 1). Prentice Hall.

Beidas, R. S., Adams, D. R., Kratz, H. E., Jackson, K., Berkowitz, S., Zinny, A., Cliggitt, L. P., DeWitt, K. L., Skriner, L., & Evans, A., Jr. (2016). Lessons learned while building a trauma-informed public behavioral health system in the City of Philadelphia. *Evaluation and Program Planning, 59,* 21–32. https://doi.org/10.1016/j.evalprogplan.2016.07.004

Beidas, R. S., & Kendall, P. C. (2010). Training therapists in evidence-based practice: A critical review of studies from a systems-contextual perspective. *Clinical Psychology: Science and Practice, 17*(1), 1–30. https://doi.org/10.1111/j.1468-2850.2009.01187.x

Cappella, E., Hamre, B. K., Kim, H. Y., Henry, D. B., Frazier, S. L., Atkins, M. S., & Schoenwald, S. K. (2012). Teacher consultation and coaching within mental health practice: Classroom and child effects in urban elementary schools. *Journal of Consulting and Clinical Psychology, 80*(4), 597–610. https://doi.org/10.1037/a0027725

Cohen, J. A., Mannarino, A. P., Kliethermes, M., & Murray, L. A. (2012). Trauma-focused CBT for youth with complex trauma. *Child Abuse & Neglect, 36*(6), 528–541.

Cohen, J. A., Deblinger, E., Mannarino, A. P., & Steer, R. A. (2004). A multisite, randomized controlled trial for children with sexual abuse-related PTSD symptoms. *Journal of the American Academy of Child & Adolescent Psychiatry, 43*(4), 393–402.

Damschroder, L. J., Aron, D. C., Keith, R. E., Kirch, S. R., Alexander, J. A., & Lowery, J. C. (2009). Fostering implementation of health services research findings into practice: A consolidated framework for advancing implementation science. *Implementation Science, 4*, 50. https://doi.org/10.1186/1748-5908-4-50

De Arellano, M. A., Lyman, D. R., Jobe-Shields, L., George, P., Dougherty, R. H., Daniels, A. S., Ghose, S. S., Huang, L., & Delphin-Rittmon, M. E. (2014). Trauma-focused cognitive-behavioral therapy for children and adolescents: Assessing the evidence. *Psychiatric Services, 65*(5), 591–602. https://doi.org/10.1176/appi.ps.201300255

De Haan, A. M., Boon, A. E., de Jong, J., & Vermeiren, R. (2018). A review of mental health treatment dropout by ethnic minority youth. *Transcultural Psychiatry, 55*(1), 3–30. https://doi-org.libproxy.temple.edu/10.1177/1363461517731702

Dorsey, S., McLaughlin, K. A., Kerns, S., Harrison, J. P., Lambert, H. K., Briggs, E. C., Revillion Cox, J., & Amaya-Jackson, L. (2017). Evidence base update for psychosocial treatments for children and adolescents exposed to traumatic events. *Journal of Clinical Child & Adolescent Psychology, 46*(3), 303–330. https://doi.org/10.1080/15374416.2016.1220309

Foa, E. B., Asnaani, A., Zang, Y., Capaldi, S., & Yeh, R. (2018). Psychometrics of the child PTSD symptom scale for DSM-5 for trauma-exposed children and adolescents. *Journal of Clinical Child & Adolescent Psychology, 47*(1), 38–46. https://doi-org.libproxy.temple.edu/10.1080/15374416.2017.1350962

Ford, J. D., & Hawke, J. (2012). Trauma affect regulation psychoeducation group and milieu intervention outcomes in juvenile detention facilities. *Journal of Aggression, Maltreatment and Trauma, 21*(4), 365–384. https://doi.org/10.1080/10926771.2012.673538

Garcia, A. R., DeNard, C., Morones, S., & Eldeeb, N. (2019). Mitigating barriers to implementing evidence-based interventions: Lessons learned from scholars and agency directors. *Children and Youth Services Review, 100*, 313–331.

Garcia, A. R., Myers, C., Morones, S., Ohene, S., & Kim, M. (2020). "It starts from the top" Caseworkers, leaders, and TripleP providers' perceptions of implementation processes and contexts. *Human Service Organizations: Management, Leadership, and Governance, 44*(3), 266–293. https://doi.org/10.1080/23303131.2020.1755759

Herschell, A. D., Kolko, D. J., Baumann, B. L., & Davis, A. C. (2010). The role of therapist training in the implementation of psychosocial treatments: A review and critique with recommendations. *Clinical Psychology Review, 30*(4), 448–466.

Modrowski, C. A., & Kerig, P. K. (2019). Investigating the association between posttraumatic risky behavior and offending in adolescents involved in the juvenile justice system. *Journal of Youth and Adolescence, 48*(10), 1952–1966. https://doi.org/10.1007/s10964-019-01120-0

Snyder, S. E. (2018). Implementation of trauma-focused cognitive–behavioral therapy in juvenile detention: A practice note from the field. *Practice Innovations, 3*(4), 284–294. https://doi-org.libproxy.temple.edu/10.1037/pri0000081

Mitton, C., Adair, C. E., McKenzie, E., Patten, S. B., & Perry, B. W. (2007). Knowledge transfer and exchange: Review and synthesis of the literature. *Milbank Quarterly, 85*(4), 729–768.

Moullin, J. C., Dickson, K. S., Stadnick, N. A., Rabin, B., & Aarons, G. A. (2019). Systematic review of the exploration, preparation, implementation, sustainment (EPIS) framework. *Implementation Science, 14*(1), 1. https://doi.org/10.1186/s13012-018-0842-6

Myers, C., Garcia, A. R., Beidas, R., & Yang, Z. (2020). Factors that predict child welfare caseworker referrals to an evidence-based parenting program. *Children and Youth Services Review, 109*, 104750.

Nutley, S. M., Walter, I., & Davies, H. T. (2007). *Using evidence: How research can inform public services.* Policy Press.

Palinkas, L. A., & Aarons, G. A. (2009). A view from the top: Executive and management challenges in a statewide implementation of an evidence-based practice to reduce child neglect. *International Journal of Child Health and Human Development, 2*(1), 47–55.

Palinkas, L. A., Garcia, A. R., Aarons, G. A., Finno-Velasquez, M., Holloway, I., Mackie, T., Leslie, L. K., & Chamberlain, P. (2016). Measuring use of research evidence: The structured interview for evidence use. *Research on Social Work Practice, 26*(5), 550–564.

Pellecchia, M., Mandell, D. S., Nuske, H. J., Azad, G., Benjamin Wolk, C., Maddox, B. B., Reisinger, E. M., Skriner, L. C., Adams, D. R., Stewart, R., Hadley, T., & Beidas, R. S. (2018). Community-academic partnerships in implementation research. *Journal of Community Psychology, 46*(7), 941–952. https://doi.org/10.1002/jcop.21981

Powell, B. J., Waltz, T. J., Chinman, M. J., Damschroder, L. J., Smith, J. L., Matthieu, M. M., Proctor, E. K., & Kirchner, J. E. (2015). A refined compilation of implementation strategies: Results from the Expert Recommendations for Implementing Change (ERIC) project. *Implementation Science, 10*(1), 21. https://doi:10.1186/s13012-015-0209-1

Ritchie, M. J., Dollar, K. M., Miller, C. J., Smith, J. L., Oliver, K. A., Kim, B., Connolly, S. L., Woodward, E., Ochoa-Olmos, T., Day, S., Lindsay, J. A., & Kirchner, J. E. (2020). *Using implementation facilitation to improve healthcare (Version 3).* Veterans Health Administration, Behavioral Health Quality Enhancement Research Initiative (QUERI). Available at https://www.queri.research.va.gov/tools/implementation/Facilitation-Manual.pdf.

Rudd, B., George, J., Cliggitt, L., Snyder, S., Whyte, M., & Beidas, R. S. (2020, September). Implementing mental health assessment in a juvenile detention behavioral health unit: Lessons learned from a community academic partnership [Conference presentation]. *Implementation Science, 15.* CAMPUS, 4 CRINAN ST, LONDON N1 9XW, ENGLAND: BMC.

Sanders, M. R. (2012). Development, evaluation, and multinational dissemination of the Triple P-Positive Parenting Program. *Annual Review of Clinical Psychology, 8*, 345–379.

Sanders, M. R., Kirby, J. N., Tellegen, C. L., & Day, J. J. (2014). The Triple P-Positive Parenting Program: A systematic review and meta-analysis of a multi-level system of parenting support. *Clinical Psychology Review, 34*(4), 337–357.

Stanley, B., & Brown, G. K. (2012). Safety planning intervention: A brief intervention to mitigate suicide risk. *Cognitive and Behavioral Practice, 19*(2), 256–264.

Stein, B. D., Jaycox, L. H., Kataoka, S. H., Wong, M., Tu, W., Elliott, M. N., & Fink, A. (2003). A mental health intervention for schoolchildren exposed to violence: A randomized controlled trial. *Journal of the American Medical Association, 290*(5), 603–611. https://doi:10.1001/jama.290.5.603

Underwood, L., & Washington, A. (2016). Mental illness and juvenile offenders. *International Journal of Environmental Research and Public Health, 13*(2), 228–242. https://doi.org/10.3390/ijerph13020228

Waltz, T. J., Powell, B. J., Fernández, M. E., Abadie, B., & Damschroder, L. J. (2019). Choosing implementation strategies to address contextual barriers: Diversity in recommendations and future directions. *Implementation Science, 14*(1), 42–57. https://doi.org/10.1186/s13012-019-0892-4

Weiss, M., Testa, S., Worley, J., Armstrong, J., Washington, A., Lawson, G., Capella, E., Hwang, S., Comeau, C., & Wolk, C. B. (2022, November). *Adaptation and implementation of the BRIDGE model in the Philadelphia School System*. Accepted for presentation at the annual meeting of the Association for Behavioral and Cognitive Therapies, New York, NY.

Wolk, A., K. T., & Proctor, E. K. (2022). Implementing evidence-based practices in nonspecialty mental health settings. *Families Systems and Health, 40*(2), 274–282. https://doi.org/10.1037/fsh0000506

Wolk, C. B., Stewart, R. E., Eiraldi, R., Cronholm, P., Salas, E., & Mandell, D. S. (2019). The implementation of a team training intervention for school mental health: Lessons learned. *Psychotherapy, 56*(1), 83–90. http://dx.doi.org/10.1037/pst0000179

CHAPTER 9

ADAPTATION

We have already discussed some of the problems practitioners have identified with implementation of ESIs. This chapter will center on some of the concerns involving the presumed rigidity associated with treatment manuals interfering with clinicians' judgment about how to meet individuals' needs, which may shift over time (Norcross et al., 2006). Most clients that social workers see do not face a single problem but rather multiple challenges. Manuals are typically devoted to one problem, leaving co-morbidity and co-occurring problems out of the equation. Further, practitioners often work with high caseloads of people across various disorders and lack time and resources to learn a specialized manual for each problem.

At the same time, there is a good reason for the use of manuals in RCT studies, as discussed in Chapter 4, so that fidelity to treatment can be tested. Many studies have shown that high-fidelity treatments perform better than their low-fidelity counterparts (e.g., Goense et al., 2016). To create more flexibility, there are certain options, including *common factors*, *common elements*, and *transdiagnostic* models. After exploring these, we will discuss making culturally relevant and sensitive adaptations to interventions.

COMMON FACTORS: RELATIONSHIP FACTORS

The school of common factors believes that all treatments can be equally effective; the critical agent of change is a good therapeutic relationship and working alliance. Wampold (2019) has defined the alliance as involving: (1) the bond between the therapist and the client and (2) the level of agreement about goals and tasks that are compatible with "the client's culture, attitudes, values, and characteristics." Wampold (2019) believes that a well-defined and -structured intervention is essential, but having satisfied that component, the working alliance is what matters. He notes that a particular type of practitioner will select a theoretical position that fits one's preference and competencies. Lambert (2013) shares the position about the necessity of the working alliance to assess the therapeutic relation with the client completing ratings at each session. The provider can use this feedback to recalibrate to the client's preferences and needs for the next session.

Some studies have examined the association between the alliance and how well clients fare at the end of treatment. Karver and colleagues (2006) found a moderate association in 49 child and adolescent treatment studies. In a more recent meta-analysis (N = 38), the relationship between the child and parent alliance with the provider and client improvement was much smaller (McLeod, 2011). Therefore, conflicting evidence exists in the meta-analyses regarding the role of alliance in youth treatment. Another variable might be the problem being treated. With depression, the working alliance between client and practitioner appears critical for adult clients to experience reductions in depression (Richardson et al., 2018). However, the working alliance does not seem as salient to achieve reductions in alcohol use for adults.

Cuijpers et al. (2012) examined "non-directive supportive therapy" as a common factor delivery of services. Nondirective supportive therapy was defined as basic counseling—reflection, empathy, encouragement, and helping people explore and express experiences and emotions. Cuijpers et al. (2012) found that common factors contributed almost 50% to outcomes, and 33% were client factors and circumstances. Lowest of the contributors was specific therapies (17%). These results seem to indicate the importance of common factors. The implication is that social workers should always attend to the relationship with clients and be skilled at fundamental helping processes, including setting goals.

COMMON ELEMENTS

Common factors and *common elements,* unfortunately sound very much the same, so it's easy to confuse them. While common factors involve therapeutic alliance and generic counseling skills, the common elements approach focuses on discrete treatment techniques. These are derived through distilling treatment manuals targeted at a similar problem into smaller numbers of practice elements or core features of that type of treatment. This can be done empirically (Hogue et al., 2019) or conceptually through content analysis of the manual with team-based coding and consensus across expert reviewers (Chorpita & Daleiden, 2009).

While manuals are complex, uniform, and disorder-specific, common elements are granular, flexible, and transdiagnostic (Hogue et al., 2019). Clinicians can more easily learn these components of treatment, and these common elements are more suited to individualizing approaches. Chorpita and colleagues (2009) coded and analyzed 615 treatments represented in 322 RCTs and found the critical components for various child disorders. See Table 9.1 for the techniques that tested favorably for particular problems. Another effort at a common elements approach through distillation and mapping was undertaken for school-based trauma treatments (Chorpita et al., 2005). The results indicated that the most effective common practice elements were (1) psychoeducation, (2) social skills training, (3) coping skills training, (4) relaxation and mind-body techniques, (5) group work, and (6) creative-expressive techniques. Chorpita and colleagues have developed a purveyor model for decision-making about modular choices,

TABLE 9.1 Common Elements of Family Therapy Techniques for Delinquency in Adolescence

Common Element	Description
Interactional change	Encourage family to interact so they can assess and direct in-session interactions to promote more effective ways of relating.
Relational frame	Transforming symptom-based or teen-focused view of problem into being fundamentally relational.
Adolescent engagement	Attempts to engage youth in therapeutic process.
Relational emphasis	Assessing systemic attributions and processes and promoting family functioning.

but free access is also granted for some materials (see https://www.practicewise.com/Community/MAP).

Another approach to identifying effective modules is to take on an empirical distillation. Hogue and colleagues (2019) examined high-fidelity sessions of manualized family therapy and distilled components conceptually, then through factor analysis for adolescent externalizing behaviors and substance use disorders. See Table 9.1 for the common factors they found, which they concluded essentially translated into structural family therapy.

Hogue and colleagues (2020) undertook a similar process for cognitive behavioral therapy (CBT) of adolescent substance use disorders and distilled six core practice elements of CBT. Table 9.2 delineates the specific CBT techniques they implemented.

For example, a social worker was employed in a setting that provided community monitoring to teens awaiting a court appearance after a criminal charge. The theoretical orientation of the program overall was CBT. Part of the program involved a group session weekly. However, because

TABLE 9.2 CBT Techniques for Adolescent Substance Use Disorders (Hogue et al., 2020)

Functional analysis of behavior problems	(a) identifying the typical scenarios in which substance misuse occurs and antecedents ("triggers"), analyzing positive and outcomes (i.e., decisional balancing, cost–benefit analysis).
Prosocial activity sampling	restructuring everyday environments "stimulus control" (a) avoid high-risk persons and situations; and (b) seek new outlets for social and recreational activities.
Cognitive monitoring and restructuring	monitoring cognitions and gaining awareness of how cognitions and core beliefs influence emotions and behaviors; learning to view events or behaviors in a new light, to use reason, and/or consider alternatives.
Emotion regulation training	Anger management and relaxation training
Problem-solving training	Identifying stressors, breaking them down into manageable problems, brainstorming solutions, analyzing and weighing the advantages and disadvantages, and selecting an option to use.
Communication training	active listening, suggest possible solutions, effective communication with role-playing

of the short-term nature of the monitoring, each teen was not able to go through a cycle of groups and rather attended only one session on average. Most empirically supported treatments for this population, although brief, involved 8–12 sessions. As a result, the social worker chose a modular approach to CBT and focused on one technique per session. That way, even if teens only attended once, they could benefit from that technique, and it was unnecessary to have built on the other techniques.

TRANSDIAGNOSTIC APPROACHES

Transdiagnostic approaches are designed to capitalize on the benefits of manualized treatments and their supporting evidence while affording greater flexibility to meet complex, individual needs, including comorbid diagnoses and other problems people may bring (Marchette & Weisz, 2017). The advantages are efficiency and cost-effectiveness and the ability to meet youths' complex and often changing needs. The *Unified Protocol for the Transdiagnostic Treatment of Emotional Disorders* (Barlow et al., 2010; McHugh et al., 2009) is a prime example, targeted for both anxiety and depression; often comorbid, these disorders share overlapping features and similar risk and protective factors. The intervention is assumed to treat the underlying common dysfunction. Variations also exist for children: *Unified Protocol for the Treatment of Emotional Disorders in Children* (Ehrenreich-May et al., 2017; Ehrenreich-May et al., 2018). These brief treatments (8–21 sessions) have the following key treatment components: enhancing emotional awareness and using mindfulness; cognitive reappraisal of distorted thoughts and attributions; and exposure to fears while understanding the harmful role of avoidance. Unfortunately, there is not a transdiagnostic approach designed for child externalizing problems, which constitute the foremost reason children are referred for treatment. However, the above-referenced manuals do mention "anger" as part of the range of problems that they address in addition to worry, depression, and stress. There is also not as much work on using transdiagnostic approaches with adult problems.

More recently, another transdiagnostic approach considers the balance of critical risk and protective factors in attaining healthy adjustment. A developing literature on youth exposed to trauma and subsequent risk and protective factors has been explored by McLaughlin and colleagues (e.g., McLaughlin et al., 2020; Weissman et al., 2020). We explored a risk and resilience framework as a possible assessment method in Chapter 2. Reducing common risk factors (e.g., low emotional awareness) and increasing protective factors (e.g., social support) involve a transdiagnostic approach that is not dependent on specific clinical disorders.

CULTURAL ADAPTATIONS

Now that we have discussed approaches to adaptation, we turn to a discussion of adapting manualized treatment to address the specific needs of your target population regarding cultural diversity. Cultural adaptation has been defined as the systematic modification of an evidence-based protocol to consider language, culture, and context in such a way that it is compatible with the individual's cultural patterns, meanings, and values (Bernal et al., 2009). Circumstances that justify adaptation include poor engagement in terms of recruitment and retention, if participants experience discrimination, and if there are unique cultural factors to the presenting problem (Barrera & Castro, 2006). Overall, studies examining culturally adapted treatment find that they compare favorably against non–culturally adapted interventions for racial/ethnic minority clients with mental health problems (Benish et al., 2011).

If these factors are present with a particular clientele, we start by searching the literature, which is always the go-to strategy for a provider who believes in the EBP process. What cultural adaptations have already been done, and are these effective? We suggest you start with the systematic reviews because, as you know from Chapter 5, they encapsulate a large body of studies at a time. In some studies, a moderator analysis is conducted to determine whether certain factors, such as race/ethnicity influences, play a role in the effects. For example, Wilson et al. (2003) found that ethnicity did not account for recidivism after adolescents involved with the juvenile justice system received treatment. The next step is to look up any recent RCTs and the qualitative research, which might help us with in-depth perceptions that we might not have heard unless we had much experience with the population.

Several conceptual frameworks have been designed to ensure adaptations are developed through a systematic process. The conceptual framework that is most used is the ecological validity model (Bernal et al., 1995) based on work with Latinx populations, and we illustrate it here the by applying it to a study. McCabe and Yeh (2009) compared the effectiveness of a culturally modified version of parent-child interaction therapy (PCIT) for Mexican American families to both standard PCIT and treatment as usual. See Tables 9.3 and 9.4.

We also show how McCabe et al. (2009) sought information and buy-in for the adaptation in Table 9.4.

CONCLUSION

This chapter's topic involved adapting existing treatments so they are relevant to your client's characteristics, as well as the real-world practice context, which includes you as the provider. There is recognition in the EBP process that interventions studied under university conditions with strict inclusion criteria for participation may not always apply to community settings; hence, the need for assessing any adaptations made by tracking progress and gathering data to understand the effects of adaptations. A theme of the chapter, as well, has been to consult the literature, as there is likely a wealth of information that can inform any changes you believe are needed to your intervention to fit the specific needs of the client and setting.

In exploring common factors, common elements, and transdiagnostic approaches, there are specific implications to take forward. One implication of common factors is that even

TABLE 9.3 Example of Bernal et al. (1995) applied to McCabe et al. (2009)

	Description	Applied to McCabe et al. (2009)
Language	Treatment is delivered in a language that is culturally appropriate and syntonic	Adapted the name of intervention to Spanish; Intervention offered in both Spanish and English; Child Behavior Check List offered in Spanish
Persons	Providers being attuned to characteristics of cultural group. Clients are comfortable with the characteristics of interventionist to include cultural match between client and provider	Therapists were either bilingual, bicultural, or extremely familiar with Mexican American traditions and values
Metaphors	Treatment uses of symbols and concepts that are shared by the cultural group	Framed program as educational and skill building instead of mental health therapy
Content	Treatments are consonant with the values, customs, traditions, and history of the cultural group	Added representation of Mexican American families to materials, such as written handouts; materials were simplified when needed
Concepts	Theoretical orientation and concepts of treatment are consonant with the cultural group	Cultural concepts were referenced throughout treatment so program was presented congruent with parent belief systems.
Goals	Treatment goals are framed within the cultural values and expectations of the cultural group	Goals were framed as building skills to assist with difficult child behavior, increase prosocial behaviors, and decrease negative behaviors
Methods	Treatment procedures are framed within the cultural values of the group	Increased time allowed in session for rapport and trust building
Context	The broader socioeconomic context	Intervention was chosen specifically due to efficacy as well as cost-effectiveness

when adaptation is necessary, social workers should always attend to the relationship with clients and be skilled at fundamental helping processes, including collaborative goal setting. A second implication, derived from common elements, is that, particularly in settings where intervention is short-term and one-off, such as schools, a modular approach to helping clients acquire a certain skill may be useful. Another implication, more specific to antisocial and externalizing youth, is that practitioners learn structural family therapy, as its essential elements cross-cut many multidimensional models that have shown effectiveness. Finally, adapting practice to apply a transdiagnostic approach is useful in considering how to reduce common risks and bolster protective factors that underlie many similar presenting issues that clients face.

TABLE 9.4 Justifying the Adaptation as Applied to PCIT

Concept	Description	Applied to McCabe et al. (2009)
Literature Search	EBP Process	Found literature to support a priori belief that PTIC intervention would be effective within Mexican American population
Assessment	Focus Groups, Interviews, Needs Assessments	Gathered information on MA families' preferences for their young children's treatment
Decision	Review interventions and decide what to adopt and/or adapt	Intervention was chosen for efficacy as well as parent preference, accessibility, and cost effectiveness
Adaptation	Pretest Methods	Families determined eligible by phone attended a 3- to 4-hr pretreatment assessment
Production	Draft of Adapted ESI	Drafting of adapted ESI was not mentioned in the chosen article.
Topical Experts	Experts offer input	Process of adapting PTIC included input from treatment developers. Not further described in article.
Integration	Integrate input from experts	Process of adapting PTIC included input from treatment developers. Not further described in article.
Training	Train those involved in testing	Interventionists were trained and received weekly supervision by primary researcher.
Testing	Conduct pilot testing	Pilot testing of materials was not discussed.

FOR YOUR PRACTICE

ACTIVITY #1: PROCESS FOR DETERMINING ADAPTATIONS

Directions: Find an RTC of a cultural adaptation for a particular population/problem. Using Bernal et al.'s framework, trace the adaptations that were made.

	Description	Applied to Study
Language	Treatment is delivered in a language that is culturally appropriate and syntonic	
Persons	Providers being attuned to characteristics of cultural group. Clients are comfortable with the characteristics of interventionist to include cultural match between client and provider	

	Description	Applied to Study
Metaphors	Treatment uses of symbols and concepts that are shared by the cultural group	
Content	Treatments are consonant with the values, customs, traditions, and history of the cultural group	
Concepts	Theoretical orientation and concepts of treatment are consonant with the cultural group	
Goals	Treatment goals are framed within the cultural values and expectations of the cultural group	
Methods	Treatment procedures are framed within the cultural values of the group	
Context	The broader socioeconomic context	
Concept	Description	Applied to Study
Literature Search	EBP Process	
Assessment	Focus Groups, Interviews, Needs Assessments	
Decision	Review interventions and decide what to adopt and/or adapt	
Adaptation	Pretest Methods	
Production	Draft of Adapted ESI	
Topical Experts	Experts offer input	
Integration	Integrate input from experts	
Training	Train those involved in testing	
Testing	Conduct pilot testing	

ACTIVITY #2:

Considering the common factors, common elements, and transdiagnostic approaches, which of thosese appeals to you, and how specifically would they be applicable at your field agency?

REFERENCES

Barlow, D. H., Ellard, K. K., & Fairholme, C. P. (2010). *Unified protocol for transdiagnostic treatment of emotional disorders: Workbook.* Oxford University Press.

Barrera, M., Jr., & Castro, F. G. (2006). A heuristic framework for the cultural adaptation of interventions. *Clinical Psychology: Science and Practice, 13*(4), 311–316.

Benish, S. G., Quintana, S., & Wampold, B. E. (2011). Culturally adapted psychotherapy and the legitimacy of myth: A direct-comparison meta-analysis. *Journal of Counseling Psychology, 58*(3), 279.

Bernal, G., Bonilla, J., & Bellido, C. (1995). Ecological validity and cultural sensitivity for outcome research: Issues for the cultural adaptation and development of psychosocial treatments with Hispanics. *Journal of Abnormal Child Psychology, 23*, 67–82.

Bernal, G., Jiménez-Chafey, M. I., & Domenech Rodríguez, M. M. (2009). Cultural adaptation of treatments: A resource for considering culture in evidence-based practice. *Professional Psychology: Research and Practice, 40*(4), 361.

Chorpita, B. F., & Daleiden, E. L. (2009). Mapping evidence-based treatments for children and adolescents: Application of the distillation and matching model to 615 treatments from 322 randomized trials. *Journal of Consulting and Clinical Psychology, 77*(3), 566–579. https://doi.org/10.1037/a0014565

Chorpita, B. F., Daleiden, E. L., & Weisz, J. R. (2005). Identifying and selecting the common elements of evidence based interventions: A distillation and matching model. *Mental Health Services Research, 7*(1), 5–20. https://doi.org/10.1007/s11020-005-1962-6

Cuijpers, P., Driessen, E., Hollon, S. D., van Oppen, P., Barth, J., & Andersson, G. (2012). The efficacy of non-directive supportive therapy for adult depression: A meta-analysis. *Clinical Psychology Review, 32*, 280–291. https://doi.org/10.1016/j.cpr.2012.01.003

Ehrenreich-May, J., Kennedy, S., Sherman, J., Bilek, E., & Barlow, D. (2017). *Unified protocol for transdiagnostic treatment of emotional disorders in children: Workbook.* Oxford University Press.

Ehrenreich-May, J., Kennedy, S. M., Sherman, J. A., Bilek, E. L., Buzzella, B. A., Bennett, S. M., & Barlow, D. H. (2018). *Unified protocols for transdiagnostic treatment of emotional disorders in children and adolescents: Therapist guide.* Oxford University Press.

Goense, P. B., Assink, M., Stams, G. J., Boendermaker, L., & Hoeve, M. (2016). Making "what works" work: A meta-analytic study of the effect of treatment integrity on outcomes of evidence-based interventions for juveniles with antisocial behavior. *Aggression and Violent Behavior, 31*, 106–115.

Hogue, A., Bobek, M., Dauber, S., Henderson, C. E., McLeod, B. D., & Southam-Gerow, M. A. (2019). Core elements of family therapy for adolescent behavior problems: Empirical distillation of three manualized treatments. *Journal of Clinical Child & Adolescent Psychology, 48*, 29–41. https://doi.org/10.1080/15374416.2018.1555762

Hogue, A., Bobek, M., MacLean, A., Miranda, R., Wolff, J. C., & Jensen-Doss, A. (2020). Core elements of CBT for adolescent conduct and substance use problems: Comorbidity, clinical techniques, and case examples. *Cognitive and Behavioral Practice, 27*(4), 426–441. https://doi.org/10.1016/j.cbpra.2019.12.002

Karver, M. S., Handelsman, J. B., Fields, S., & Bickman, L. (2006). Meta-analysis of therapeutic relationship variables in youth and family therapy: The evidence for different relationship variables in the child and adolescent treatment outcome literature. *Clinical Psychology Review, 26*(1), 50–65.

Lambert, M. J. (2013). The efficacy and effectiveness of psychotherapy. In M. J. Lambert (Ed.), *Bergin and Garfield's handbook of psychotherapy and behavior change* (6th ed., pp. 169–218). Wiley.

Marchette, L. K., & Weisz, J. R. (2017). Practitioner review: Empirical evolution of youth psychotherapy toward transdiagnostic approaches. *Journal of Child Psychology and Psychiatry, 58*(9), 970–984. https://doi.org/10.1111/jcpp.12747

McCabe, K., & Yeh, M. (2009). Parent–child interaction therapy for Mexican Americans: A randomized clinical trial. *Journal of Clinical Child & Adolescent Psychology, 38*(5), 753–759. https://doi.org/10.1080/15374410903103544

McHugh, R. K., Murray, H. W., & Barlow, D. H. (2009). Balancing fidelity and adaptation in the dissemination of empirically-supported treatments: The promise of transdiagnostic interventions. *Behaviour Research and Therapy, 47*(11), 946–953.

McLaughlin, K. A., Colich, N. L., Rodman, A. M., & Weissman, D. G. (2020). Mechanisms linking childhood trauma exposure and psychopathology: A transdiagnostic model of risk and resilience. *BMC Medicine, 18*(1), 96–96. https://doi.org/10.1186/s12916-020-01561-6

McLeod, B. (2011). Relation of the alliance with outcomes in youth psychotherapy: A meta- analysis. *Clinical Psychology Review, 31*(4), 603–616. https://doi.org/10.1016/j.cpr.2011.02.001

Norcross, J. C., Beutler, L. E., & Levant, R. F. (2006). *Evidence-based practices in mental health: Debate and dialogue on the fundamental questions.* American Psychological Association.

Richardson, D., Adamson, S., & Deering, D. (2018). Therapeutic alliance predicts mood but not alcohol outcome in a comorbid treatment setting. *Journal of Substance Abuse Treatment, 91,* 28–36. https://doi.org/10.1016/j.jsat.2018.04.007

Wampold, B. E. (2019). *The basics of psychotherapy: An introduction to theory and practice* (2nd ed.). American Psychological Association. https://doi.org/10.1037/0000117-000

Weissman, D. G., Nook, E. C., Dews, A. A., Miller, A. B., Lambert, H. K., Sasse, S. F., Somerville, L. H., & McLaughlin, K. A. (2020). Low emotional awareness as a transdiagnostic mechanism underlying psychopathology in adolescence. *Clinical Psychological Science, 8*(6), 971–988. https://doi.org/10.1177/2167702620923649

Wilson, J., Lipsey, M., & Soydan, H. (2003). Are mainstream programs for juvenile delinquency less effective with minority youth than majority youth? A meta-analysis of outcomes research. *Research on Social Work Practice, 13*(1), 3–26. https://doi.org/10.1177/1049731502238754

FURTHER RESOURCES

Butler, A. M., & Titus, C. (2015). Systematic review of engagement in culturally adapted parent training for disruptive behavior. *Journal of Early Intervention, 37*(4), 300–318. https://doi.org/10.1177/1053815115620210

Degnan, A., Baker, S., Edge, D., Nottidge, W., Noke, M., Press, C. J., Husain, N., Rathod, S., & Drake, R. J. (2018). The nature and efficacy of culturally-adapted psychosocial interventions for schizophrenia: A systematic review and meta-analysis. *Psychological Medicine, 48*(5), 714–727. https://doi.org/10.1017/S0033291717002264

van Mourik, K., Crone, M. R., de Wolff, M. S., & Reis, R. (2017). Parent training programs for ethnic minorities: A meta-analysis of adaptations and effect. *Prevention Science, 18*(1), 95–105. https://doi.org/10.1007/s11121-016-0733-5

BLACK/AFRICAN AMERICAN

van Mourik, K., Crone, M. R., de Wolff, M. S., & Reis, R. (2017). Parent training programs for ethnic minorities: A meta-analysis of adaptations and effect. *Prevention Science, 18*(1), 95–105. https://doi.org/10.1007/s11121-016-0733-5.

Gregory, V. L., Jr. (2016). Cognitive-behavioral therapy for depressive symptoms in persons of African descent: A meta-analysis. *Journal of Social Service Research, 42*(1), 113–129. https://doi.org/10.1080/01488376.2015.1084973

Gregory, V. L., Jr. (2019). Cognitive-behavioral therapy for anxious symptoms in persons of African descent: A meta-analysis. *Journal of Social Service Research, 45*(1), 87–101. https://doi.org/10.1080/01488376.2018.1479344

LATINX

Casas, J. B., Benuto, L. T., & González, F. (2020). Latinos, anxiety, and cognitive behavioral therapy: A systematic review. *International Journal of Psychology and Psychological Therapy, 20*(1), 91–104.

CHAPTER 10

EVALUATING CLIENT PROGRESS

Review and Critique of Methods to Evaluate Practice

David, an 8-year-old Latino male, was referred to the Crisis Treatment Center within the school-based therapeutic services at an elementary school. David was referred due to difficulty regulating emotions, conflict with peers, falling asleep in class, an over-focus on violence and guns, frequent sad moods, and poor grades. During the biopsychosocial assessment (refer to Chapter 2 for review), the social work intern learned that he was born and raised in Mexico and moved to an urban area in the Northeast several years ago following the sudden death of his father from acute alcohol poisoning. Before his father's death, he had witnessed him verbally and physically abuse his mother. After an evaluation, David received the diagnosis of adjustment disorder.

The PICO question the social work intern posed was: Among first-generation Latino students, does TF-CBT compared to school-based services as usual, improve social, emotional, and behavioral problems rooted in exposure to trauma? During the search and critical review process, the intern learned that TF-CBT would likely be effective, especially given that it has been shown to reduce trauma symptoms and subsequent externalizing behaviors among Latino males (refer to Allison & Ferreira, 2017). The treatment plan outlines the following three goals: (1) David will experience a decrease in negative feelings, thoughts, and behaviors related to violence and aggression; (2) David will stay focused in class and follow his teacher's instructions without distracting his peers (and thereby improve his grades); and (3) David will develop appropriate communication and social skills to improve positive peer relations.

In this chapter, we will illuminate the numerous ways you could monitor client progress and ensure that the issues of concern are being addressed. Many of our students in the past experienced challenges identifying the "best" method to monitor client progress. Given David's age and circumstances, we will review the pros and cons of several methods and describe how the social work intern from the case study above selected and justified one of those methods. To further your understanding, we will present other case studies delineating the process for developing a plan for monitoring client progress.

WHY MONITOR CLIENT PROGRESS?

You may recall from Chapter 2 that the assessment phase, while it has not garnered much attention in the EBP process, is a critical component. Much of Chapter 2 focused on tools or frameworks to rely on when first meeting with clients to identify issues of concern, strengths, and sources of resiliency. In this chapter, we cover questionnaires or measures you can use to assess and monitor client progress over time to see whether the intervention plan is addressing issues of concern. In addition to the term "evidence-based practice" (EBP), you will also hear about "evidence-based assessment," which means that standardized measurements are used for assessment. It is equally essential to ensure the measures you use to assess clients' progress are valid, reliable, and normed for the populations or clients you are working with.

What happens when your assessment unveils an issue of concern? What specific measures will you use to track whether David's symptoms of trauma are reduced over time? This chapter will offer information on a menu of different ways you could monitor client progress, exploring the strengths and weaknesses for each method, and the case in particular.

Besides knowing whether or not your intervention and case planning is achieving intended outcomes, monitoring client progress offers you and your client opportunities to reflect on progress. How empowering is it for clients to know they are making headway on achieving their goals, even if just a little progress has been made? If progress is not moving along as planned, what then could be the source? Keep in mind that it may not be necessary to revamp the intervention plan completely. Instead, the context or circumstances may need to be modified. Perhaps your client, for example, experienced other extenuating events that impacted their mood or ability to focus on intervention strategies. If progress is not achieved after a while, it may be indicative that you and your client need to discuss modifying intervention strategies. Besides the fundamental value of maintaining accountability and knowing whether your intervention plan is effective, tracking progress is often required by agencies and third-party payers. Despite these advantages of monitoring client progress and recent studies showing that clients value receiving feedback (e.g., Jensen-Doss et al., 2018), this last step of the EBP process is often overlooked. The time you devote to provide feedback on your clients' progress could greatly increase their satisfaction with treatment and their progress.

STANDARDIZED MEASURES

In your previous research courses, you may have encountered studies that rely on measures to evaluate whether a particular intervention or program is effective. They rely on and "score" these measures to derive or assign a "numerical value" to whether progress is being made. In other words, they are operationalizing concepts into numerical quantities (Corcoran & Secret, 2013). The reliance on standardized measures helps us achieve this goal. While many students are eager to develop their own measures, we remind them that newly developed measures have not been subjected to the scientific process. Standardized measures have gone through the arduous process of being normed or tested on a large number of people, and the results have been statistically analyzed to determine the reliability and validity of the measure. To that end, when you use a standardized measure, you will not have to establish reliability and validity or figure out how to score the instrument and interpret what they mean.

A common challenge is finding a brief standardized measure that can be used weekly without clients experiencing "survey fatigue." As well, brief measures can encompass a variety of topics, ranging from screeners to assess if further assessment is warranted, readiness for change measures, nondiagnostic measures (self-esteem, social support, parenting stress, conflict tactics, client attitudes, and personality traits), and outcome measures that assess effectiveness of services (Baer & Blais, 2010; Beidas et al., 2015; Meier, 2014). They usually can be completed in 15 minutes or less without interfering with the treatment process. Ideally, scoring is straightforward, and in many cases, clients can score them when self-administered. Examples of brief measures include the Global Assessment Functioning (GAF), Zung Self-Rating Anxiety Scale, Beck Depression Inventory, Zung Self-Rating Depression Inventory, Marital Happiness Scale, and Dyadic Adjustment Scale, to name a few (Levitt & Reid, 1981). As for the case study, a rapid assessment instrument (RAI) that might be appropriate for David's case is the Student Life Satisfaction Scale (SLSS). The SLSS scale is a general measure of subjective well-being (Casas, 2016; Casas & Rees, 2015). The scale consists of six items that measure overall life satisfaction. Children are asked to denote their level of agreement on an 11-point scale (0 "Not at all agree" to 10 "Totally agree"), with higher scores indicating more overall life satisfaction. Examples of items they respond to are: "My life is going well," "I have a good life," and "The things in my life are excellent." As for the case study, the SLSS would not take as long as the Strengths and Difficulties Questionnaire (SDQ) to administer, is easy to score, and could even be completed by David.

LOCATING STANDARDIZED MEASURES

Measurement instruments can be expensive given that some purveyors charge by the person for each survey administered. Thus, agencies may not have them readily accessible. However, there are several freely available standardized measures that have been identified and compiled for both adult (Beidas et al., 2015) and youth mental health disorders (Becker-Haimes et al., 2020). Aside from these, you can peruse other publications that have compiled various instruments. Fischer et al. (2020a, 2020b) are social work academics with two volumes of measures for individuals, children, couples, and families. For child and adolescent problems, the interested reader is urged to consult Youngstrom et al. (2020), who provide a comprehensive discussion of various self-report instruments, rating scales for teachers and parents, and behavioral observational measures. Early and Newsome (2005) discuss measures that emphasize strengths, and Johnson et al. (2008) specifically address family assessment in relation to child welfare.

The following websites also have information on standardized measures:

- http://www.yorku.ca/rokada/psyctest/
- http://www.psywww.com/resource/bytopic/testing.html
- http://www.caps.ucsf.edu/tools/surveys/
- http://www.muhlenberg.edu/depts/psychology/Measures.html
- https://www.psychiatry.org/psychiatrists/practice/dsm/educational-resources/assessment-measures

Finally, as highlighted in *Ratings of Psychometric Support for Frequently Used Scales to Monitor Client Progress* (see Appendix A) we provide a rating of "psychometric support" for numerous scales assessing the following issues of concern: disruptive behavior, ADHD, anxiety, depression, traumatic stress, disordered eating, suicidality, bipolar/mania, and substance use. For each scale, we listed the number of items, whom the measure is completed by, the ages that the scale has been normed for, and a link and citation to the measure.

CRITIQUING THE MEASURE

After identifying a list of potential measures to use, the next step is to determine whether indeed the measure is reliable, valid, and applicable. While our list of measures could be a valuable resource, you will still need to critique the utility of the scale for your clients. Suppose the scale fails to derive the same results with the same client within a short period (reliability) or does a poor job of actually measuring what it is purported to measure (validity). In that case, you will not be able to gauge your clients' progress with treatment accurately. While other textbooks have delved into lengthy discussions about the different types of reliability and validity, we offer a brief summation of key concepts in Tables 10.1 and 10.2.

TABLE 10.1 Types of Reliability

Type of Reliability	Description
Internal consistency	Extent to which items are intercorrelated.
Split-half reliability	Scale items are divided in half (randomly or odd/even) and both halves correlate together.
Test-retest reliability	Have participants take the instrument at two different times and see if scores stay consistent.
Interrater (interobserver) reliability	The extent to which different interviewers or observers using the same measure get equivalent results.
Parallel forms	Two forms of the same instrument (reorder items on the 2nd measure to reduce item response error) should be equivalent.

TABLE 10.2 Types of Validity

Types of Validity	Description	Example from Studies
Face validity	Scale appears to measure what it is designed to measure. On its "face," it looks valid.	
Content Validity	Concerns the extent to which a measure adequately represents all facets of a concept	Consider a series of questions that serve as indicators of depression (don't feel like eating, lost interest in things usually enjoyed, etc.). If there were other kinds of common behaviors that mark a person as depressed that were not included in the index, then the index would have low content validity since it did not adequately represent all facets of the concept
Criterion (gold standard)	Establish validity by showing a correlation between a measurement device and some other criterion or standard that we believe accurately measures the variable under consideration. Known-groups—Are the scores different from a group of participants without the presenting issues of concern(s)?	*Concurrent*—comparing the measure to a criterion (diagnosis, indicator) when both measures are taken at the same time. *Predictive*—an instrument is used to predict a future state of affairs such as using GPA to predict how well a student will do in college — Concurrent validity was supported by the correlation between the PTSD Symptom Scale-Self Report (PSS-SR) and similar measures of PTSD (Foa et al., 1993) Elliott et al. (1985) showed that the Self-Report Delinquency Scale has predictive validity with chronic offenders (Dunford & Elliott, 1984) and serious offenders (Elliott et al., 1985)
Construct	The extent to which the measure in question taps into the theoretical construct that it was designed to measure.	*Convergent*—Are scores correlated with other relevant variables or other measures that are theoretically linked to our construct *Divergent*—Are scores uncorrelated from other irrelevant variables or phenomena? The scale of interest is not related to another scale that is supposed to measure a completely different construct or phenomena that are theoretically different. — In the Davidson Trauma Scale (Davidson et al., 1997), good convergent validity was found as it correlated strongly with other trauma measures. In the Brown Attention-Deficit Disorder Scales for Children and Adolescents (BADDS; Brown et al., 2001), divergent validity is shown by lower correlations between BADDS and internalizing measures.

To summarize, *reliability* grapples with whether we get the same results under the same conditions and circumstances. In contrast, validity delves into whether the survey measures what we intend to measure. While many of the scales we cite in Appendix A, "Ratings of Psychometric Support for Frequently Used Scales to Monitor Client Progress," and other standardized measures, may be deemed reliable and valid, it is important also to consider "measurement invariance" when selecting a scale to monitor client progress. Measurement invariance refers to whether the assessment method works the same way or has the same meaning across diverse groups (gender, culture, race/ethnicity, sexual orientation, etc.; Stevanovic et al., 2017). In a recent systematic review of 26 scales that assessed measurement invariance, Stevanovic and colleagues (2017) concluded that most of them are not valid or applicable across cultures (e.g., Child Behavior Checklist, Eyeberg Child Behavior Inventory, Vanderbilt ADHD Teacher Rating Scale, Social Emotional Questionnaire). Many of the remaining studies demonstrated only a moderate level of evidence for measurement invariance (e.g., Youth Self-Report, Disruptive Behavior Rating Scale, Revised Child Anxiety and Depression Scale). To that end, we encourage you to be critical and assess whether the scale "works" for your clients. You will want to ideally administer a scale that has been normed for the client(s) you are working with. Has the measure been tested among populations that reflect your client(s)' identity (race/ethnicity, gender, age, immigration status, sexual orientation) and presenting issues of concern? If the measure is psychometrically robust but does not reflect your client's positionality or situation, it might still be advantageous to consider other measures or methods for measuring progress. If you do proceed to use the measure, keep in mind the limitations of lack of validity and applicability.

Other weaknesses may stand in the way of opting for a standardized measure. For example, the language used for some of these measures may be "too wordy" or hard to understand for those who experience literacy or language barrier challenges. Some scales are cumbersome to administer, given the length and time it takes to complete them. Some measures, for example, take up to 30 minutes to complete. As noted above, the scale may not have been normed for your client population; thus, cultural sensitivity or responsiveness may be questioned. Finally, they may be too expensive, given that some purveyors charge by the person for each survey administered. Thus, agencies may not have them readily accessible. Alternative measures, however, may address some of these weaknesses.

RELATING CONCEPTS TO THE CASE

To grapple with the challenges of engaging with the EPB process, our students are tasked with locating a standardized measure; critiquing it in terms of its reliability, validity, and applicability; and justifying the selection of the most appropriate method to monitor progress for one of the clients they are assigned to engage with at their field internship. As noted in the intern's appraisal below, the standardized measure, while psychometrically well demonstrated, does not apply to David's positionality. Here is the intern's critique of the Strengths and Difficulties Questionnaire as it applies to David, his 8-year-old client.

Based on David's clinical presentation, treatment plan, and the agency setting within a school, an applicable standardized measure would be the Strengths and Difficulties

Questionnaire (SDQ). The SDQ measures psychosocial problems and strengths in children ages 2–16 and is intended to be completed by a parent or teacher. The SDQ is a 25-item measure that produces a total difficulties score and 5 subscale scores (emotional symptoms, conduct problems, hyperactivity/inattention, peer relationship problems, prosocial behavior). The intern found a systematic review of the properties of the SDQ (Stone et al., 2010) from which he pulled the following information.

RELIABILITY

The systematic review reported that the SDQ exhibited good internal consistency for total difficulties for parent ($\alpha = 0.80$) and teacher ($\alpha = 0.82$) informants. However, for parent informants, the subscales revealed internal consistencies below 0.70. The review also found stable test-retest reliability for teacher informants in the subscales and overall score (mean correlation = 0.84). Yet, the retest reliability for parent informants in the subscales and overall score were less stable (mean correlation = 0.76). Correspondingly, the interrater reliability between parents and teachers shows only modest correlations ranging from 0.37–0.62. Parallel forms were not discussed in Stone et al.'s (2010) review.

VALIDITY

Based on clinical judgment, the SDQ has face validity in that it measures children's psychosocial functioning. Stone et al. (2010) report that the SDQ does have construct validity at the total scales level, as it appears to have high correlations with the well-supported Child Behavior Checklist. Additionally, Stone et al. (2010) used factor analysis to determine that the SDQ has factorial validity. The authors note that construct validity is less apparent at the subscale level. In terms of criterion validity, the review found that among the three studies that examined predictive validity, all three showed that the SDQ predicted help-seeking for children with psychosocial problems.
Similarly, it was found that the SDQ has known-group validity in that it correctly discerns children who are diagnosed with a disorder versus those who do not have a diagnosis. As noted above, however, we must consider measurement invariance. Stevanovic et al. (2017) concluded that measurement invariance for the SDQ self-report is conflicting, weak for the parent report version, and strong for the teacher version.

ANALYSIS

The review by Stone et al. (2010) was comprehensive as it included 48 studies, which yielded a total sample of N = 131,233. The quality of the SDQ appears to be good, particularly in measuring teacher-report total difficulties. Regarding feasibility, the SDQ can be administered at no cost since it is available on a website that also contains scoring information (http://www.sdqinfo.org/). Moreover, the questionnaire is only 25 questions and can easily be completed by David, a teacher, or his parent in a few minutes. Although gathering data from the SDQ would be informative, it has its limitations, including (1) it cannot monitor all of David's presenting issues of concern, and (2) as noted above, measurement invariance is called into question, depending on who completes the measure (Stevanovic et al., 2017). Thus, administering the SDQ is recommended so as long as additional measures are administered to monitor David's progress effectively.

ALTERNATIVE MEASURES

Relying on alternative measures is another option to consider if there are concerns about feasibility, ability, preference, or access to standardizes measures. Alternative measures may include individualized rating scales, behavioral observation, client logs, and unobtrusive measures.

INDIVIDUALIZED RATING SCALES

Clinicians may opt to monitor client progress by developing a scale with the client to measure progress with meeting goals. Self-anchored scales involve establishing a range (e.g., 1–5 or 1-10) that focuses on the intensity or the problem (degree of anxiety) as perceived by the client (Bloom et al., 2021). Rating scales are like self-anchored scales, albeit another individual scores it for the client. Referring to the case study above, one approach to monitoring client progress is to ask the teacher or school counselor to rate the intensity of David's sadness and conflict with peers every week.

BEHAVIORAL OBSERVATION AND CLIENT LOGS

Direct observation of overt or covert behaviors is another option to measure client progress. In these cases, a student or clinician may ask a teacher to track how many times a student engages in prosocial behaviors or completes a homework assignment on time within a given time frame, and to assess if these behaviors increase over time. Sometimes, you might recommend your clients track their actions or behaviors. Regardless, you will want to think about whether you want behaviors to increase or decrease and if you expect them to occur within a specified period. Orme and Combs-Orme (2012) provide different versions of observation forms, including forms that focus on documenting or logging (1) number of times a behavior occurred, (2) length of time a behavior occurred, and (3) behaviors, antecedents, and consequences. You may request your client to maintain a log of activities, and their thoughts, and reactions to them. Keep in mind that while these methods are generally reliable, they are often time-consuming and only capture behavior during a set period when observation occurs. In David's case, the teacher could document the number of times he bullies or fights with peers in a week, does homework, and feels happy instead of down and worthless. Table 10.3 offers examples of applying observation data to David's case.

TABLE 10.3 Measures of Observation

Level of Change	Definition	Measure	David
Frequency	Number of times	Count	Number of days in the week David completes his homework. David will decrease the number of days he bullies his peers.
Duration	Amount of time a behavior that is not discrete and lasts for varying amounts of time occurs.	Time	David may increase time on homework by 30 minutes.
Intensity	Degree to which an emotion is experienced (pervasiveness, strengths, amount it interferes with other experiences)	The Subjective Units of Disturbance or Distress Scale, first created by Wolpe (1990), is usually constructed as a 1–10 scale with 1 as "no distress" and 10 "severe distress."	The intensity of feeling down and worthless will decrease from an "8" (on a scale from 1–10) to a "7" within two weeks.

UNOBTRUSIVE MEASURES

In other cases, you may rely on unobtrusive measures to avoid the overuse of scales during each visit with a client. Data, for example, grades and attendance via schools, probation records, or medical records, would not require any interaction with clients and would offer insight into important dimensions of well-being. In Table 10.4, we have listed various settings where social workers are employed and the data that is often available.

For David, one of the concerns is his inability to stay focused in class, which likely impacts his grades. Thus, keeping tabs on his grades would be an additional data point to assess whether the treatment plan is effective. While providing information about his academic functioning, this method would fall short when it comes to monitoring his psychosocial functioning.

GOAL ATTAINMENT SCALING

After gaining more familiarity with the aforementioned methods, many students enrolled in applied or direct research practice courses raise critical questions:

1. What if I want to select more than one method?
2. If I use more than one method, how can I "combine" or consider all findings, especially when they conflict?

TABLE 10.4 Key Outcomes at Agency Settings

Settings	Common Outcomes
Child Welfare	• Length of time case is open • Reoccurrence of maltreatment • Safety/risk assessment • Length of foster care stay • Number of foster care placements
Criminal Justice	• Recidivism (arrests or convictions) • Domestic violence police calls
Schools	• Academic performance (grades) • Attendance • Discipline referrals
Mental Health	• Hospitalization • Volunteer work/Employment • Medication compliance • Diagnosis • Length of treatment
Health	• Hospitalization • Compliance with treatment • Diagnosis • Length of treatment

3. How can I ensure buy-in or acceptability among my clients?
4. How can I be sure this process is culturally responsive? With the support of clinicians, using the Goal Attainment Scale (GAS) provides clients an opportunity to be in the driver's seat as they set the parameters for defining, measuring, and monitoring their goals. The beauty of goal attainment scaling (Bloom et al., 2021) is that it aligns well with social work values—the process meets clients where they are. As clinicians, we work collaboratively to establish concrete, measurable goals. On that note, and in alignment with core social work values, the GAS serves as a tool that imbues cultural relevancy, as the core concepts are derived from how clients define their issues of concern and how they believe they could be addressed. The formal evaluation system involves these key processes: (1) identifying problems and establishing measurable goals and an intervention plan to address goals, (2) assigning weights to those problems, based on client preferences about which goals are more important, (3) estimating expected outcomes, based on where the client stands at baseline, and (4) readministering the same measures over time to examine whether those outcomes are achieved.

STEP 1: IDENTIFY THE PROBLEM AND ESTABLISH AN INTERVENTION PLAN TO ADDRESS GOALS

In the first step, clients identify the problems or issues of concern—they could be normative (problem behaviors, social dysfunction, work problems, legal issues), therapeutic (depressed mood, anxiety), or most likely both. During this phase, we encourage students to rely on the "Concerns, Goals, and Interventions" table (see Appendix B) to document the following:

1. Client concerns: These are the concerns reported by clients.
2. Collect baseline data. Recall that baseline scores refer to scores on assessments or scales gathered before implementing the intervention plan. These data are critical, as they will help you determine where the client is at—and provide you with a benchmark for what is realistic for your client to achieve during treatment.
3. Goals Defined: Not only are clients encouraged to articulate what they hope to achieve to overcome concerns, but they are also offered guidance on numerically operationalizing how much progress they hope to achieve within a given time frame. The baseline data can help you and your client gauge hoped-for outcomes within a specified amount of time. For example, a client may work toward praising their child or spouse at least once a day for 3 days each week for 2 months. State precisely what the client will be doing. How will you know when the goal will be reached? Additionally, specify how well or how often the behavior must occur. As you reflect on the process, assess whether goals and tasks are realistic. Consider client motivation and your abilities, time, and resources. At the same time, it is imperative to continually assess whether the goals are important for your clients to achieve and what or how much progress they would consider successes.
4. Verifying Source: Here, the client and clinician decide who is going to collect the data to monitor progress toward meeting goals.
5. Goal of the Intervention: Clients articulate what will be accomplished by engaging in treatment to achieve goals.
6. Intervention Methods: The precise techniques or strategies that will be implemented to achieve goals of the intervention are noted. While empirically supported interventions (ESIs) are often discussed, our students are tasked to educate clients about the therapeutic strategies used for each ESI and to document what those are.

Like all methods of monitoring client progress, goal attainment scaling comes replete with weaknesses, too, including: (1) clients may not be in a stable mindset to predict what "success" looks like; (2) someone may need to act as a proxy, if, for example, age, ability, or other circumstances prevent the client from engaging in the process; and (3) it may take a significant amount of time upfront to develop goals and the scoring procedures.

Despite these drawbacks, the social work intern selected the GAS to monitor David's progress. David's "Concerns, Goals, and Interventions" table (see Table 10.5) is included here. While completing his table, the social work intern gathered baseline scores. In the past week, David could not focus in class, completed his homework on time one day, did not practice verbalizing positive comments with peers, felt happy one day, and received a "difficult" score of 25 on the SDQ. Notice all baseline data applies to what happened within the past week. You will also want to be consistent with the timing across all the outcomes you are measuring. While time-consuming, completing the table will help you delineate the necessary steps to define specific, measurable goals and applicable intervention methods to support your clients' journey toward achieving them.

TABLE 10.5 David's Concerns, Goals, and Interventions Plan

Case Study—David's Concerns, Goals, and Interventions

Client Concerns	Goal Defined	Verifying Source	Goal of the Intervention	Intervention Methods
Per the teacher, David often loses focus in the classroom and becomes easily distracted	David will remain focused and attentive in the classroom for two hours each day.	Teacher will complete an individualized rating of how often David remains focused in class.	David will stay focused in class and follow his teacher's instructions without distracting his peers.	TF-CBT involves teaching relaxation techniques (focused breathing and progressive muscle relaxation).
David is performing below average in class due to lack of attentiveness.	David will complete his homework on time three days per week.	Teacher will provide weekly grade reports.	David will earn at least a "C" in all of his coursework by the end of the semester.	The school counselor will link David up with in-home tutoring two times per week.
Per the teacher, when in groups, David makes sarcastic comments intended to create humor. The comments lead to misunderstanding and physical aggression toward peers.	David will develop effective communication skills. He will practice verbalizing positive comments with peers three times during the week.	Teacher will complete the SDQ and an individualized rating of positive comments and interactions with peers each week.	David will develop appropriate communication and social skills to improve positive peer relations.	David will engage in affective expression and regulation as part of TF-CBT treatment.
Per the mother, David's mood fluctuates from being aggressive to feeling down and saddened by lack of friends. David reports feeling sad every day.	Goal A: David will report feeling happy three days per week. Goal B: Mother will report a 10% reduction in a "difficulties" score and a 10% increase in "strengths" each week.	A: David will complete the SLSS each week. B: Mother will complete the SDQ each week. The teacher will complete an individualized rating of David's mood each week.	Improve David's mood and ability to regulate emotions.	As part of TF-CBT, David will gradually recount the domestic violence he witnessed and receive support in modifying cognitive distortions. He will also learn to understand the connections between thoughts, feelings, and behaviors.

STEP 2: WEIGHT AND PRIORITIZE GOALS

Based on the baseline scores, you would then collaboratively gauge, with the client and/or proxy, the expected or hoped-for outcomes within a specified amount of time. During this process, each issue of concern is weighted. Simply put, they are assigned "numbers," based on what the client finds most pressing or imperative to focus on. For each item, a standard scale is introduced (-2, -1, 0, +1, +2), where 0 represents what would be expected if the goal was achieved.

STEP 3: ESTIMATING EXPECTED OUTCOMES

In Step 3, the client is asked to think about where they would be with goals if they achieved somewhat more than expected (+1), much more than expected (+2), expected level of outcome (0), somewhat less than expected (−1), and much less than expected (−2). In this regard, each goal is weighted equally. If a client finds some goals more important than others, you may assign individual weights to each item. While any numerical system could be implemented, we often suggest students think of having to sum up their score to 100 points. If you have three goals to work with, how would the client allocate those 100 points? For example, goal #1 could be assigned 50 points, whereas goals 2 and 3 could each be assigned 25 points. At this stage, the treatment plan and scoring procedures are solidified.

STEP 4: MONITORING CLIENT PROGRESS

The final step involves collecting data over time, using the same "verifying sources" (or methods to assess outcomes) to examine whether outcomes are achieved due to implementing the intervention methods and strategies. In the goal attainment scaling framework, you could incorporate several different ways for monitoring client progress for each goal—standardized instruments, rapid assessments, or any of the other alternative measures we discussed in this chapter. The data could be collected as often as needed, albeit we encourage students to consider how long treatment will last and survey fatigue. If treatment, for example, will last only 4 weeks, it might make sense to collect data weekly. If longer—say 3 months, every other week might be considered. If collecting records, think about how long it will take to access them. Make sure you collect data simultaneously for each outcome you measure (e.g., once a week, once a month, etc.).

In this final step, we find that some students are perplexed about scoring procedures after data are collected for each goal. The easiest way to explain the scoring process is to refer to David's case. Based on the expected outcomes we outlined in the "Goals Defined" column of his "Concerns, Goals, and Interventions" table, we delineated in the GAS scoring template below in Table 10.6 what it would look like if David met, exceeded, or did not meet his goals. Note herein that the "Goals Defined" description is also elucidated in the "Expected Level of Outcome" (score 0).

With the template developed, you would readminister the same "verifying sources" the following week and rely on the data to score the GAS accordingly. As highlighted in David's

TABLE 10.6 David's Goal Attainment Scaling Scoresheet

Level Of Attainment	Goal 1 Baseline: Not Focused at all Weight: 10	Goal 2 Baseline: 1 day Weight: 10	Goal 3 Baseline: No practice Weight: 10	Goal 4A Baseline: 1 day Weight: 40	Goal 4A Baseline: 25 Weight: 30	Total
Much less than expected −2	David will not remain focused and attentive in the classroom at all during the week.	David will not complete his homework during the week.	David will not practice verbalizing positive comments with peers during the week.	David will report feeling happy 0–1 days per week	Mother will report an increase in a SDQ "difficulties" score for the week.	
Somewhat less than expected −1	David will remain attentive in class 1 hour per day during the week.	David will complete his homework 2 days per week.	David will practice verbalizing positive comments with peers 1–2 times per week.	David will report feeling happy 2 days per week	Mother will report a 0%–9% decrease in a SDQ "difficulties" score per week.	
Expected level of outcome 0	David will remain attentive in class 2 hours per day during the week.	David will complete his homework on time 3 days per week.	David will practice verbalizing positive comments with peers 3 times per week.	David will report feeling happy 3 days per week	Mother will report a 10% decrease in a SDQ "difficulties" score per week.	
Somewhat more than expected +1	David will remain attentive in class 3 hours per day during the week.	David will complete his homework on time 4 days per week.	David will practice verbalizing positive comments with peers 4 times per week.	David will report feeling happy 4 days per week.	Mother will report a 11%–15% decrease in a SDQ "difficulties" score per week.	
Much more than expected +2	David will remain attentive in class 4 hours per day during the week.	David will complete his homework on time 5 days per week.	David will practice verbalizing positive comments with peers 5 times per week.	David will report feeling happy 5–7 days per week.	Mother will report a 16%–20% decrease in a SDQ "difficulties" score per week.	
Actual Level	0	−1	+1	0	−1	−1
Weighted Level	0*10 = 0	−1*10 = −10	1*10 = 10	0*40 = 0	−1*30 = −30	−30

GAS scoring sheet, a week later, he scored "as expected" for Goal 1 (score of 0), somewhat less than expected for Goal 2 (score of -1), somewhat more than expected for Goal 3 (score of +1), and as expected for Goal 4A and somewhat less than expected for Goal 4B. If we opt to treat each goal on equal footing, the total scores would be -1, which would bring his total GAS score across all goals to "-1, or somewhat less than expected." As weighted, Goals 1–3 account for 10 points each, based on teacher and mother preferences. Goal 4A accounts for 40 points (40 would be multiplied by the actual raw score of 0 = 0), and Goal 4B equates to 30 points; so 30*-1= -30., bringing his total score to -30 points below what is expected when the goals are weighted.

WHY DID THE SOCIAL WORK INTERN SELECT THE GAS?

Due to David's age, the social work intern completed the GAS in collaboration with David's mother and teacher. The verifying sources for progress will come from David's reports of global subjective well-being (via the SLSS scale), teacher reports (SDQ and individualized ratings of David's ability to stay focused, as well as his mood and interactions with peers while at school), mother-reports (SDQ), and a nonobtrusive measure (i.e., weekly grade reports). The GAS was selected for several reasons. First, the GAS allows the intern to integrate a mixed methods approach to tracking David's progress. Each method explained above may have pros and cons, but collectively, with input from all parties involved, they help paint a clear picture of David's psychosocial functioning and well-being. Second, it would be informative for David's mother and teacher, as they will actively monitor David's progress and receive updates on his scores. Third, because the GAS is tailored to David's specific case, its cultural relevance and applicability are greater than solely relying on the SDQ or grades. Fourth, although the SDQ measures psychosocial functioning, it does not holistically capture all his specific challenges (e.g., peer conflict, grades), as the GAS does.

Moreover, the GAS is practical as it would only require that the social work intern check in with David's mother and teacher for a few minutes each week. Finally, the GAS is amendable—it targets concerns that are specific to David and can be modified if need be. The intern plans to collect the data for the GAS from David's mother and teacher each week and will formulate David's score on the GAS and report findings to David, his mother, and his teacher.

CASE STUDY #2: MONITORING JACK'S PROGRESS

In this following example, we present a case study from one of our students, Clara. Clara was grappling with the best approach to monitoring client progress for her client, Jack, who is seeking help to address his cocaine addiction and symptoms of depression.

PART I: CLIENT INFORMATION AND DESIRED OUTCOMES

As a social work intern at the Treatment and Research Center (TRC) at the University Hospital, Clara meets with participants in studies on effective treatments for people with cocaine and alcohol dependence. The current study tests whether a medication called Chantix, along with cognitive behavioral therapy (CBT), affects cocaine cravings and use. All participants in the Chantix study have been evaluated during an intake, and it has been determined that they meet criteria for DSM-IV cocaine dependence (304.20). The study is 13 weeks and requires weekly CBT sessions (with social workers and interns) and triweekly appointments with the nursing staff, where there is a physical exam and medication dispensation.

Jack is an 18-year-old African American male who has lived in the city his whole life with his mother. Jack's father left his household when Jack was 4 years old and has had no contact with him since. Jack said he spends $100 to $200 on cocaine a week, and it is getting "out of control." He also describes feeling as though he "has lost a lot of good things in his life because of his drug use." He reports a sense of shame (in part because drug use is heavily frowned on in his family/background/culture), difficulty concentrating on tasks, and daily sadness, along with regret, and guilt. He completed the Beck Depression Inventory (BDI) and scored a "32." The following guidelines have been suggested to interpret the BDI: no or minimal depression = 0–9, mild depression = 10–18, moderate depression = 19–29, and severe depression = 30–63 (Beck et al., 1988). Thus, per these guidelines, Jack meets criteria for severe depression. Jack's goals for the entire 13 weeks are broken up into stages. The *desired outcomes/goals* for Jack for the *first 6 weeks* are:

1. decrease BDI score to 25 (moderate depression).
2. decrease cocaine use by 70% (approximately $45 per week would be the cocaine use goal), which would be a work in progress toward a goal of complete abstinence for the 13 weeks.

This data will be collected to determine the effects of CBT intervention with medication on his goals of decreasing BDI scores and cocaine use.

PART II: USING SCALES TO MEASURE CHANGE

Two scales are used to *measure the progress* of each of Jack's goals. Each of these scales will be used weekly, once during each CBT session. These scales are the Beck Depression Inventory (BDI) and the Functional Analysis (FA) worksheet (CBT). The BDI scale (21 items are measured) is used to track changes regarding symptoms of depression, and the FA measures 5 items including (1) situations in which there is a craving and/or use, (2) thoughts and feelings (3) actions/behaviors in response to cravings, and use, (4) negative consequences of use (e.g., felt guilty, increased conflict with relatives), and (5) positive consequences (e.g., less pain).

Studies demonstrate that the BDI scores has strong validity and reliability. A 2002 psychometric meta-analytic review of the BDI demonstrated that it has high test-retest reliability

(.93) and internal consistency (.90) (Aben et al., 2002). The review also found evidence of strong content and criterion-based validity in various settings and populations. A 2006 meta-analytic study found that the test's use of specific depressive symptoms within a consistent line of questioning has made it a reliable and valid measure of depression (Shafer, 2006). Studies point to the BDI examining the "appropriate criteria" for assessing depression and have verified the reliability by testing these measures with various populations over time (Storch et al., 2004, p. 187).

One of the core principles of the use of FA within substance dependence treatment is the acknowledgment of powerful negative and positive reinforcements that can enable or prohibit future behaviors from occurring. Studies on the reliability and validity of FA locate concerns with the aspect of self-reporting substance use (Devilly, 2002). In the case of self-reported data, several factors can jeopardize client data's validity and reliability, including; reporter (client) bias (especially if there are concerns of self-esteem and shame regarding substance use) and the client's psychological state when filling out the FA. Other reasons for nondisclosure could be tied to cultural norms surrounding "keeping certain information private" (Devilly, 2002, p. 3). For this reason, there are concerns about interobserver reliability and current criterion validity with this scale. On the other hand, the FA is an important, low-cost and efficient tool for obtaining data and, when used correctly, gives an accurate display of use, cravings, and reactions over time in the client's own words.

PART III: GAS AND ANALYSIS

The Goal Attainment Scale, or GAS, focuses on Jack's two goals, decrease his cocaine use by 70% and the BDI score by 30%. These goals are prioritized by their weight (70 for cocaine use and 30 for BDI score). Jake came to the TRC with the main goal of decreasing his cocaine use, so this is listed as Goal 1. Seventy percent reduction in cocaine use is appropriate given his long- term goal of 100% abstinence. Jake's participation in therapy and check-ins at the TRC support this goal. If cocaine use is reported honestly (urine samples would verify this information), GAS scores would be reliable. Given the consistency of testing over time planned for Jack and the tested reliability of the BDI, it is proposed that the GAS's reliability would be high for BDI. In light of Jack's goal of decreasing depressive symptoms, his BDI goal for 6 weeks is a 25 (moderate depression).

PART IV: GAS VERSUS OTHER MEASURES: A COMPARISON

Based on the analysis of BDI, Functional Analysis, and the GAS, it is recommended that the GAS be used to measure client outcomes. The GAS uses weighted scores based on the client's beliefs about the importance of the goals, which would better inform treatment and track progress. The nursing staff at TRC and/or the social work staff can collect the GAS. BDI administration and scoring are typically completed by social workers at TRC. Measurements of the GAS score would be in both dollar amount (relating to cocaine use weekly) and the BDI score and would lead to an accurate measurement of progress.

FOR YOUR PRACTICE

ACTIVITY #1:

Using the information from the chapter, come up with ways that you could track progress for your clients, using the different ways to assess change.

Level of Change	Client Example
Frequency	
Duration	
Intensity	

ACTIVITY #2: MULTIPLE-CHOICE QUESTIONS

1. Parents completed the Child Behavior Checklist and then at another point 6 weeks later. Results at each time point were correlated together. This describes:
   A. Internal validity.
   B. Internal consistency
   C. Convergent validity.
   D. Test-retest reliability
   E. None of the above.

2. You are provided with this information about the Reiss Screen for Maladaptive Behavior (Reiss, 1988). Internal consistency was .92 for the total score. The scale is highly correlated with the Aberrant Behavior Checklist and patterns of service use. What can you say about this scale? (pick best answer)
   A. It is reliable.
   B. It is valid.
   C. It is reliable and valid.
   D. It is neither reliable nor valid.

3. What is NOT necessarily a part of goal attainment scaling?
   A. It involved collaborating with clients to identify goals or hoped-for outcomes and to estimate how much progress to aim for within a specified amount of time.
   B. Goals are measurable, specific, and align with addressing issues of concern.
   C. They must involve administering and scoring a standardized measure.
   D. They can incorporate behavioral observation and client logs.

4. Which scenario IS NOT a way to use client logs as a method for monitoring client progress?
   A. Ask a teacher to track how many times a day a student bullies their peers.
   B. Ask a parent to log how many times the child conveys good manners at home (says thank you, you're welcome, please, etc).
   C. To request your client to maintain a log of times, events, and places when she feels sad.

    D.   To assess whether the client no longer meets DSM criteria for anxiety.
5. You are provided with the following information about the Beck Anxiety Inventory. Correlations of .58 were found when adolescents completed both the Beck Anxiety Inventory and the Revised Children's Manifest Anxiety Scale.
What type of psychometric testing is involved here?

    A.   Internal reliability
    B.   Inter-rater reliability
    C.   Convergent validity
    D.   Content validity

ACTIVITY #3: MONITORING LUCAS'S PROGRESS

Turn your attention to the case presented in Chapter 2. Recall 8-year-old Lucas had been placed in foster care for 18 months and was subsequently diagnosed with posttraumatic stress disorder (PTSD–309.81 (F43.10)). Lucas learned that his father had sexually abused his brother, and he had been separated from his family by child protective services due to safety concerns. Like the social work intern assigned to David, Lucas's social worker selected TF-CBT as part of his intervention plan and needs consultation about which method(s) to rely on to ensure TF-CBT is addressing his symptoms of PTSD. The social worker has limited time to monitor client progress during therapy sessions, albeit wants to use a measure that is reliable, valid, and assesses his symptoms of PTSD every other week during the 4 months he is in treatment. Consider a measure that requires a child and a collateral contact (e.g., teacher, caretaker, mentor) to complete it.

ACTIVITY #4:

Think about a prior or current case you have been assigned to, either as the lead social worker or while shadowing a seasoned social worker. Rely on that case to complete a "Concerns, Goals, and Interventions" table. See Appendix B for a template to work from.

ACTIVITY #5:

Select and critique a standardized measure that you could administer to address an issue of concern for your target population.

REFERENCES

Allison, A. C., & Ferreira, R. J. (2017). Implementing cognitive behavioral intervention for trauma in schools (CBITS) with Latino youth. *Child and Adolescent Social Work Journal, 34*(2), 181–189. https://doi.org/10.1007/s10560-016-0486-9

Aben, I., Verhey, F., Lousberg, R., Lodder, J., & Honig, A. (2002). Validity of the Beck Depression Inventory, Hospital Anxiety and Depression Scale, SCL-90, and Hamilton Depression Rating Scale as screening instruments for depression in stroke patients. *Psychosomatics, 43*(5), 386–393.

Baer, L., & Blais, M. A. (2010). *Handbook of clinical rating scales and assessment in psychiatry and mental health.* Humana Press.

Beidas, R. S., Stewart, R. E., Walsh, L., Lucas, S., Downey, M. M., Jackson, K., Fernandez, T., & Mandell, D. S. (2015). Free, brief, and validated: Standardized instruments for low-resource mental health settings. *Cognitive and Behavioral Practice, 22*(1), 5–19. https://doi.org/10.1016/j.cbpra.2014.02.002.

Beck, A. T., Steer, R. A., & Garbin, M. G. (1988). Psychometric properties of the Beck Depression Inventory: Twenty-five years of evaluation. *Clinical Psychology Review, 8*(1), 77–100.

Becker-Haimes, E. M., Tabachnick, A. R., Last, B. S., Stewart, R. E., Hasan-Granier, A., & Beidas, R. S. (2020). Evidence Base Update for Brief, Free, and Accessible Youth Mental Health Measures. *Journal of Clinical Child and Adolescent Psychology, 49*(1), 1–17. https://doi.org/10.1080/15374416.2019.1689824

Bloom, M., Fischer, J., & Orme, J. G. (2021). *Evaluating practice: Guidelines for the accountable professional* (6th ed.). Prentice-Hall.

Brown, R. T., Freeman, W. S., Perrin, J. M., Stein, M. T., Amler, R. W., Feldman, H. M., Pierce, K., & Wolraich, M. L. (2001). Prevalence and assessment of attention-Deficit/Hyperactivity disorder in primary care settings. *Pediatrics (Evanston), 107*(3), e43–e43. https://doi.org/10.1542/peds.107.3.e43

Casas, F. (2016). Children, adolescents and quality of life: The social sciences perspective over two decades. In Maggino, F. (ed.), *A life devoted to quality of life* (pp. 3–21). Springer. https://doi.org/10.1007/978-3-319-20568-7_1

Casas, F., & Rees, G. (2015). Measures of children's subjective well-being: Analysis of the potential for cross-national comparisons. *Child Indicators Research, 8*(1), 49–69.

Corcoran, J., & Secret, M. (2013). *Social work research skills workbook: A step-by-step guide to conducting agency-based research.* Oxford University Press.

Davidson, J. R., Book, S. W., Colket, L. A., Tupler, L. A., Roth, S., David, D., Hertzberg, M., Mellman, T., Beckham, J. C., Smith, R. D., & Davison, R. M. (1997). Assessment of a new self-rating scale for post-traumatic stress disorder. *Psychological Medicine, 27*(1), 153–160.

Devilly, G. J. (2002). Clinical intervention, supportive counseling and therapeutic methods: A clarification and direction for restorative treatment. *International Review of Victimology, 9*(1), 1–14.

Dunford, F., & Elliott, D. (1984). Identifying career offenders using self-reported data. *Journal of Research in Crime and Delinquency, 21*, 57–86.

Early, T. J., & Newsome, W. S. (2005). 15 Measures for assessment and accountability in practice with families from a strengths perspective. In J. Corcoran (Ed.), *Building strengths and skills: A collaborative approach to working with clients* (pp. 359–393). Oxford University Press.

Elliott, D., Huizinga, D., & Ageton, S. (1985). *Explaining delinquency and drug use.* Sage.

Fischer, J., Corcoran, K., & Springer, D. W. (2020a). *Measures for clinical practice and research: A sourcebook: Couples, families, and children, Vol. 1.* Oxford University Press.

Fischer, J., Corcoran, K., & Springer, D. W. (2020b). *Measures for clinical practice and research: A sourcebook: Adults, Vol. 2.* Oxford University Press.

Foa, E. B., Riggs, D. S., Dancu, C. V., Rothbaum, B. O. (1993). Reliability and validity of a brief instrument for assessing post-traumatic stress disorder. *Journal of Traumatic Stress, 6*, 459–473. https://doi.org/10.1002/jts.2490060405

Jensen-Doss, A., Becker Haimes, E. M., Smith, A. M., Lyon, A. R., Lewis, C. C., Stanick, C. F., & Hawley, K. M. (2018). Monitoring treatment progress and providing feedback is viewed favorably but rarely used in practice. *Administration and Policy in Mental Health and Mental Health Services Research, 45*(1), 48–61. https://doi.org/10.1007/s10488-016-0763-0

Johnson, M. A., Stone, S., Lou, C., Vu, C. M., Ling, J., Mizrahi, P., & Austin, M. J. (2008). Family assessment in child welfare services: Instrument comparisons. *Journal of Evidence-Based Social Work, 5*(1-2), 57–90.

Levitt, J., & Reid, W. (1981). Rapid-assessment instruments for practice. *Social Work Research and Abstracts, 17*, 13–19. https://doi.org/10.1093/swra/17.1.13

Meier, S. T. (2014). *Incorporating progress monitoring and outcome assessment into counseling and psychotherapy: A primer.* Oxford University Press.

Orme, J. G., & Combs-Orme, T. (2012). *Outcome-informed evidence-based practice.* Boston: Pearson.

Reiss, S. (1988). *Reiss screen for maladaptive behavior: Test manual.* IDS Publishing Corporation.

Sachser, C., Berliner, L., Holt, T., Jensen, T. K., Jungbluth, N., Risch, E., Rosner, R., & Goldbeck, L. (2017). International development and psychometric properties of the Child and Adolescent Trauma Screen (CATS). *Journal of Affective Disorders, 210*, 189–195.

Shafer, A. B. (2006). Meta-analysis of the factor structures of four depression questionnaires: Beck, CES-D, Hamilton, and Zung. *Journal of Clinical Psychology, 62*(1), 123–146.

Stevanovic, D., Jafari, P., Knez, R., Franic, T., Atilola, O., Davidovic, N., Bagheri, Z., & Lakic, A. (2017). Can we really use available scales for child and adolescent psychopathology across culture? A systematic review of cross-cultural measurement invariance data. *Transcultural Psychiatry, 54*(1), 125–152. https://doi.org/10.1177/1363461516689215

Stone, L. L., Otten, R., Engels, R. C., Vermulst, A. A., & Janssens, J. M. (2010). Psychometric properties of the parent and teacher versions of the strengths and difficulties questionnaire for 4- to 12-year-olds: A review. *Clinical Child and Family Psychology Review, 13*(3), 254–274.

Storch, E. A., Roberti, J. W., & Roth, D. A. (2004). Factor structure, concurrent validity, and internal consistency of the Beck Depression Inventory—Second Edition in a sample of college students. *Depression and Anxiety, 19*(3), 187–189.

Wolpe, J. (1990). *The practice of behavior therapy* (4th ed.). Pergamon Press.

Youngstrom, E. A., Prinstein, M. J., Mash, E. J., & Barkley, R. A. (Eds.). (2020). *Assessment of Disorders in Childhood and Adolescence.* Guilford Publications.

APPENDIX A

RATINGS OF PSYCHOMETRIC SUPPORT FOR FREQUENTLY USED SCALES TO MONITOR CLIENT PROGRESS

Measures of Disruptive Behavior (n = 10)

Psychometric Support	Measure Name	# of Items	Completed by:[a]	Ages[c]	Link to Measure	Citation
Excellent	IOWA Conners (Loney & Milich, 1982)	10	P, T	School aged	https://osf.io/wa5hb/	Milich, R., Loney, J., & Landau, S. (1982). Independent dimensions of hyperactivity and aggression: A validation with playroom observation data. Journal of Abnormal Psychology, 91(3), 183–198. https://doi.org/10.1037/0021-843X.91.3.183
Excellent	Swanson, Nolan, and Pelham Rating Scale (SNAP-IV; Swanson et al., 2001)	18 or 26 versions	P, T	5-17	http://www.shared-care.ca/toolkits-adhd	Swanson, J. M., Kraemer, H. C., Hinshaw, S. P., Arnold, L. E., Conners, C. K., Abikoff, H. B., . . . Hechtman, L. (2001). Clinical relevance of the primary findings of the MTA: success rates based on severity of ADHD and ODD symptoms at the end of treatment. Journal of the American Academy of Child and Adolescent Psychiatry, 40(2), 168–179.
Good	Inventory Callous and Unemotional Traits (ICU; Essau et al., 2006)*	12 or 24	Y, P, T	3-18	http://labs.uno.edu/developmental-psychopathology/ICU.html	Essau, C. A., Sasagawa, S., & Frick, P. J. (2006). Callous-unemotional traits in a community sample of adolescents. Assessment, 13(4), 454-469.
Good	Behavior Problems Inventory-Short Form (BPI-S; Rojahn et al., 2012a and Rojahn et al., 2012b)*	30	P	2+	http://bpi.haoliang.me/pdf/BPI-S/BPI-S%20English.pdf	Rojahn, J., Rowe, E. W., Sharber, A. C., Hastings, R., Matson, J. L., Didden, R., . . . Dumont, E. L. M. (2012). The Behavior Problems Inventory-Short Form for individuals with intellectual disabilities: Part I: Development and provisional clinical reference data. Journal of Intellectual Disability Research, 56(5), 527–545. Rojahn, J., Rowe, E. W., Sharber, A. C., Hastings, R., Matson, J. L., Didden, R., . . . Dumont, E. L. M. (2012). The Behavior Problems Inventory-Short Form for individuals with intellectual disabilities: Part II: Reliability and validity. Journal of Intellectual Disability Research, 56(5), 546–565.

Good	Disruptive Behavior Disorders Rating Scale (DBDRS; Pelham et al., 1992)*	45	P, T	3–13	https://ccf.fiu.edu/about/resources/index.html	Pelham, W. E., Jr, Gnagy, E. M., Greenslade, K. E., & Milich, R. (1992). Teacher ratings of DSM-III-R symptoms for the disruptive behavior disorders. Journal of the American Academy of Child and Adolescent Psychiatry, 31(2), 210–218.
Good	Children's Scale of Hostility and Aggression: Reactive/Proactive (C-SHARP; Farmer & Aman, 2010)*	48	P	3–21	https://psychmed.osu.edu/index.php/instrument-resources/c-sharp/	Farmer, C. A., & Aman, M. G. (2010). Psychometric properties of the children's scale of hostility and aggression: Reactive/proactive (C-SHARP). Research in Developmental Disabilities, 31(1), 270–280.
Adequate	Conduct Disorder Rating Scale (CDRS; Waschbusch & Elgar, 2007 and Fabiano et al., 2006)	12 or 15	P, T	5–12	http://www.midss.org/content/conduct-disorder-rating-scale-teachers-cdrs-t http://www.midss.org/content/conduct-disorder-rating-scale-parents-cdrs-p	Waschbusch, D. A., & Elgar, F. J. (2007). Development and validation of the conduct disorder rating scale. Assessment, 14(1), 65–74. Fabiano, G. A., Pelham, W. E., Jr., Waschbusch, D. A., Gnagy, E. M., Lahey, B. B., Chronis, A. M., ... Burrows-MacLean, L. (2006). A practical measure of impairment: Psychometric properties of the impairment rating scale in samples of children with attention deficit hyperactivity disorder and two school-based samples. Journal of Clinical Child & Adolescent Psychology, 35(3), 369–385.
Adequate	Modified Overt Aggression Scale (MOAS; Sorgi et al., 1991)	16	P, T	Children and adolescents[d]	https://www.thereachinstitute.org/trainees/ppp-trainees/rating-scales-1	Sorgi, P., Ratey, J. J., Knoedler, D. W., Markert, R. J., & Reichman, M. (1991). Rating aggression in the clinical setting: A retrospective adaptation of the Overt Aggression Scale: Preliminary results. Journal of Neuropsychiatry and Clinical Neurosciences, 3(2), S52–S56. .
Adequate	Outburst Monitoring Scale (OMS; Kronenberger et al., 2007)	20	P	12–17	http://www.cpack.org/screening-tools-for-kids/	Kronenberger, W. G., Giauque, A. L., & Dunn, D. W. (2007). Development and validation of the outburst monitoring scale for children And adolescents. Journal of Child and Adolescent Psychopharmacology, 17(4), 511–526.

Measures of Disruptive Behavior (*n* = 10)

Adequate	Delinquent Activities Scale (DAS; Reavy et al., 2012)	37	Y	Adolescents[d]	http://www.midss.org/sites/default/files/mbq.doc	Reavy, R., Stein, L. A., Paiva, A., Quina, K., & Rossi, J. S. (2012). Validation of the delinquent activities scale for incarcerated adolescents. Addictive Behaviors, 37(7), 875-879.

[a] Completed by: Y = Youth, P = Parent/Caregiver, C = Clinician, T = Teacher.
[b] Intended Clinical Use: S = Screening, D = Diagnostic Aid or Treatment Planning, O = Outcome Monitoring
[c] Exact age range for specific forms (e.g., self-report, parent report) may vary.
[d] Exact age range not specified.
* Available in multiple languages.
Note. Table adapted from Becker-Haimes, E. M., Tabachnick, A. R., Last, B. S., Stewart, R. E., Hasan-Granier, A., & Beidas, R. S. (2020). Evidence base update for brief, free, and accessible youth mental health measures. *Journal of Clinical Child & Adolescent Psychology, 49*(1), 1-17.

Measures of ADHD (*n* = 4)

Psychometric Support	Measure Name	# of Items	Completed by:[a]	Ages[c]	Link to Measure	Citation
Excellent	Strengths and Weaknesses of ADHD Symptoms and Normal-behavior scale (SWAN; Swanson et al., 2012)	18	P,T	Children and adolescents[d]	https://www.phenxtoolkit.org/protocols/view/121502	Swanson, J. M., Schuck, S., Porter, M. M., Carlson, C., Hartman, C. A., Sergeant, J. A., ... Wigal, T. (2012). Categorical and dimensional definitions and evaluations of symptoms of ADHD: History of the SNAP and the SWAN Rating Scales. *International Journal of Educational and Psychological Assessment, 10*(1), 51-70.
Excellent	Swanson, Nolan, and Pelham Rating Scale (SNAP-IV; Swanson et al., 2001)	18 or 26 versions	P,T	5-17	http://www.shared-care.ca/toolkits-adhd	Swanson, J. M., Kraemer, H. C., Hinshaw, S. P., Arnold, L. E., Conners, C. K., Abikoff, H. B., ...Hechtman, L. (2001). Clinical relevance of the primary findings of the MTA: success rates based on severity of ADHD and ODD symptoms at the end of treatment. *Journal of the American Academy of Child and Adolescent Psychiatry, 40*(2), 168-179.

| Excellent | Vanderbilt ADHD Diagnostic Teacher Rating Scale (VADTRS; Wolraich et al., 2003) | 43 | T | 4–12 | https://www.nichq.org/resource/nichq-vanderbilt-assessment-scales | Wolraich, M. L., Lambert, W., Doffing, M. A., Bickman, L., Simmons, T., & Worley, K. (2003). Psychometric properties of the Vanderbilt ADHD diagnostic parent rating scale in a referred population. Journal of Pediatric Psychology, 28(8), 559–568. |
| Good | Children's Scale of Hostility and Aggression: Reactive/Proactive (C-SHARP; Farmer & Aman, 2010)* | 48 | P | 3–21 | https://psychmed.osu.edu/index.php/instrument-resources/c-sharp/ | Farmer, C. A., & Aman, M. G. (2010). Psychometric properties of the children's scale of hostility and aggression: Reactive/proactive (C-SHARP). Research in Developmental Disabilities, 31(1), 270–280. |

[a] Completed by: Y = Youth, P = Parent/Caregiver, C = Clinician, T = Teacher.
[b] Intended Clinical Use: S = Screening, D = Diagnostic Aid or Treatment Planning, O = Outcome Monitoring
[c] Exact age range for specific forms (e.g., self-report, parent report) may vary
[d] Exact age range not specified.
* Available in multiple languages
Note. Table adapted from Becker-Haimes, E. M., Tabachnick, A. R., Last, B. S., Stewart, R. E., Hasan-Granier, A., & Beidas, R. S. (2020). Evidence base update for brief, free, and accessible youth mental health measures. Journal of Clinical Child & Adolescent Psychology, 49(1), 1–17.

Measures of Anxiety (n = 11)

Psychometric Support	Measure Name	# of Items	Completed by:[a]	Ages[c]	Link to Measure	Citation
Excellent	Spence Children's Anxiety Scale (SCAS; Spence, 1998)*	38	Y, P	7–19	https://www.scaswebsite.com/	Spence, S. H. (1998). A measure of anxiety symptoms among children. Behaviour Research and Therapy, 36(5), 545–566.

Measures of Anxiety (n = 11)

Rating	Measure	Items	Age	Reporter	URL	Reference
Excellent	Screen for Child Anxiety-41 Related Emotional Disorders (SCARED; Birmaher et al., 1999)*	41	7–17	Y, P	https://www.pediatricbipolar.pitt.edu/resources/instruments	Birmaher, B., Brent, D. A., Chiappetta, L., Bridge, J., Monga, S., & Baugher, M. (1999). Psychometric properties of the Screen for Child Anxiety Related Emotional Disorders (SCARED): a replication study. Journal of the American Academy of Child and Adolescent Psychiatry, 38(10), 1230–1236.
Excellent	Revised Child Anxiety and Depression Scale (RCADS/RCADS-P; Chorpita et al., 2005)*	47/25	Grade 3–12 [d]	Y, P	https://www.childfirst.ucla.edu/resources/	Chorpita, B. F., Moffitt, C. E., & Gray, J. (2005). Psychometric properties of the Revised Child Anxiety and Depression Scale in a clinical sample. Behaviour Research and Therapy, 43(3), 309–322.
Good	Short OCD Screener (SOCS; Uher et al., 2007)	7	9–19	Y	https://primarycare.ementalhealth.ca/index.php?m=survey&ID=14	Uher, R., Heyman, I., Mortimore, C., Frampton, I., & Goodman, R. (2007). Screening young people for obsessive-compulsive disorder. British Journal of Psychiatry, 191(4), 353–354.
Good	Penn State Worry Questionnaire-Child version (PSWQ-C; Chorpita et al., 1997)*	14	7–17	Y	https://www.childfirst.ucla.edu/resources/	Chorpita, B. F., Tracey, S. A., Brown, T. A., Collica, T. J., & Barlow, D. H. (1997). Assessment of worry in children and adolescents: An adaptation of the Penn State Worry Questionnaire. Behaviour Research and Therapy, 35(6), 569–581.

Quality	Measure	Items	Respondent	Age	URL	Reference
Good	School Anxiety Scale-Teacher Report (SAS-TR; Lyneham et al., 2008)*	16	T	5–12	https://www.mq.edu.au/research/research-centres-groups-and-facilities/healthy-people/centres/centre-for-emotional-health-ceh/resources	Lyneham, H. J., Street, A. K., Abbott, M. J., & Rapee, R. M. (2008). Psychometric properties of the school anxiety scale—Teacher report (SAS-TR). Journal of Anxiety Disorders, 22(2), 292–300.
Good	Child Anxiety Life Interference Scale-Parent/Child, form and preschool Version (CALIS/CALIS-PV; Lyneham et al., 2013)*	19, 10, 18	Y, P	3–17	https://www.mq.edu.au/research/research-centres-groups-and-facilities/healthy-people/centres/centre-for-emotional-health-ceh/resources	Lyneham, H. J., Sburlati, E. S., Abbott, M. J., Rapee, R. M., Hudson, J. L., Tolin, D. F., & Carlson, S. E. (2013). Psychometric properties of the child anxiety life interference scale (CALIS). Journal of Anxiety Disorders, 27(7), 711–719.
Good	Preschool Anxiety Scale-28 Revised (PAS; Edwards et al., 2010)*	28	P	3–5	https://www.mq.edu.au/research/research-centres-groups-and-facilities/healthy-people/centres/centre-for-emotional-health-ceh/resources	Edwards, S. L., Rapee, R. M., Kennedy, S. J., & Spence, S. H. (2010). The assessment of anxiety symptoms in preschool-aged children: the revised Preschool Anxiety Scale. Journal of Clinical Child & Adolescent Psychology, 39(3), 400–409.
Adequate	Social Worries Questionnaire (SWQ; Spence, 1995)	10	Y, P, T	8–17	http://www.scaswebsite.com/index.php?p=1_57	Spence, S. H. (1995). The social worries questionnaire. Social skills training: Enhancing social competence with children and adolescents. Windsor: NFER-Nelson.

Measures of Anxiety (n = 11)

Adequate	Hamilton Anxiety Rating Scale-A (Hamilton, 1959)*	14	C	Adolescents [d]	https://dcf.psychiatry.ufl.edu/files/2011/05/HAMILTON-ANXIETY.pdf	Hamilton, M. A. X. (1959). The assessment of anxiety states by rating. *British Journal of Medical Psychology*, 32(1), 50–55.
Adequate	Patient-Reported Outcomes Measurement Information System (PROMIS Anxiety; DeWalt et al., 2015)*	15	Y, P	8 to 17	http://www.healthmeasures.net/administrator/components/com_instruments/uploads/15-09-01_02-00-50_Neuro-QOLv1.0-PediatricAnxietySF_03-14-2014.pdf	DeWalt, D. A., Gross, H. E., Gipson, D. S., Selewski, D. T., DeWitt, E. M., Dampier, C. D., ... Varni, J. W. (2015). PROMIS(®) pediatric self-report scales distinguish subgroups of children within and across six common pediatric chronic health conditions. *Quality of Life Research*, 24(9), 2195–2208. https://doi.org/10.1007/s11136-015-0953-3

[a] Completed by: Y = Youth; P = Parent/Caregiver, C = Clinician, T = Teacher.
[b] Intended Clinical Use: S = Screening, D = Diagnostic Aid or Treatment Planning, O = Outcome Monitoring
[c] Exact age range for specific forms (e.g., self-report, parent report) may vary
[d] Exact age range not specified.
* Available in multiple languages

Note. Table adapted from Becker-Haimes, E. M., Tabachnick, A. R., Last, B. S., Stewart, R. E., Hasan-Granier, A., & Beidas, R. S. (2020). Evidence base update for brief, free, and accessible youth mental health measures. *Journal of Clinical Child & Adolescent Psychology*, 49(1), 1–17.

Measures of Depression (n = 13)

Psychometric Support	Measure Name	# of Items	Completed by:[a]	Ages[c]	Link to Measure	Citation
Excellent	Mood and Feelings Questionnaire (MFQ; Angold et al., 1995)*	13 or 33	Y, P	6–17	https://devepi.duhs.duke.edu/measures/the-mood-and-feelings-questionnaire-mfq/	Messer, S. C., Angold, A., Costello, E. J., Loeber, R., Van Kammen, W., & Stouthamer-Loeber, M. (1995). Development of a short questionnaire for use in epidemiological studies of depression in children and adolescents: Factor composition and structure across development. International Journal of Methods in Psychiatric Research, 5, 251–262.
Excellent	Patient Health Questionnaire-9 (PHQ-9; Johnson et al., 2002)*	9	Y	13+	https://www.amerihealthcaritasla.com/pdf/provider/behavioral-health/depression-toolkit-adolescent-questionnaire.pdf See phqscreeners.com for translations	Johnson, J. G., Harris, E. S., Spitzer, R. L., & Williams, J. B. (2002). The patient health questionnaire for adolescents: Validation of an instrument for the assessment of mental disorders among adolescent primary care patients. Journal of Adolescent Health, 30(3), 196–204.
Excellent	Positive and Negative Affect Scale for Children (PANAS-C; Laurent et al., 1999)	27	Y	9–17	https://www.phenxtoolkit.org/protocols/view/180502#Source	Laurent, J., Catanzaro, S. J., Joiner Jr, T. E., Rudolph, K. D., Potter, K. I., Lambert, S., ... Gathright, T. (1999). A measure of positive and negative affect for children: scale development and preliminary validation. Psychological Assessment, 11(3), 326.
Excellent	Revised Child Anxiety and Depression Scale (RCADS/RCADS-P; Chorpita et al., 2005)*	47/25	Y, P	Grade 3–12 [d]	https://www.childfirst.ucla.edu/resources/	Chorpita, B. F., Moffitt, C. E., & Gray, J. (2005). Psychometric properties of the Revised Child Anxiety and Depression Scale in a clinical sample. Behaviour Research and Therapy, 43(3), 309–322.

Measures of Depression (n = 13)

Good	Center for Epidemiological Studies-Depression Scale for children (CES-DC; Faulstich et al., 1986)	20	Y	6–18	Faulstich, M. E. (1986). Depression–pediatric. Psychiatry, 143, 1024–1027. https://www.brightfutures.org/mentalhealth/pdf/professionals/bridges/ces_dc.pdf
Good	Depression Self-Rating Scale (DSRS; Birelson, 1981)*	18	Y	8–14	Birleson, P. (1981). The validity of depressive disorder in childhood and the development of a self-rating scale: A research report. Journal of Child Psychology and Psychiatry, 22(1), 73–88. http://www.childrenandwar.org/projectsresources/measures/
Good	Hopelessness Scale for Children (HSC/HPLS; Kazdin et al., 1986)	17	Y, C	6–13	Kazdin, A. E., Rodgers, A., & Colbus, D. (1986). The Hopelessness Scale for Children: Psychometric characteristics and concurrent validity. Journal of Consulting and Clinical Psychology, 54(2), 241. https://www.phenxtoolkit.org/protocols/view/640601#Source
Good	Hospital Anxiety and Depression Scale (HADS; Snaith, 2003)	14	Y	12+	Snaith, R. P. (2003). The hospital anxiety and depression scale. Health and Quality of Life Outcomes, 1(1), 29. https://www.svri.org/sites/default/files/attachments/2016-01-13/HADS.pdf
Good	Kutcher Adolescent Depression Scale (KADS; Brooks et al., 2003)*	6 or 11	Y	12–17	Brooks, S. J., Krulewicz, S. P., & Kutcher, S. (2003). The Kutcher Adolescent Depression Scale: Assessment of its evaluative properties over the course of an 8-week pediatric pharmacotherapy trial. Journal of Child and Adolescent Psychopharmacology, 13(3), 337–349. 6 item: https://teenmentalhealth.org/wp-content/uploads/2014/09/6-KADS.pdf 11 item: https://teenmentalhealth.org/wp-content/uploads/2014/08/CAPN_11Item_KADS.pdf

Good	Preschool Feelings Checklist (PFC; Luby et al., 2004)[e]	16	P	3–6	https://medicine.tulane.edu/centers-institutes/tecc/provider-resources/problem-screens	Luby, J. L., Heffelfinger, A., Koenig-McNaught, A. L., Brown, K., & Spitznagel, E. (2004). The preschool feelings checklist: A brief and sensitive screening measure for depression in young children. Journal of the American Academy of Child & Adolescent Psychiatry, 43(6), 708–717.
Adequate	Depression Anxiety and Stress Scale (DASS-21; Henry & Crawford, 2005)*	21	Y	12+	http://www2.psy.unsw.edu.au/dass/	Henry, J. D., & Crawford, J. R. (2005). The short-form version of the Depression Anxiety Stress Scales (DASS-21): Construct validity and normative data in a large non-clinical sample. British Journal of Clinical Psychology, 44(2), 227–239.
Adequate	Mental Health Problems Self Report Questionnaire (SRQ-20; Beusenberg & Orley, 1994)*	20	Y	Adolescents	https://www.infontd.org/content/srq-self-reporting-questionnaire	Beusenberg, M., Orley, J. H., & World Health Organization. (1994). A user's guide to the self reporting questionnaire (SRQ) (No. WHO/MNH/PSF/94.8. Unpublished). Geneva: World Health Organization.
Adequate	PROMIS Depression (DeWalt et al., 2015)*	8	Y, P	5–17	http://www.healthmeasures.net/index.php?Itemid=992	DeWalt, D. A., Gross, H. E., Gipson, D. S., Selewski, D. T., DeWitt, E. M., Dampier, C. D., ...Varni, J.W. (2015). PROMIS® pediatric self-report scales distinguish subgroups of children within and across six common pediatric chronic health conditions. Quality of Life Research, 24(9), 2195–2208.

[a] Completed by: Y = Youth, P = Parent/Caregiver, C = Clinician, T = Teacher.
[b] Intended Clinical Use: S = Screening, D = Diagnostic Aid or Treatment Planning, O = Outcome Monitoring
[c] Exact age range for specific forms (e.g., self-report, parent report) may vary
[d] Exact age range not specified.
[e] A 20-item version of this measure exists with more psychometric support (particularly for outcome monitoring) but was not identified as freely or accessibly available
* Available in multiple languages

Note. Table adapted from Becker-Haimes, E. M., Tabachnick, A. R., Last, B. S., Stewart, R. E., Hasan-Granier, A., & Beidas, R. S. (2020). Evidence base update for brief, free, and accessible youth mental health measures. Journal of Clinical Child & Adolescent Psychology, 49(1), 1–17.

Measures of Traumatic Stress (n = 7)

Psychometric Support	Measure Name	# of Items	Completed by:[a]	Ages[c]	Link to Measure	Citation
Excellent	Child Post-Traumatic Cognitions Inventory (CPTCI; Maiser-Stedman et al., 2009)*	25	Y	6–18	http://www.childrenandwar.org/projectsresources/measures/	Meiser-Stedman, R., Smith, P., Bryant, R., Salmon, K., Yule, W., Dalgleish, T., & Nixon, R. D. (2009). Development and validation of the child post-traumatic cognitions inventory (CPTCI). Journal of Child Psychology and Psychiatry, 50(4), 432–440.
Good	Children's Revised Impact of Event Scale (CRIES; Perrin et al., 2005)*	8 or 13	Y	8–18	http://www.childrenandwar.org/projectsresources/measures/	Perrin, S., Meiser-Stedman, R., & Smith, P. (2005). The Children's Revised Impact of Event Scale (CRIES): Validity as a screening instrument for PTSD. Behavioural and Cognitive Psychotherapy, 33(4), 487–498.
Good	Child and Youth Resilience Measure Revised (CYRM; Jefferies et al., 2018)*	17	Y, P	5–23	http://cyrm.resilienceresearch.org/download/	Jefferies, P., McGarrigle, L., & Ungar, M. (2019). The CYRM-R: A Rasch-validated revision of the Child and Youth Resilience Measure. Journal of Evidence-Based Social Work, 16(1), 70–92.
Good	Child and Adolescent Trauma Screen (CATS; Sachser et al., 2017)*	20	Y, P	3–17	https://depts.washington.edu/hcsats/PDF/TF-%20CBT/pages/assessment.html	Sachser, C., Berliner, L., Holt, T., Jensen, T. K., Jungbluth, N., Risch, E., . . . Goldbeck, L. (2017). International development and psychometric properties of the Child and Adolescent Trauma Screen (CATS). Journal of Affective Disorders, 210, 189–195.
Good	Child PTSD Symptom Scale (CPSS-5-SR; Foa et al., 2018)*	6 or 24	Y	8–18	http://www.midss.org/content/child-ptsd-symptom-scale-cpss	Foa, E. B., Asnaani, A., Zang, Y., Capaldi, S., & Yeh, R. (2018). Psychometrics of the Child PTSD Symptom Scale for DSM-5 for trauma-exposed children and adolescents. Journal of Clinical Child & Adolescent Psychology, 47(1), 38–46.
Adequate	ChildTrauma Screen (CTSQ; Kenardy et al., 2006)	10	Y	7–16	https://www.nctsn.org/measures/child-trauma-screening-questionnaire	Kenardy, J. A., Spence, S. H., & Macleod, A. C. (2006). Screening for posttraumatic stress disorder in children after accidental injury. Pediatrics, 118(3), 1002–1009.

	Child Stress Disorders Checklist (CSDC; Saxe et al., 2003)	36	P	2–18	https://www.nctsn.org/measures/child-stress-disorders-checklist	Saxe, G., Chawla, N., Stoddard, F., Kassam-Adams, N., Courtney, D., Cunningham, K., . . . King, L. (2003). Child Stress Disorders Checklist: A measure of ASD and PTSD in children. Journal of the American Academy of Child and Adolescent Psychiatry, 42(8), 972–978.
Adequate						

[a] Completed by: Y = Youth, P = Parent/Caregiver, C = Clinician, T = Teacher.
[b] Intended Clinical Use: S = Screening, D = Diagnostic Aid or Treatment Planning, O = Outcome Monitoring
[c] Exact age range for specific forms (e.g., self-report, parent report) may vary
* Available in multiple languages

Note. Table adapted from Becker-Haimes, E. M., Tabachnick, A. R., Last, B. S., Stewart, R. E., Hasan-Granier, A., & Beidas, R. S. (2020). Evidence base update for brief, free, and accessible youth mental health measures. *Journal of Clinical Child & Adolescent Psychology, 49*(1), 1–17.

Measures of Disordered Eating (*n* = 12)

Psychometric Support	Measure Name	# of Items	Completed by:[a]	Ages[c]	Link to Measure	Citation
Excellent	Eating Disorder Diagnostic Scale (EDDS; Stice et al., 2000)	22	Y	13+	http://www.ori.org/sticemeasures	Stice, E., Telch, C. F., & Rizvi, S. L. (2000). Development and validation of the Eating Disorder Diagnostic Scale: A brief self-report measure of anorexia, bulimia, and binge-eating disorder. Psychological Assessment, 12(2), 123.
Excellent	Bulimic Investigatory Test, Edinburgh (BITE; Henderson & Freeman, 1987)	33	Y	12+	http://www.wales.nhs.uk/sitesplus/866/opendoc/224740	Henderson, M., & Freeman, C. P. L. (1987). A self-rating scale for bulimia the "bite." British Journal of Psychiatry, 150(1), 18–24.
Good	Ideal Body Stereotype Scale-Revised (IBSS-R; Stice et al., 2001)*	6	Y	Adolescents[d]	http://www.ori.org/sticemeasures	Stice, E., Chase, A., Stormer, S., & Appel, A. (2001). A randomized trial of a dissonance-based eating disorder prevention program. International Journal of Eating Disorders, 29(3), 247–262.

Measures of Disordered Eating (n = 12)

Good	Children's Eating Attitudes Test (ChEAT; Maloney et al., 1988)	26	Y	8–13	http://www.1000livesplus.wales.nhs.uk/sitesplus/documents/1011/ChEAT.pdf	Maloney, M. J., McGuire, J. B., & Daniels, S. R. (1988). Reliability testing of a children's version of the Eating Attitude Test. Journal of the American Academy of Child and Adolescent Psychiatry, 27(5), 541–543.
Good	Eating Attitudes Test (EAT; Garner et al., 1982)	26 or 40	Y	13+	https://www.eat-26.com/	Garner, D. M., Olmsted, M. P., Bohr, Y., & Garfinkel, P. E. (1982). The eating attitudes test: Psychometric features and clinical correlates. Psychological Medicine, 12(4), 871–878.
Good	Body Checking Questionnaire (BCQ; Netemeyer and Williamson, 2002)	23	Y	15+	https://www.phenxtoolkit.org/toolkit_content/supplemental_info/mhr_eating_disorders/measures/Body_Checking_Questionnaire.doc	Reas, D. L., Whisenhunt, B. L., Netemeyer, R., & Williamson, D. A. (2002). Development of the body checking questionnaire: A self-report measure of body checking behaviors. International Journal of Eating Disorders, 31(3), 324–333.
Adequate	Eating Disturbances in Youth Questionnaire (EDY-Q; Kurz et al., 2015)*	14	Y	8–13	http://ul.qucosa.de/api/qucosa%3A14486/attachment/ATT-0/	Kurz, S., Van Dyck, Z., Dremmel, D., Munsch, S., & Hilbert, A. (2015). Early-onset restrictive eating disturbances in primary school boys and girls. European Child and Adolescent Psychiatry, 24(7), 779–785.
Adequate	Clinical Impairment Assessment (CIA; Bohn et al., 2008)	16	Y	Adolescents[d]	http://www.wales.nhs.uk/sitesplus/documents/866/CIA.pdf	Bohn, K., & Fairburn, C. G. (2008). The clinical impairment assessment questionnaire (CIA 3.0). In C. Fairburn (Ed.), Cognitive Behavioral Therapy for Eating Disorders, 315–317. New York: Guilford Press.
Adequate	Physical Appearance State and Trait Anxiety Scale (PASTAS; Reed et al., 1991)	17	Y	13+	https://sites.google.com/site/bodyimageresearchgroup/measures/physical-appearance-state-and-trait-anxiety-scale---state-and-trait-versions-pastas	Reed, D. L., Thompson, J. K., Brannick, M. T., & Sacco, W. P. (1991). Development and validation of the physical appearance state and trait anxiety scale (PASTAS). Journal of Anxiety Disorders, 5(4), 323–332.

Psychometric Support	Measure Name	# of Items	Completed by:[a]	Ages[c]	Link to Measure	Citation
Adequate	Dimensional Yale Food Addiction Scale for Children 2.0 (YFAS-C; Gearhardt et al., 2013)	25	Y	13+	https://fastlab.psych.lsa.umich.edu/yale-food-addiction-scale/	Gearhardt, A. N., Roberto, C. A., Seamans, M. J., Corbin, W. R., & Brownell, K. D. (2013). Preliminary validation of the Yale Food Addiction Scale for children. Eating Behaviors, 14(4), 508–512.
Adequate	Sociocultural Attitudes Towards Appearance Questionnaire-4 (SATAQ-4; Thompson et al., 2000)	30	Y	Adolescents[d]	https://sites.google.com/site/bodyimageresearchgroup/measures	Cattarin, J. A., Thompson, J. K., Thomas, C., & Williams, R. (2000). Body image, mood, and televised images of attractiveness: The role of social comparison. Journal of Social and Clinical Psychology, 19(2), 220–239.
Adequate	Body Shape Questionnaire (BSQ; Cooper et al., 1987)*	8, 16, or 34	Y	14+	https://www.psyctc.org/tools/bsq/	Cooper, P. J., Taylor, M. J., Cooper, Z., & Fairburn, C. G. (1987). The development and validation of the Body Shape Questionnaire. International Journal of Eating Disorders, 6(4), 485–494.

[a] Completed by: Y = Youth, P = Parent/Caregiver, C = Clinician, T = Teacher.
[b] Intended Clinical Use: S = Screening, D = Diagnostic Aid or Treatment Planning, O = Outcome Monitoring
[c] Exact age range for specific forms (e.g., self-report, parent report) may vary
[d] Exact age range not specified.
* Available in multiple languages

Note. Table adapted from Becker-Haimes, E. M., Tabachnick, A. R., Last, B. S., Stewart, R. E., Hasan-Granier, A., & Beidas, R. S. (2020). Evidence base update for brief, free, and accessible youth mental health measures. Journal of Clinical Child & Adolescent Psychology, 49(1), 1–17.

Measures of Suicidality (n = 6)

Psychometric Support	Measure Name	# of Items	Completed by:[a]	Ages[c]	Link to Measure	Citation
Excellent	Alexian Brothers Urge to Self-Injure Scale (ABUSI; Washburn et al., 2010)	5	Y	Adolescents[d]	https://itriples.org/measures/	Washburn, J. J., Juzwin, K. R., Styer, D. M., & Aldridge, D. (2010). Measuring the urge to self-injure: Preliminary data from a clinical sample. Psychiatry Research, 178(3), 540–544.

Measures of Suicidality (n = 6)

Good	Columbia Suicide Screen Severity Rating Scale (C-SSRS; Posner et al., 2008)*	19	C	5-18	http://cssrs.columbia.edu/	Posner, K., Brent, D., Lucas, C., Gould, M., Stanley, B., Brown, G., . . . Mann, J. (2008). Columbia-suicide severity rating scale. Columbia University.
Adequate	Ask Suicide-Screening Questions (ASQ; Horowitz et al., 2012)*	4	C	10-24	https://www.nimh.nih.gov/research/research-conducted-at-nimh/asq-toolkit-materials/index.shtml	Horowitz, L. M., Bridge, J. A., Teach, S. J., Ballard, E., Klima, J., Rosenstein, D. L., . . . Joshi, P. (2012). Ask Suicide-Screening Questions (ASQ): A brief instrument for the pediatric emergency department. Archives of Pediatrics and Adolescent Medicine, 166(12), 1170–1176.
Adequate	Depressive Symptom Inventory Suicidality Subscale (DSI-SS; Joiner et al., 2002)	4	Y	15+	https://psy.fsu.edu/~joinerlab/resources.html	Joiner, T. E., Jr, Pfaff, J. J., & Acres, J. G. (2002). A brief screening tool for suicidal symptoms in adolescents and young adults in general health settings: Reliability and validity data from the Australian National General Practice Youth Suicide Prevention Project. Behaviour Research and Therapy, 40(4), 471–481.
Adequate	Suicidal Behaviors Questionnaire Revise (SBQ-R; Osman et al., 2001)	4	C	Older adolescents[d]	https://www.integration.samhsa.gov/images/res/SBQ.pdf	Osman, A., Bagge, C. L., Gutierrez, P. M., Konick, L. C., Kopper, B. A., & Barrios, F. X. (2001). The Suicidal Behaviors Questionnaire-Revised (SBQ-R): Validation with clinical and nonclinical samples. Assessment, 8(4), 443–454.
Adequate	Functional Assessment of Self-Mutilation (FASM; Lloyd-Richardson et al., 2007)	40	Y	Adolescents[d]	https://itriples.org/measures/	Klonsky, E. D., & Muehlenkamp, J. J. (2007). Self-injury: A research review for the practitioner. Journal of Clinical Psychology, 63(11), 1045–1056.

[a] Completed by: Y = Youth, P = Parent/Caregiver, C = Clinician, T = Teacher.
[b] Intended Clinical Use: S = Screening, D = Diagnostic Aid or Treatment Planning, O = Outcome Monitoring
[c] Exact age range for specific forms (e.g., self-report, parent report) may vary
[d] Exact age range not specified.
* Available in multiple languages

Note. Table adapted from Becker-Haimes, E. M., Tabachnick, A. R., Last, B. S., Stewart, R. E., Hasan-Granier, A., & Beidas, R. S. (2020). Evidence base update for brief, free, and accessible youth mental health measures. *Journal of Clinical Child & Adolescent Psychology*, 49(1), 1–17.

Measures of Bipolar/Mania (*n* = 6)

Psychometric Support	Measure Name	# of Items	Completed by:[a]	Ages[c]	Link to Measure	Citation
Excellent	Child Mania Rating Scale-Parent Version (CMRS-P; Pavuluri et al., 2006)	21	P	5–17	http://www.midss.org/content/child-mania-rating-scale-parent-version-cmrs-p	Pavuluri, M. N., Henry, D. B., Devineni, B., Carbray, J. A., & Birmaher, B. (2006). Child mania rating scale: Development, reliability, and validity. Journal of the American Academy of Child and Adolescent Psychiatry, 45(5), 550–560.
Good	10-item Mania General Behavior Inventory (PGBI-10M; Youngstrom et al., 2008)	10	P	5–17	https://osf.io/ub8h7/	Youngstrom, E. A., Frazier, T. W., Demeter, C., Calabrese, J. R., & Findling, R. L. (2008). Developing a ten item mania scale from the parent general behavior inventory for children and adolescents. Journal of Clinical Psychiatry, 69(5), 831.
Good	Mood Disorder Questionnaire-Parent Version (P-MDQ; Wagner et al., 2006)	13	P	12–17	bipolarnews.org/wp-content/uploads/2012/08/Mood-Disorder-Questionnaire-for-Parents-of-Adolescents.pdf	Wagner, K. D., Hirschfeld, R., Emslie, G. J., Findling, R. L., Gracious, B. L., & Reed, M. L. (2006). Validation of the Mood Disorder Questionnaire for bipolar disorders in adolescents. Journal of Clinical Psychiatry, 67(5), 827–830.

Measures of Bipolar/Mania (*n* = 6)

	Measure	# items	Completed by[a]	Age range[c]	Link	Reference
Good	Young Mania Rating Scale (YMRS; Young et al., 1978, 2000; McIntyre et al., 2004)	11	Y, P, C	5–17	https://www.outcometracker.org/library/YMRS.pdf https://www.tn.gov/content/dam/tn/mentalhealth/documents/Pages_from_CY_BPGs_483-488.pdf	Young, R. C., Biggs, J. T., Ziegler, V. E., & Meyer, D. A. (1978). A rating scale for mania: Reliability, validity and sensitivity. British Journal of Psychiatry, 133(5), 429–435. Young, R. C., Biggs, J. T., Ziegler, V. E., & Meyer, D. A. (2000). Young mania rating scale. Handbook of Psychiatric Measures, 540–542. McIntyre, R. S., Mancini, D. A., Srinivasan, J., McCann, S. M., Konarski, J. Z., & Kennedy, S. H. (2004). The antidepressant effects of risperidone and olanzapine in bipolar disorder. Journal of Population Therapeutics and Clinical Pharmacology, 11(2), e218–e226.
Good	Washington Early Recognition Center Affectivity and Psychosis Screen (WERCAP; Mamah et al., 2014)*	16	Y	15–24	http://werc.wustl.edu/Home/ScreeningInstruments	Mamah, D., Owoso, A., Sheffield, J. M., & Bayer, C. (2014). The WERCAP screen and the WERC stress screen: Psychometrics of self-rated instruments for assessing bipolar and psychotic disorder risk and perceived stress burden. Comprehensive Psychiatry, 55(7), 1757–1771.
Adequate	7 Up 7 Down Inventory (Brief General Behavior Inventory; Jenkins & Youngstrom, 2016)	14	P	5–18+	https://cls.unc.edu/files/2014/06/7u7d_self_english_v1.pdf	Jenkins, M. M., & Youngstrom, E. A. (2016). A randomized controlled trial of cognitive debiasing improves assessment and treatment selection for pediatric bipolar disorder. Journal of Consulting and Clinical Psychology, 84(4), 323.

[a] Completed by: Y = Youth, P = Parent/Caregiver, C = Clinician, T = Teacher.
[b] Intended Clinical Use: S = Screening, D = Diagnostic Aid or Treatment Planning, O = Outcome Monitoring
[c] Exact age range for specific forms (e.g., self-report, parent report) may vary
* Available in multiple languages

Note. Table adapted from Becker-Haimes, E. M., Tabachnick, A. R., Last, B. S., Stewart, R. E., Hasan-Granier, A., & Beidas, R. S. (2020). Evidence base update for brief, free, and accessible youth mental health measures. *Journal of Clinical Child & Adolescent Psychology, 49*(1), 1–17.

Measures of Substance Use (*n* = 13)

Psychometric Support	Measure Name	# of items	Completed by:[a]	Ages[c]	Link to Measure	Citation
Excellent	Hooked on Nicotine Checklist (HONC; DiFranza et al., 2002)	10	Y	12+	https://cancercontrol.cancer.gov/brp/tcrb/guide-measures/honc.html	DiFranza, J. R., Savageau, J. A., Fletcher, K., Ockene, J. K., Rigotti, N. A., McNeill, A. D., . . . Wood, C. (2002). Measuring the loss of autonomy over nicotine use in adolescents: The DANDY (Development and Assessment of Nicotine Dependence in Youths) study. Archives of Pediatrics and Adolescent Medicine, 156(4), 397–403.
Good	Fagerstrom Test for Nicotine Dependence (FTND; Prokhorov et al., 1996, and Heatherton et al., 1991)	7	Y	Adolescents[d]	http://bit.ly/FTND_inst	Prokhorov, A. V., Pallonen, U. E., Fava, J. L., Ding, L., & Niaura, R. (1996). Measuring nicotine dependence among high-risk adolescent smokers. Addictive Behaviors, 21(1), 117–127. Heatherton, T. F., Kozlowski, L. T., Frecker, R. C., & Fagerström, K. O. (1991). The Fagerström test for nicotine dependence: A revision of the Fagerstrom Tolerance Questionnaire. British Journal of Addiction, 86(9), 1119–1127.
Good	Car-Relax-Alone-Forget-Family-and-Friends-Trouble (CRAFFT; Knight et al., 1999)*	9	Y, C	14–18	https://crafft.org/get-the-crafft/	Knight, J. R., Shrier, L. A., Bravender, T. D., Farrell, M., Vander Bilt, J., & Shaffer, H. J. (1999). A new brief screen for adolescent substance abuse. Archives of Pediatrics and Adolescent Medicine, 153(6), 591–596.
Good	Cannabis Use Problems Identification Test (CUPIT; Bashford et al., 2010)	16	Y	13+	http://www.massey.ac.nz/massey/learning/departments/school-of-psychology/research/cupit/clinicians/clinicians_home.cfm	Bashford, J., Flett, R., & Copeland, J. (2010). The Cannabis Use Problems Identification Test (CUPIT): Development, reliability, concurrent and predictive validity among adolescents and adults. Addiction, 105(4), 615–625.

Measures of Substance Use (n = 13)

Good	Adolescent Cannabis Problems Questionnaire (CPQ-A; Gates and Swift, 2006)	12 and 27	Y	14–18	http://bit.ly/CPQ-A_inst https://cannabissupport.com.au/files/media/4564/adolescent-cannabis-problems-questionnaire.pdf	Martin, G., Copeland, J., Gilmour, S., Gates, P., & Swift, W. (2006). The adolescent cannabis problems questionnaire (CPQ-A): Psychometric properties. Addictive Behaviors, 31(12), 2238–2248.
Adequate	CAGE-Adapted to Include Drugs (AID; Couwenbergh et al., 2009, and Brown et al., 1995)	4	Y, P	Dec-18	http://bit.ly/CAGE-AID_inst	Couwenbergh, C., Van Der Gaag, R. J., Koeter, M., De Ruiter, C., & Van den Brink, W. (2009). Screening for substance abuse among adolescents validity of the CAGE-AID in youth mental health care. Substance Use and Misuse, 44(6), 823–834. Brown, R. L., & Rounds, L. A. (1995). Conjoint screening questionnaires for alcohol and other drug abuse: Criterion validity in a primary care practice. Wisconsin Medical Journal, 94(3), 135–140.
Adequate	Severity Dependence Scale (SDS; Gossop et al., 1995)*	5	Y	14+	http://adai.washington.edu/instruments/pdf/Severity_of_Dependence_Scale_397.pdf	Gossop, M., Darke, S., Griffiths, P., Hando, J., Powis, B., Hall, W., & Strang, J. (1995). The Severity of Dependence Scale (SDS): Psychometric properties of the SDS in English and Australian samples of heroin, cocaine and amphetamine users. Addiction, 90(5), 607–614.
Adequate	Cannabis Use Disorder Identification Test-Revised (CUDIT-R; Loflin et al., 2018)	8	Y	Adolescents[d]	http://bit.ly/CUDIT_inst	Loflin, M., Babson, K., Browne, K., & Bonn-Miller, M. (2018). Assessment of the validity of the CUDIT-R in a subpopulation of cannabis users. American Journal of Drug and Alcohol Abuse, 44(1), 19–23.

Adequate	Brief Screener for Tobacco Alcohol and Other Drugs (BSTAD; Kelly et al., 2014, and Levy et al., 2014)	11	Y	12–17	https://www.drugabuse.gov/nidamed-medical-health-professionals/screening-tools-resources/screening-tools-for-adolescent-substance-use	Kelly, S. M., Gryczynski, J., Mitchell, S. G., Kirk, A., O'Grady, K. E., & Schwartz, R. P. (2014). Validity of brief screening instrument for adolescent tobacco, alcohol, and drug use. Pediatrics, 133(5), 819–826. Levy, S. J., & Williams, J. F. (2016). Substance use screening, brief intervention, and referral to treatment. Pediatrics, 138(1), e20161211.
Adequate	TCU Drug Screen (Knight et al., 2014)*	15	Y	13–19	https://ibr.tcu.edu/forms/drug-use-and-crime-risk-forms-adol/s	Knight, D. K., Blue, T. R., Flynn, P. M., & Knight, K. (2018). The TCU drug screen 5: Identifying justice-involved individuals with substance use disorders. Journal of Offender Rehabilitation, 57(8), 525–537.
Adequate	Rutgers Alcohol Problem Index (RAPI; White & Labouvie, 1989)	10, 18, or 23	Y, C	12–18+	http://bit.ly/RAPI_inst	White, H. R., & Labouvie, E. W. (1989). Towards the assessment of adolescent problem drinking. Journal of Studies on Alcohol, 50(1), 30–37.
Adequate	Risks and Consequences Questionnaire (RCQ; Stein et al., 2010)	26	Y	14–19	http://www.midss.org/content/risks-and-consequences-questionnaire-rcq	Stein, L. A., Lebeau, R., Clair, M., Rossi, J. S., Martin, R. M., & Golembeske, C. (2010). Validation of a measure to assess alcohol- and marijuana-related risks and consequences among incarcerated adolescents. Drug and Alcohol Dependence, 109(1–3), 104–113.
Adequate	Adolescents' Need for Smoking Scale (ANSS; Richardson et al., 2007)	35	Y	Adolescents[d]	http://www.chrisgrichardson.ca/anss/about-the-anss/get-the-anss/	Richardson, C. G., Johnson, J. L., Ratner, P. A., Zumbo, B. D., Bottorff, J. L., Shoveller, J. A., & Prkachin, K. M. (2007). Validation of the Dimensions of Tobacco Dependence Scale for adolescents. Addictive Behaviors, 32(7), 1498–1504.

[a] Completed by: Y = Youth, P = Parent/Caregiver, C = Clinician, T = Teacher.
[b] Intended Clinical Use: S = Screening, D = Diagnostic Aid or Treatment Planning, O = Outcome Monitoring
[c] Exact age range for specific forms (e.g., self-report, parent report) may vary
[d] Exact age range not specified.
* Available in multiple languages

Note. Table adapted from Becker-Haimes, E. M., Tabachnick, A. R., Last, B. S., Stewart, R. E., Hasan-Granier, A., & Beidas, R. S. (2020). Evidence base update for brief, free, and accessible youth mental health measures. Journal of Clinical Child & Adolescent Psychology, 49(1), 1–17.

APPENDIX B

CLIENT CONCERNS, GOALS, AND INTERVENTIONS

CLIENT CONCERNS	GOAL DEFINED	VERIFYING SOURCE	GOAL OF THE INTERVENTION	INTERVENTION METHODS

CHAPTER 11

REVIEW AND CONCLUSION

The premise of this textbook was to illustrate through case studies and real-life circumstances the complexity of engaging in the evidence-based practice (EBP) process. As we highlighted in each chapter, social workers must grapple with simultaneously balancing (1) client needs and preferences, (2) the best available evidence, and (3) the implementation context. We provided a framework for aligning these three essential ingredients of the EBP process and presented case studies and activities to increase your confidence in applying and translating evidence to practice.

While the EBP process is not a new concept, our inclusion of the assessment process as part of the initial stages of the EBP process is novel. As Chapter 2 illustrated, the methods and skills you use to collect data from your clients could very well impact what and how much information you gather from your clients—and, by extension, how relevant, applicable, and specified your PICO questions are (see Chapter 2). As you move forward in the EBP process, you will find that your PICO question will likely impact what articles and sources you gather (INPUT stage). As exemplified in Chapter 3, the sources you gather will set the stage for the broad range of information you will have to address your PICO question. The challenging part of this process is weeding out the sources that are not applicable to your target population and their issues of concern and the evidence that may not apply under those circumstances (PROCESS stage). Section 2 (Chapters 4–6) provided an overview of types of research designs you may come across. While knowing the pros and cons of each research design is imperative, we illustrated with real-life case studies that each one of them must be considered in the context of "real-life" considerations and client preferences. We provided examples and strategies on how to grapple with challenges, such as being unable to find studies that include samples of the diverse client groups you're working with or finding treatment plans that don't align with client preferences or agency procedures. We then presented strategies to either modify the context to address implementation barriers or adapt the treatment plan in Section 3 (Chapters 7–9). Many of our students who engaged in the EBP process were later discouraged as they learned after engaging in the input and process stages that the implementation context (or OUTPUT stage) may not always be conducive to adhering to the ideal treatment plan. We conclude here by offering a couple of case studies that illustrate the complexity of the EBP process and draw on the strategies and tools we introduced throughout this book. Again, we find that students grasp this process more effectively by learning from case studies.

CASE STUDY #1: MADISON—ALCOHOL USE DISORDER

By Jaclyn Rales

STEP 1: ASSESSMENT

Madison is a 21-year-old African American straight cis-female who presents for treatment following her reported behavior of heavy drinking daily. Madison resides in a shelter that serves young people ages 21 and under experiencing homelessness and has been living there for the past 21 days since she was kicked out of the family home for drinking. She reports drinking half to a whole fifth (750 mL) of hard liquor per day and will "do whatever it takes" to have consistent access to alcohol. She states that her preferred choice of alcohol is vodka; she began drinking at age 14, but her consumption level escalated at 18 when she began having roughly 7 drinks a day. Madison was diagnosed with an alcohol use disorder (AUD) by the on-site drug and alcohol specialist, with whom she completed the shelter's standard biopsychosocial assessment. Madison reports that the alcohol is "numbing" and allows her to tolerate "everything inside [her] head." She hopes to reduce the amount of alcohol she is drinking "without going cold turkey." Her goal is to become less dependent on a substance to get through each day. She expressed that once she can better manage her alcohol use, she can exit homelessness and reunite with her family at their home.

STEP 2: DEVELOPMENT OF WELL-FORMED QUESTIONS (PICO)

P = African American woman
I = Harm reduction model
C = None or no intervention
O = Decreased alcohol use

For an African American woman who is homeless, what is an effective harm reduction model (compared to no intervention) to reduce alcohol use?

STEP 3: EVIDENCE SEARCH

To identify relevant studies pertinent to the PICO question, the student searched 4 electronic databases, EMBASE, PsycINFO, the Cochrane Database of Systematic Reviews, and Google Scholar, for randomized control trials (RCTs), systematic reviews, meta-analyses, and metasyntheses. Search terms included "homeless," "homelessness," "shelter," "harm reduction," "alcohol," "alcohol use disorders," "housing first," "substance use," "substance abuse," and "substance use disorders."

The student located an RCT to measure the effectiveness of a short-term harm reduction model for alcohol (HaRT-A) in treating individuals experiencing homelessness, as well as alcohol use disorders (AUDs) (Collins et al., 2019). Participants (N = 169) were randomized to 4 sessions of HaRT-A or treatment as usual. Over half (58%) identified as Black/African American, and three-quarters were male. Compared to the control group at 3 months, HaRT-A participants showed statistically significant changes in several outcomes: alcohol-related harm, number of AUD symptoms, more continuous abstinence, no days drinking to intoxication, and increased emotional health-related quality of life.

STEP 4: CRITICAL APPRAISAL

The student summarized the study (Table 11.1); the information informed her answers for impact, rigor of study, and applicability.

> **Impact:** The short-term harm reduction intervention produced statistically significant changes on several alcohol-related measures over the treatment-as-usual control group.
>
> **Rigor of study:** The student conducted a critical appraisal (Table 11.2) and found that the study had a number of strengths. Concerns were that the study period was only 3 months, although this was a follow-up after only four sessions of intervention.
>
> **Applicability:** Collins et al.'s (2019) study was predominantly male (76% of sample); therefore, the applicability to women such as Madison are unknown. At the same time, the sample was also predominantly African American (58%), as Madison identifies. The intervention was specific to alcohol, which is Madison's drug of choice. She stays at a shelter, where the harm reduction program was delivered. The length of stay ranges from 1 to 3 months, the length of the study period.

STEP 5: SELECTING AND IMPLEMENTING THE INTERVENTION

Due to the rigor of the study and the match in terms of PICO factors, the student chose the HaRT-A intervention.

> **Provider Context:** The student had also spent her foundation year at this placement in a different role, so she had the support and guidance of not only her field supervisor but also the clinical psychologist and the drug and alcohol specialist. The

TABLE 11.1 Study Summary: Collins et al. (2019)

Author(s) (year) Purpose and Hypotheses Theoretical orientation	Research Design	Sampling N [method recruited from demographic info]	Measure	Results [related to hypotheses]
Collins, S., Clifasefi, S., Nelson, L., Stanton, J., Goldstein, S., Taylor, E., Hoffmann, G., King, V., Hatsukami, A., Cunningham, Z., Taylor, E., Mayberry, N. Malone, D., & Jackson, T. (2019). Randomized control trial of harm reduction treatment for alcohol (HaRT-A) for people experiencing homelessness and alcohol use disorder. International Journal of Drug Policy, 67, 24-33. The purpose of this study was to measure and assess the initial effectiveness of a short-term harm reduction model for alcohol (HaRT-A) in treating individuals experiencing homelessness with diagnosed alcohol use disorders (AUDs) when compared to their services-as-usual counterparts.	This study was a 3-month long randomized control trial (RCT) with one intervention group (receiving HaRT-A treatment) and one control group (receiving treatment as usual).	N = 169 participants Participants experiencing homelessness with AUD diagnoses were recruited from 3 community-based, social services agencies; participants interested in the study were selected by organizational staff and screened by research staff. In the total sample, over half of the participants identified as Black/African American (58%); 22% identified as white/European, 12% as American Indian/Alaska Native/First Nations Most of the sample includes males.	The Alcohol Quantity and Use Assessment (AQUA) Addiction Severity Index–5th edition The Structured Clinical Interview for the DSM-5 The Short Inventory of Problems Ethyl glucuronide (EtG) to detect heavier alcohol use RAND 36-Item Short Form Health Survey	"Compared to their services-as-usual control counterparts, HaRT-A participants showed statistically significant improvements on alcohol outcomes, including reductions in peak alcohol quantity, alcohol-related harm, number of AUD symptoms, and alcohol-positive EtG tests" (p. 31). HaRT-A did **not** have a significant effect on physical health-related quality of life ($p > .40$), but it did, importantly, have a statistically significant effect on emotional health-related quality of life ($p = .003$).

TABLE 11.2 Critical Appraisal for Collins et al. (2019)

Were they properly randomized into group using concealed assignment?	Interested individuals who met inclusion criteria were randomly assigned to either the intervention or control group using stratified block randomization.
What is the method of randomization?	
Was everyone involved in the study (participants and researchers) "blind" to treatment? In other words, were they not privy about which interventions participants received?	
Was randomization blind?	It does not explicitly state in the study whether randomization was blind, despite the control group not receiving HaRT-A treatment. Participants still met with research staff for the same number of sessions as the HaRT-A group. Moreover, services as usual were also still offered to both groups for the duration of the study, and the intervention did not interfere with these sites existing services. Given this information, it appears that randomization is blind but that is not explicitly confirmed.
Are the people who implement the measures (both pre and post) blind to the treatment condition?	This was not explicitly stated in the study. However, the authors' mentioning that the interventionists' (a registered nurse, psychologist, and social worker) fidelity training included review of the HaRT-A manual evinces that they were not blind to the treatment condition.
Were intervention and control groups similar at the start of the trial?	
Were the differences between groups tested at baseline? Were there differences?	Treatment groups did not significantly differ on baseline demographics (specifically in terms of age, birth sex, race, and ethnicity) or outcome variables.
Fidelity: Was the treatment implemented as it was designed?	
What were the methods used to ensure fidelity?	Research staff underwent several online trainings regarding the ethical conduct of research participants as well as study-specific in-person training. Staff who would be assessment interviewers received >20 hours of training, a review of written guidelines, on-site shadowing, and mock interviews with feedback given. Interventionists received 20 hours of in-person training, shadowing, role-plays, review of the HaRT-A manual, and received feedback. Additionally, all staff at these sites received weekly supervision, which included regularly reviewing audiorecorded sessions with an experienced clinical psychologist who specializes in research on alcohol interventions.

(continued)

TABLE 11.2 Continued

Were results reported on fidelity?	Yes; adherence was high, with HaRT-A interventionists on average providing approximately 99% of the treatment model's expected components. Moreover, spanning the four competence scales (informativeness, direction, authoritativeness, and warmth), participant ratings ranged between "high" and "top 10 percent of clinicians" levels for each of the scales. These characteristics of treatment integrity were measured using the HaRT-A Adherence and Competence Coding Scale, which also assessed interventionists' adherence to manualized components of the HaRT-A model.
Are all the participants who entered the trial accounted for at its conclusion?	
Were the outcomes all reported?	Yes, all outcomes were reported and elaborated on in the study—both primary and secondary outcome analyses were discussed, including the outcomes that didn't support their hypothesis (i.e., health-related quality of life). The "missingness" mechanism related to outcome variables for this study was deemed "ignorable" in the context of their primary analyses (Collins et al., 2019, p. 28).
Was there differential attrition between the groups?	Yes, but not much—the final Month 3 session was attended by 76% of the HaRT-A group ($n = 65$); $n = 21$ participants did not complete the study. On the other hand, 72% of the control group ($n = 60$) attended the final Month 3 session; $n = 23$ participants did not complete the study.
Intent to treat?	One individual was stated to not have been included in analysis due to having received treatment and follow-up assessments outside of the research design's timeline because of administrative errors. The authors do not otherwise indicate any exclusion of participants not completing treatment from the analyses.

student said that her placement allowed time for online trainings, so she had time to devote to the training for HaRT-A (below).

Client Values and Preferences: Given Madison's reporting that she does not want to "quit cold turkey" and only desires to reduce her alcohol intake, HaRT-A would offer autonomy in setting goals that make the most sense for her in a supportive and safe environment. The student would frame the intervention to Madison by explaining that it is specifically designed for individuals who want to limit their alcohol use and would reiterate its compassionate, nonjudgmental orientation.

Training, Supervision, and Fidelity: The student learned that interventionists for the research received 20 hours of in-person training, which entailed shadowing role plays, reviewing the HaRT-A manual (offered as an appendix to the article), and receiving feedback on their practice. The student believed, with the support of the interdisciplinary team at the shelter, that she could deliver the intervention with Madison. She also committed to using the HaRT-A Adherence and Competence Coding Scale.

Adaptations: The student thought the applicability level was high, and there was no need for adaptations in this case.

STEP 6: MONITOR CLIENT PROGRESS

To monitor Madison's progress, the student chose the Alcohol Use Disorders Identification Test (AUDIT), a 10-item screening tool that assesses alcohol consumption, alcohol-related problems, and drinking behaviors. A clinician can administer the AUDIT as an oral interview or a self-report questionnaire; a score of 8 or higher implies harmful or dangerous alcohol use. The AUDIT is both reliable and valid, has been consistently tested across gender and racial lines, and is available in 40 languages, suggesting its universality as a measurement scale (Daeppen et al., 2000). During a once-weekly check-in, the client would complete this brief scale at the beginning of each session to assess her alcohol intake, experience of alcohol-related harm, and potential dependence on alcohol.

This case exemplifies how social workers can align the three essential stages of the EBP process—honoring client needs and preferences, using the best available evidence, and considering the implementation process and context. In the next case study, we offer a more detailed glimpse of how to screen for issues of concern from an agency-wide perspective (versus for an individual client).

CASE STUDY #2: CASE MANAGEMENT FOR DEPRESSION

STEP 1: ASSESSMENT

A first-year MSW student was placed in a means-tested home-visiting program for pregnant or early postpartum women. The intern's role was to provide support and case management for the women on her caseload. The intern noticed that the women she worked with complained of low energy and mood and seemed depressed. She wondered how many of them were clinically depressed, how they could best be screened, and whether help for depression could be provided as part of home visiting or whether a separate referral was needed and for what kind of treatment.

STEP 2: DEVELOPMENT OF WELL-FORMED QUESTIONS (PICO)

One of the student's PICO questions was, *How effective is screening participants in home visiting for depression and referring, when necessary, to treatment?*

STEP 3: EVIDENCE SEARCH

To answer this PICO, the student did a search on PubMed with the following search strategy:

((("Postpartum Period"[Mesh] OR "Postnatal Care"[Mesh] OR "Pregnancy"[Mesh] OR pregnan*) AND depression) OR "Depression, Postpartum"[Mesh] OR "postpartum depression")

AND

("Home Environment"[Mesh] OR "Home Health Nursing"[Mesh] OR "Home Care Services"[Mesh] OR "House Calls"[Mesh] OR "home visit*")

AND

((y_5[Filter]) AND (english[Filter]))

The student found a study reporting a quasi-experimental design with this population/problem area in *Addressing Maternal Depression, Substance Use, and Intimate Partner Violence in Home Visiting: A Quasi-Experimental Pilot Test of a Screen-and-Refer Approach* (Dauber et al., 2019).

STEP 4: CRITICAL APPRAISAL

The student analyzed the study for *impact and rigor* by relying on a template for quantitative studies (discussed further in Chapter 4 [RCTs]) (see Table 11.3 below). The critical appraisal was drawn from the Johanna Briggs checklist for quasi-experimental studies (see Table 11.4 below). The study was also assessed for *applicability*.

TABLE 11.3 Template for Quantitative Studies—Case Example

Author and Purpose	Research Design	Sampling	Measures	Results
Dauber et al. (2019) Purpose: to compare a screen and refer approach for depression (and intimate partner violence and substance use) in a home-visiting context to home visiting only on screening, identification, and referrals	Quasi-experimental design: experimental group that had screen and refer program (4 counties in a state) compared to other 5 counties who did not have the screen and refer program, which involved screening, motivational interviewing, and case management	4 counties in a state compared to other 5 demographically matched counties; Counties were selected by convenience on whether they had strong enough leadership to sustain the changes.	identification of risk, discussion, and referral to services	Identification and referral practices were low in experimental group (30% and 10%, respectively for depression). The experimental condition: home visitors had more discussions about depression than did the control group home visitors. Fidelity was low: less than half of positive-screening clients received motivational interviewing or case management.

TABLE 11.4 JBI Critical Appraisal Checklist for Quasi-Experimental Studies (nonrandomized experimental studies)

Critical Appraisal Questions	Answers: Yes, No, Unclear or Not/Applicable	Dauber et al., 2019
1. Is it clear in the study what is the "cause" and what is the "effect" (i.e., there is no confusion about which variable comes first)?	Yes	The "cause" is the HELP intervention. The "effect" is the impact of the HELP intervention on three outcomes that are routinely tracked by home visitors (1) risk identification of SU, MD, and IPV; (2) discussion of SU, MD, and IPV during home visits; and (3) referrals to treatment for SU, MD, and IPV.
2. Were the participants included in any comparisons similar?	Yes	Due to the larger size of the comparison counties, their HV programs were contracted to serve more families, accounting for the disparity in sample size across conditions: 394 HELP clients and 771 non-HELP clients met eligibility criteria and were included in study analyses. There were no significant baseline differences between HELP and non-HELP clients.
3. Were the participants included in any comparisons receiving similar treatment/care, other than the exposure or intervention of interest?	Yes	The comparison and intervention conditions received similar treatment/care—home visits, screenings, discussions on risks/issues, and referral.
4. Was there a control group?	Yes	The comparison condition received the Healthy Families HV model.
5. Were there multiple measurements of the outcome both pre and post intervention/exposure?	Yes	The outcomes were not applicable at pretest because they involved behaviors on the part of the home visitors. However, the *Identify* phase included standardized screening for MD, SU, and IPV during the first 3 months of HV and again at 6 months.
6. Was followup complete and if not, were differences between groups in terms of their follow up adequately described and analyzed?	Yes	Risk identification and referral outcomes were missing for 31% and 39% of the HELP and non-HELP samples respectively. Analyses on risk-identification outcomes excluded the 356 clients with missing data. Referral outcomes were coded from referral forms that could be completed during any home visit and 452 clients who had at least 1 home visit had no referral forms completed. The authors conducted a sensitivity analysis in which results were analyzed with and without these cases. The results were equivalent.

7. Were the outcomes of participants included in any comparisons measured in the same way?	Yes	There were three study outcomes (risk identification, risk discussion, referral) (p. 1243). Trained family assessment workers or home visitors collected data in clients' homes using the state's standardized forms and subsequently entered the data into the management information system. All study outcome measures were extracted from the Healthy Families management information system. (pp. 1236–1237)
8. Were outcomes measured in a reliable way?	No	Fidelity to the HELP protocol was low, and this included the ability to record risk identification and referral outcomes, which were missing for 31% and 39% of the HELP and non-HELP samples respectively.
9. Was appropriate statistical analysis used?	Yes	Propensity weights were used in all analyses to account for potential imbalance between conditions. Weighted logistic regressions were conducted to compare HELP and non-HELP clients on the three study outcomes in each of the three risk domains (MD, SU, and IPV). All analyses were conducted as intent-to-treat, including all clients in the HELP condition regardless of dosage. Odds ratios were presented as measures of effect size.
Overall appraisal:		Given the low fidelity to HELP, it is difficult to disentangle whether the lack of HELP impact is due to the intervention itself being ineffective or to clients receiving an insufficient dosage of the intervention. The administrative outcomes, while pragmatic, lack sensitivity and specificity. Risk identification and referral within home visiting (HV) are complex processes that are not adequately captured (p. 1241).

Review and Conclusion • 225

Applicability: Although the student was concerned about the lack of impact of the protocol on paraprofessionals' behavior, she did find that the study intervention matched her role (case management) and the setting (home visiting). The student was attentive to the fact that the home visitors could not implement the intervention as planned, as this had implications for feasibility issues in potentially any home-visiting setting.

Additional Context: With the example from the student in the home-visiting program, a prevalence question might be: How many women who are in means-tested home-visiting programs for pregnant and postpartum mothers suffer from depression?

Dauber et al. (2019) used existing data on 735 participants in Wisconsin home-visiting programs. The student noted that the number of participants was large but that the authors presumably collected their data by convenience sampling; the home-visiting programs involved 15 counties and 4 tribal regions in Wisconsin, but it wasn't explained why these were the areas selected. Despite the sampling limitation, the student learned that a significant proportion of women—24% screened positive for either minor or major depression. She also found out this was much higher than the rate of depression found in a nationally representative sample of women (11%) (Brody et al., 2018), confirming her observation that there was a high level of such symptoms in the women she saw in her field placement.

STEP 5: SELECTING AND IMPLEMENTING THE INTERVENTION

Provider Context: The student concluded that the practitioner context differed, given that she lacked the life experience and community involvement of the paraprofessional home visitors.

Client Values and Preferences: Values and preferences will be assessed as women engage in treatment if the screening phase detects it is indeed warranted.

Training, Supervision, and Fidelity: Through her MSW program, the student was developing the knowledge and skills to enable her to do clinical assessment of depression, as well as substance abuse and intimate partner violence, and provide motivational interviewing.

STEP 6: MONITOR CLIENT PROGRESS

A measurement question might involve finding the best (feasible, economical, reliable, and valid) instrument to screen, assess, or evaluate a particular problem. An example might be: *What is the most accurate (sensitive) screening instrument to use to find out if women who are low-income and pregnant/postpartum experience depression?* Psychometric studies on measurement instruments with certain populations (see Chapter 10) and systematic reviews of these types of studies (see Chapter 5) can answer these questions. In this example, the student found a systematic review titled *Screening for Perinatal Depression with the Patient Health Questionnaire Depression Scale* (PHQ-9) (Wang et al., 2021), which concluded that both the Edinburgh Postnatal Depression Scale (Cox et al., 1987) or the PHQ were appropriate for use with this population. Both were short (10 or fewer items), freely accessible, reliable, and valid.

CASE SUMMARY

To recap, the student formulated several PICO questions, as illustrated throughout the chapter. She learned in answer to *How many women who are in means-tested home visiting programs for pregnant and postpartum mothers suffer from depression* that about one-quarter of the program's clients might score at clinical levels on a screening inventory for depression. The student could present this information to agency stakeholders to discuss the need to address the problem programmatically. The student also learned from the diagnostic question about the appropriate measures to assess for depression and found that both the Edinburgh Postpartum Depression Screening and the PHQ were acceptable screening tools that participants could complete and practitioners could score quickly during intake and periodic home assessments. In answer to the main PICO question, the effectiveness of screening, she found that training and support were necessary so that home visitors could identify depression and refer for services.

CONCLUSION

Overall, the chapter encapsulates the multifaceted nature of the EBP process through the lens of real-life scenarios, offering a comprehensive understanding of how social workers can navigate the intricacies of addressing client needs, utilizing the best evidence, and accounting for implementation challenges. The chapter concludes with several practice-related activities to help you integrate key concepts we presented in this book.

REFERENCES

Brody, D. J., Pratt, L. A., & Hughes, J. P. (2018). Prevalence of depression among adults aged 20 and over: United States, 2013–2016. *NCHS Data Brief*, (303), 1–8.

Collins, S. E., Clifasefi, S. L., Nelson, L. A., Stanton, J., Goldstein, S. C., Taylor, E. M., Hoffmann, G., King, V. L., Hatsukami, A. S., Cunningham, Z. L., Taylor, E., Mayberry, N., Malone, D. K., & Jackson, T. R. (2019). Randomized controlled trial of harm reduction treatment for alcohol (HaRT-A) for people experiencing homelessness and alcohol use disorder. *The International Journal on Drug Policy*, 67, 24–33. https://doi.org/10.1016/j.drugpo.2019.01.002

Cox, J. L., Holden, J. M., & Sagovsky, R. (1987). Detection of postnatal depression. Development of the 10-item Edinburgh Postnatal Depression Scale. *The British Journal of Psychiatry: The Journal of Mental Science*, 150, 782–786. https://doi.org/10.1192/bjp.150.6.782

Daeppen, J. B., Yersin, B., Landry, U., Pécoud, A., & Decrey, H. (2000). Reliability and validity of the alcohol use disorders identification test (AUDIT) imbedded within a general health risk screening questionnaire: Results of a survey in 332 primary care patients. *Alcoholism, Clinical and Experimental Research, 24*(5), 659. https://doi.org/10.1111/j.1530-0277.2000.tb02037.x

Dauber, S., Hogue, A., Henderson, C. E., Nugent, J., & Hernandez, G. (2019). Addressing maternal depression, substance use, and intimate partner violence in home visiting: A quasi-experimental pilot test of a screen-and-refer approach. *Prevention Science, 20*(8), 1233–1243. https://doi.org/10.1007/s11121-019-01045-x

Wang, L., Kroenke, K., Stump, T. E., & Monahan, P. O. (2021). Screening for perinatal depression with the Patient Health Questionnaire depression scale (PHQ-9): A systematic review and meta-analysis. *General hospital psychiatry, 68*, 74–82. https://doi.org/10.1016/j.genhosppsych.2020.12.007

FOR YOUR PRACTICE

1. Identify the following types of PICO questions from this list:

• Intervention	• The lived experience
• Prevalence	• Prediction/correlation
• Measurement	• Cost-effectiveness

   a. Is reminiscence therapy a more effective treatment than music therapy for reducing agitation and anxiety in individuals with Alzheimer's disease?

   b. Is parent-involved trauma-focused cognitive behavioral therapy (TF-CBT) more effective in reducing symptoms of PTSD in sexually abused children as opposed to child only TF-CBT?

   c. Do individuals experiencing incarceration who live with family members upon reentry have lower rates of recidivism than those who live alone or with non-family-members?

   d. Do men who are incarcerated and participate in GED programs experience higher rates of employment and lower rates of recidivism one year after reentry than those who do not participate in GED programs?

Take one of the PICO questions that interest you, and work through the EBP process. The steps needed to complete each of the six steps of the EBP process are outlined in the case studies above and could be used as a template as you engage in the process. If applicable, please refer to the consolidated framework for implementation research (CFIR) observation tool (see Chapter 8) to assess whether your agency is prepared to implement an ESI or a novel intervention in your agency.

2. As a capstone project to integrate the book's material, interview your field instructor, executive director, or other person involved in the administration of your agency and find out the types of answers they would like to know about the clientele being served. Because they likely have not been taught to formulate PICO questions, translate their issues of concern into PICO questions.

Translating Agency Needs into Answerable Questions

Issue of Concern	PICO Question

Choose one of the PICO questions to work through the EBP process as you've been taught through this book. Present the findings to your agency personnel. What is their reaction? Discuss the barriers and how you will overcome them.

INDEX

For the benefit of digital users, indexed terms that span two pages (e.g., 52–53) may, on occasion, appear on only one of those pages.

Tables, figures, and boxes are indicated by an italic *t*, *f*, or *b* following the page/paragraph number.

* (asterisks), 33

Aberrant Behavior Checklist, 190
ACF (Administration for Children and Families), 102
adaptation
    CBT techniques for adolescent substance use disorders, 170*t*
    child-centered play therapy (CCPT), 55
    common elements, 169–70
    common elements family therapy techniques, 170*t*
    cultural adaptations, 171–72
    example of Bernal (1995) applied to McCabe (2009), 173*t*
    justifying as applied to PCIT, 174*t*
    overview of, 172–73
    pros and cons of treatment manuals, 168
    relationship factors, 168–69
    transdiagnostic approaches, 171
Administration for Children and Families (ACF), 102
adolescents
    CBT techniques for adolescent substance use disorders, 170*t*
    common elements family therapy techniques, 170*t*
aggregated results, 92
alpha level, 46
alternative measures, 185–87, 186*t*

American Psychological Association (APA)
    criteria for ESIs, 6
    Division 12 Task Force compilation, 37–39
    DSM classification system, 16–18
answer key, 13
APA. *See* American Psychological Association
APA Division 12 Task Force compilation, 37–39
applicability, 50
archival documents, 84
asterisks (*), 33
ATLAS.ti, 85

Beck Anxiety Inventory. Correlations, 196
biopsychosocial-spiritual assessment, 18–22, 20*t*, 25, 111
Boolean logic, 32–35

California Evidence-Based Clearinghouse (CEBC)
    accessing, 40
    criteria for evidence-supported/informed intervention, 6
    rankings awarded by, 39
Campbell Collaboration, 62, 68
case studies
    adults (negligent treatment and interpersonal violence), 106–10
    case management for depression, 230–32
    college-age students
        issues to address, 61
        systematic reviews, 69*b*, 70–71

case studies (*cont.*)
  David
    concerns, goals, and interventions plan, 189*t*
    goal attainment scaling scoresheet, 191*t*
    issues to address, 178
    relating concepts to case, 183–85
  Elisa (abuse, neglect, and parenting issues), 111–12
  evidence-based parenting, 110–12
  JBI critical appraisal checklist for quasi-experimental studies, 228*t*
  Lucas
    DSM diagnoses, 17–18
    goal setting, 22
    issues to address, 15–16
    monitoring progress, 196
    PICO questions, 23
    risk and resilience assessment, 21*t*
  Madison (alcohol use disorder), 225–30
  Morris
    client assessment, 51
    critically appraising sudies and reviews, 53–54
    evidence search, 51
    issues to address, 45
    monitoring client progress, 55
    PICO questions, 51
    selecting and implementing interventions, 54–55
  school-aged children (PTSD and depression), 9
  study summary and critical appraisal: Collins (2019), 223*t*
  template for quantitative studies, 227*t*
  Tyrone (PTSD and depression), 3
  youth (trauma and sexual abuse), 79
CBITS. *See* cognitive behavioral intervention for trauma in schools
CBT. *See* cognitive behavioral therapy
CCPT. *See* child-centered play therapy
CEBC. *See* California Evidence-Based Clearinghouse
CFIR. *See* consolidated framework for implementation research
CFIR observation tool, 163
characteristics of individuals involved domain (CFIR)
  barriers to implementation, 105
  child welfare contexts, 152
  juvenile justice and behavioral health, 161
  multiple systems, 118–35
  as one of five critical domains, 105
  school mental health context, 158
Child Behavior Checklist, 183, 184, 195

child-centered play therapy (CCPT), 51, 52*t*, 53*t*, 54–55
Child Posttraumatic Symptom Scale (CPSS), 12
CINAHL (Cumulative Index to Nursing and Allied Health Literature), 31
client assessment and goal setting (Step 1)
  applied to case management for depression, 230
  applied to Madison (alcohol use disorder), 225
  applied to Morris (inattention and anger), 51
  applied to negligent treatment and interpersonal violence, 106–7
  biopsychosocial-spiritual assessment, 18–22
  biopsychosocial-spiritual assessment template, 25
  brief overview of, 8–9
  "Concerns, Goals, and Interventions" table, 187–88
  DSM classification system, 16–18
  formulating goals, 22
  main approaches to, 16
  overview of, 24–25
  PICO question example (familial sexual abuse), 23
  PICO question formulation, 22
  PICO question guide, 23*t*
  practice activities answer key, 13
  risk and resilience biopsychosocial-spiritual assessment, 20*t*
client logs, 185–87
client monitoring, evaluation, and feedback (Step 6)
  alternative measures, 185–87
  applied to alternative case planning, 110
  applied to case management for depression, 232
  applied to negligent treatment and interpersonal violence, 108
  brief overview of, 12
  case study: David (concerns, goals, and interventions plan), 189*t*
  case study: David (goal attainment scaling scoresheet), 191*t*
  case study: David (regulating emotions, peer conflict, falling asleep, focus on violence), 178, 183–85
  case study: Jack (cocaine addiction and depression), 192–94
  case study: Madison (alcohol use disorder), 230
  critiquing measures, 181–83
  identifying problems and addressing goals, 187–88
  key outcomes at agency settings, 187*t*
  measures of observation, 186*t*
  practice activities answer key, 13
  reasons for monitoring client progress, 179
  relating concepts to cases, 183–85

standardized measures, 179–81
types of reliability, 181*t*
types of validity, 182*t*
client perspective PICO questions, 80
client system, 57
client values and preferences
  alcohol use disorder case study (Madison), 226–30
  case management for depression, 232
  child-centered play therapy (CCPT), 54
  evidence-based practice (EBP) process, 8*t*
  intervention selection and implementation (Step 5), 54
Cochrane Collaboration, 68
Code of Ethics, 7
coding, 85
cognitive behavioral intervention for trauma in schools (CBITS)
  for PTSD in school-aged children, 9–11
  school mental health context, 157–59
cognitive behavioral therapy (CBT)
  for adolescent substance use disorders, 170*t*
  critical appraisal, 10–11
  evidence-based designations, 38
Cohen's d, 63
common elements, 169–70, 170*t*
common factors, 168–69
"Concerns, Goals, and Interventions" table, 187–88
consolidated framework for implementation research (CFIR)
  applied to Garcia (2019, 2020) child welfare contexts, 151–56
  applied to juvenile justice and behavioral health, 159–62
  applied to school mental health context, 156–59
  applied to Waltz (2019) multiple systems, 118–35
  applying to science and real-world practice, 112
  barriers to implementation, 105
  case scenario (negligent treatment and interpersonal violence), 106–8
  case scenario #1 (alternative case planning), 108–10
  case scenario #2 (evidence-based parenting), 110–12
  popularity of, 105
  uses for, 103–4
controlled vocabulary terms, 31–32
cost-effectiveness PICO questions, 24*t*
CPSS. *See* Child Posttraumatic Symptom Scale
critical agent of change, 168–69
critical appraisal (Step 4)
  applied to alternative case planning, 109

  applied to case management for depression, 231–32
  applied to David (regulating emotions, peer conflict, falling asleep, focus on violence), 184–85
  applied to Elisa (abuse, neglect, and parenting issues), 112
  applied to Madison (alcohol use disorder), 226
  applied to negligent treatment and interpersonal violence, 107–8
  brief overview of, 10–11
  of qualitative studies, 88–89
  of randomized controlled trials, 53–54
  of systematic reviews, 68, 69*b*, 76
  tools for, 74
critical paradigm, 81
cross-sectional research, 58
cultural adaptations, 171–72
cultural exchanges, 153–54
Cumulative Index to Nursing and Allied Health Literature (CINAHL), 31

data analysis
  in qualitative research, 85–86
  software for, 85
databases. *See* library databases
deductive approach, 79–80
de-implementing old practices, 103
Diagnostic and Statistical Manual of Mental Disorders (DSM), 16–18
Diffusion of Innovations theory, 105
Digital Dissertations/ Dissertation Abstracts Online, 31–37
direct observation, 185, 186*t*
disease model of abnormality, 17
Division 12 Task Force compilation, 37–39

EBP process. *See* evidence-based practice (EBP) process
Educational Resources Information Center
effect sizes
  odds ration (OR), 65–66
  SMD (standardized mean difference), 63–65
empirical distillation, 169–70
empirically supported interventions (ESIs)
  addressing barriers to, 117
  criteria for, 6–7
  EBP process and, 101–3
  myths versus facts concerning, 8*t*
  selecting, 103–6
empowerment paradigm, 81
EPIS. *See* exploration preparation implementation and sustainment

epistemology, 81–82
ERIC (Educational Resources Information Center), 31–37
ESI. *See* empirically supported interventions
ethnography, 82–83
evaluation stage, 12
evidence-based clearinghouses, 10
evidence-based practice (EBP) process
   advantages of, 7
   applications for, 5
   approach to learning, 4–5
   brief overview of, 7–12
   challenges of, 6–7
   defining as an outcome versus a process, 6–7
   definition of evidence, 81–82
   integrating into routine practice, 5
   myths versus facts concerning, 8*t*
   organizational structure of chapters, 5*f*
   overview of, 221
evidence-based repositories, 37–40
evidence maps, 71
evidence search (Step 3)
   applied to alternative case planning, 109
   applied to case management for depression, 231
   applied to Elisa (abuse, neglect, and parenting issues), 112
   applied to Madison (alcohol use disorder), 225–26
   applied to Morris (inattention and anger), 51
   applied to negligent treatment and interpersonal violence, 107
   brief overview of, 10
   evidence-based repositories, 37–40
   library databases, 30–37
   practice activities answer key, 13
   RCT summary, 52*t*
   terms used in search strategies by database, 36*t*
   tracking search process, 37*t*
   See also randomized controlled trials; systematic reviews
evidence-supported/informed intervention, 6–7
exosystem factors, 101
exploration preparation implementation and sustainment (EPIS), 103–4
external sources, reliable. *See* evidence search

Family First Prevention Services Act (FFPSA), 102
family therapy, 170*t*

Goal Attainment Scale (GAS), 187, 188–92
goal-setting
   formulating goals, 22
   goal attainment scaling, 186–87
   See also client assessment and goal setting
Google Scholar, 9–10
grounded theory, 82–83

holistic approach, 18–22
homogeneous sampling, 84–85
HyperRESEARCH, 85

ILS (Implementation Leadership Scale), 163
impact, 50
implementation barriers
   addressing, 117
   CFIR domains, 118–35
   example #2 (child welfare contexts), 151–56
   example #3 (school mental health context), 156–59
   example #4 (juvenile justice behavioral health), 159–62
   implementation process (CFIR), 142*t*
   individuals involved (CFIR), 139*t*
   inner contextual factors from the CFIR, 125*t*
   intervention characteristics from the CFIR, 119*t*
   key themes across projects, 162–63
   outer contextual factors from the CFIR, 136*t*
   practice activities answer key, 13
   tools for agency leaders/directors, 163
Implementation Leadership Scale (ILS), 163
implementation outcomes, 103–4
Implementation Process domain (CFIR)
   barriers to implementation, 105
   child welfare contexts, 154–56
   juvenile justice and behavioral health, 161–62
   multiple systems, 142*t*
   school mental health context, 158–59
implementation science
   key terms, 104–5
   platform provided by, 104
   role in implementation practice, 105
   See also intervention selection and implementation
individualized rating scales, 185
inductive approach, 79–80
Inner Setting domain (CFIR)
   barriers to implementation, 105
   child welfare contexts, 152–53
   juvenile justice and behavioral health, 160
   multiple systems, 125*t*, 135
   school mental health context, 157
INPUT stage, 10. *See also* client assessment and goal setting
instructors, note for, 13
internal consistency, 181*t*
interpretive data analytic approaches, 92

interrater (interobserver) reliability, 181t
Intervention Characteristics domain (CFIR)
    barriers to implementation, 105
    child welfare contexts, 151–52
    juvenile justice and behavioral health, 160–61
    multiple systems, 118, 119t
    school mental health context, 157–58
intervention selection and implementation (Step 5)
    applied to alternative case planning, 109–10
    applied to case management for depression, 232
    applied to Madison (alcohol use disorder), 226–30
    applied to Morris (inattention and anger), 54–55
    applied to negligent treatment and interpersonal violence, 108
    applying CFIR to science and real-world practice, 112
    brief overview of, 11–12
    case scenario (negligent treatment and interpersonal violence), 106–8
    case scenario #1 (alternative case planning), 108–10
    case scenario #2 (evidence-based parenting), 110–12
    frameworks, models, and strategies, 103–6
    overview of, 101–3
    practice activities answer key, 13
    role in EBP process, 101–3
intraorganizational cultural exchanges, 153–54

Joanna Briggs Checklist for Systematic Reviews, 76
Joanna Briggs Institute (JBI), 62, 68, 228t
Joanna Briggs tool for RCTs, 53t, 53–54

library databases
    conceptualizing search terms, 31–32
    databases available, 31
    formulating search strings, 32–35
    organizing and tracking searches, 35
    running search strategies, 35–37
    terms used in search strategies by database, 36t
    tracking search process, 37t, 41
lived experience PICO questions, 24t, 80
logs, 185–87

macrosystem factors, 101
manuals. *See* adaptation; treatment manuals
maximum variation sampling, 84–85
measurement instruments, 179–83, 185–87
measurement PICO questions, 24t
measures of observation, 186t
Mesh Terms (Medical Subject Headings), 31–32
mesosystem, 101

meta-analysis, 62, 63–66, 65t
metasynthesis, 92
methodologies, 82–85
microsystem level, 101
monitoring. *See* client monitoring, evaluation, and feedback

narrative approaches, 82–83
NASW. *See* National Association of Social Work
National Association of Social Work (NASW), 6–7
non-directive supportive therapy, 169
NVivo, 85

observation, measures of, 186t
odds ratio (OR), 65–66
OR (odds ratio), 65–66
Outer Setting or Context domain (CFIR)
    barriers to implementation, 105
    child welfare contexts, 154
    juvenile justice and behavioral health, 159–60
    multiple systems, 135, 136t
    school mental health context, 156–57
OUTPUT stage, 11–12. *See also* intervention selection and implementation
overview of reviews, 71

PAR (participatory action research), 82–83
parallel forms, 181t
parent-child interaction therapy (PCIT), 109, 151, 172, 174t
participatory action research (PAR), 82–83
PCIT. *See* parent-child interaction therapy
phenomenology, 81, 82–83
philosophical approaches, 81–82
PICO (population, intervention, comparison, outcomes) questions
    applied to David (regulating emotions, peer conflict, falling asleep, focus on violence), 178
    applied to Elisa (abuse, neglect, and parenting issues), 111
    applied to Lucas (familial sexual abuse), 23
    applied to Morris (inattention and anger), 51
    applied to youth (trauma and sexual abuse), 95
    brief overview of, 8–9
    formulating, 22–23
    PICO question guide, 23t
    practice activities answer key, 13
    role of qualitative research in, 80
    types of, 24t
    See also practice-based research questions
positivist perspective, 81
postmodern/poststructural perspectives, 81
postpositivism, 81

Index • 235

posttest-only study design, 56
practice activities
    client assessment and goal setting (Step 1), 25–28
    client monitoring, evaluation, and feedback (Step 6), 195–96
    evidence search (Step 3), 40–41
    implementation barriers, 164
    implementation science, 112–13
    intervention selection and implementation (Step 5), 112–13
    PICO (population, intervention, comparison, outcomes) questions, 27, 40–41, 234–35
    qualitative research, 95–97
    randomized controlled trials (RCTs), 59
    research designs, 59
    self-assessments, 113
    systematic reviews, 75–77
practice-based research questions (Step 2)
    applied to case management for depression, 231
    applied to Madison (alcohol use disorder), 225
    applied to negligent treatment and interpersonal violence, 107
    brief overview of, 8–9
    See also PICO questions
practice wisdom, 80
pragmatism, 81
prediction/correlational PICO questions, 24t
pre-experimental research design, 56–57
pretest/posttest study design, 56–57
prevalence PICO questions, 24t
PRISMA (Preferred Reporting Items for Systematic Reviews and Meta-Analyses), 69, 76
probably efficacious evidence, 37–38
PROCESS stage, 10–11. See also critical appraisal
program directors, note for, 13
ProQuest, 34
PROSPERO, 68, 72
protective factors, 19–22
psychometric support, 181
PsycINFO (Psychological Abstracts)
    locating research in, 31–37
    search terms fo PTSD in school-aged children, 9–10
publication bias, 61–62
PubMed search, 33–34
p-value, 46

qualitative research
    analysis of a qualitative study, 86–92
    application to case study, 95
    characteristics of, 80–81
    critical appraisal for QR synthesis and application to Neelakantan (2019), 94t
    data analysis, 85–86
    definition of, 79–80
    evidence produced by, 81–82
    example summary of qualitative study, 87t
    meta-synthesis of, 62
    methodologies, 82–85
    overview of, 95
    practice activities answer key, 13
    qualitative research synthesis, 92
    role in EBP process, 80, 92
    summary of systematic review/metasynthesis example, 93t
    template of critical appraisal and sample, 90t
quantitative studies
    deductive approach, 79–80
    meta-analysis of, 62
    versus qualitative research, 81
quasi-experimental research designs, 56, 228t

RAI (rapid assessment instrument), 180
randomized controlled trials (RCTs)
    brief review of, 45–46
    case study example, 51–55
    critical appraisal for quantitative studies, 49
    impact, rigor of study, and applicability, 50
    Joanna Briggs tool for RCTs, 53t
    practice activities answer key, 13
    RCT study summary template, 48t
    RCT summary, 52t
    reading and summarizing, 46
    threats to internal validity, 47t
Randomized Controlled Trials: Design and Implementation for Community-Based Psychosocial Interventions (Solomon), 46
rapid assessment instrument (RAI), 180
rapid reviews, 72
reflexivity, 82
Reiss Screen for Maladaptive Behavior, 195
relationship factors, 168–69
reliability, types of, 181t, 181–83
representative samples, 58
research, translating into practice, 104
research designs
    practice activities answer key, 13
    pre-experimental, 56–57
    quasi-experimental, 56
    single-system designs, 57
    surveys, 58
    See also qualitative research; randomized controlled trials; systematic reviews
research questions. See practice-based research questions
rigor of study, 50

risk and resilience biopsychosocial-spiritual assessment, 20t, 25

sampling, 84–85
scoping reviews, 71
SDQ. *See* Strengths and Difficulties Questionnaire
search process
search strategy
   recording for each database, 35
   running, 35–37
   tracking search process, 37t
search strings, 32–35
search terms
   for case management for depression, 231
   conceptualizing for library databases, 31–32
   locating qualitative research, 92
   locating systematic reviews, 63
   for PTSD in school-aged children, 9–10
   terms used in search strategies by database, 36t
self-anchored scales, 185
Short Mood and Feelings Questionnaire (SMFQ), 12
significance level, 46
single-system research design, 57
SIRC (Society for Implementation Research Collaboration), 163
SLSS (Student Life Satisfaction Scale), 180
SMD (standardized mean difference), 63
SMD effect size, 63–65
SMFQ. *See* Short Mood and Feelings Questionnaire
Society for Implementation Research Collaboration (SIRC), 163
Sociological/Social Services (Social Work) Abstracts, 31–37
Solomon, P., 46
split-half reliability, 181t
standardized mean difference (SMD), 63
standardized measures, 179–83
Step 1. *See* client assessment and goal setting
Step 2. *See* practice-based research questions
Step 3. *See* evidence search
Step 4. *See* critical appraisal
Step 5. *See* intervention selection and implementation
Step 6. *See* client monitoring, evaluation, and feedback
Strengths and Difficulties Questionnaire (SDQ), 110, 180, 183–85
Student Life Satisfaction Scale (SLSS), 180
subjectivism/interpretivism, 81–82
substance use disorders, 170t
survey fatigue, 180
survey research design, 58

synthesized results
   qualitative research, 92
   quantitative studies, 62
systematic reviews
   case study example, 70–71
   critical appraisal of, 68
   critical appraisal tools, 74
   goal of, 72
   handling multiple, 72–74
   locating, 62–63
   meta-analysis, 63–66
   overview of, 74
   practice activities answer key, 13
   process of, 61–62
   purpose of, 61
   reading and understanding, 66–68
   sample critical appraisal, 69b
   sample summary of (meta-analysis), 65t
   tables and figures explaining, 75
   variations of, 71–72

test-retest reliability, 181t
TF-CBT. *See* trauma-focused cognitive behavioral therapy
Title IV-E Prevention Services Clearinghouse, 102
transdiagnostic approaches, 171
trauma-focused cognitive behavioral therapy (TF-CBT)
   versus CBITS, 9–11
   components of, 3
   implementation, 11–12
   PICO question application, 95
   PICO question formulation, 79
trauma-informed services, 161–62
treatment manuals, pros and cons of, 168. *See also* adaptation

umbrella reviews, 71
universal assessment, 18–22
unobtrusive measures, 186
unpublished literature searches, 61–62
unrepresentative samples, 58

validity
   applied to David (regulating emotions, peer conflict, falling asleep, focus on violence), 184
   threats to internal, 47t
   types of, 182t

well-established evidence, 6, 37
well-formed questions. *See* PICO questions
wild-card truncations, 33